# TALKING
# GUITARS

Printed and bound in Great Britain by MPG Books Ltd, Bodmin

Published by: Sanctuary Publishing Limited, Sanctuary House, 45-53 Sinclair
Road, London W14 0NS, United Kingdom
www.sanctuarypublishing.com

Photos on pp. 36, 99, 110, 135, 161, 177, 180, 189, 261, 291 and 310 courtesy
of James Cumpsty
Photos on pp. 67, 91, 140, 146, 146, 156, 164, 185, 191, 193, 221, 231, 247,
253, 258, 279, 317, 328, 341, and 345 courtesy of Carol Farnworth
Photos on pp. 15, 49, 85, 197, 240, 285 and 297 courtesy of Redferns

ISBN: 1-86074-620-9

# TALKING GUITARS

## A Masterclass with the World's Greats

David Mead

Sanctuary

Dad —

read this book and
you'll be talking guitars -
not that you don't!

Rosie xx

# CONTENTS

**The Acoustic Players**

# INTRODUCTION

## PLAYING THE GAME

To say that this book has been something of a labour of love would be an understatement. It represents a 12-year phase out of a lifetime's love affair with the guitar, during which I had both the pleasure and privilege to sit down to talk to some of the finest players on the planet whilst working for *Guitarist* and *Guitar Techniques* magazines.

I've played guitar since I was 14 and always had something of an insatiable desire to find out as much about the instrument and its players as I could. In those days I would buy any guitar magazine I came across and was always drawn towards interviews with players I knew about – and even more drawn towards those with players I didn't. I discovered so many great players through those pages. The way they learned, joined bands, chose equipment and their general philosophies about the instrument helped me form my own impressions about a world I desperately wanted to become part of myself. I considered it all invaluable research and I don't think I could possibly have known that one day it would be me holding the microphone and asking the questions.

It's a fact that artists place a lot of value on interviews being published in magazines, but, as with everything, there is a time and a place. Usually, the time is when they've got something new to talk about – an album or tour, or something like that. Other than at those times, we guitar writers have absolutely no general access whatsoever. I mention this because we were always being harangued by readers as to why we'd never interviewed certain players; I suppose they imagined that all we had to do was make a couple of calls and that would be that. But in reality, interviews, particularly with the big names, were nearly always a lot harder to come by...

The game we had to play was the game of PR: public relations offices, management companies or press people at record companies were usually the first point of contact if we were chasing someone in particular. Often the answer was an outright 'no' and you gained the impression that, in many cases, the artists themselves were never even consulted. For instance, recently I had the chance to meet Jimmy Page and he asked me why he'd never been asked to do an interview in any of the UK guitar magazines. Now, I have several diaries here that show that I was at one time asking Jimmy's management every month or so for that very same thing. One very powerful manager told me that he had to employ someone in the office just to say 'no' on the phone to people who wanted his artist to do a magazine interview, open a supermarket or visit someone's granny in hospital. I guess you have to see it from both sides.

So, a lot of the time, it was a frustrating business, but always ultimately a rewarding one – hounding this or that artist until you hit upon that rare instance when they wanted to talk to you at the same moment you wanted to talk to them!

Obviously, when these interviews were carried out, the thought that they would one day form a collection was something far from my mind. Reading them together now, though, it's interesting to see how many similarities there are between these individuals who have all achieved status on their instrument. Check out how many times The Shadows guitarist Hank Marvin is cited as being the inspiration for picking up the guitar in the first place. Hank was something of a UK phenomenon – when talking to players from America, it seems to have been The Beatles who ignited the appropriate touch-paper, their celebrity having perhaps been more global.

It's surprising, too, just how many of the players in this collection started out as drummers, or at least having an interest in playing drums. This would include guitarists as diverse as Frank Zappa and Eddie Van Halen, for example.

Many state that they started off with instruments that they liken to medieval instruments of torture – with high playing actions and other ghastly attributes that would put off the faint-hearted for good. Should those among us who are new to the instrument then crank up the bridges on their guitars and try to follow suit? I don't think so. Life's hard enough, after all...

Other conclusions we can draw from reading through these pages include how few slide players actually use commercially available slides. It seems that bottles, motorcycle handlebars or plumber's yard pipe have formed the bedrock of this particular style – keeping up the tradition established by the old Delta slide players to whom, of course, such things as pre-packaged slides were not available.

Overall, I think that what Mark Knopfler says about gentlemen of the press never being able to get to the bottom of an individual's personality holds true. A lot of the true nature of some of the world's best players thus remains hidden from the probing eye of the public at large. Lots of people would ask me what so-and-so was like after carrying out an interview and I would always liken the relationship of the interviewer with the interviewee to that of meeting someone in a lift or on a train. You get to know them on purely a superficial level and can't pretend to have had anything other than a glimpse into the inner recesses of their make-up.

Nevertheless, I hope that reading through this book allows a general overview of what makes the great guitarists tick and that, not unlike a mosaic, the reader is able to put together a 'bigger picture' of what counts for virtuosity in the world of music.

All of the interviews in this book have been re-edited from the original published versions, and for many of them I went back to the original interview tapes and added material that was never previously published – a sort of a 'director's cut' if you will. We were always confined by space in the magazines;

it's great to have the freedom at long last to publish some of these conversations in full.

These interviews were an absolute joy to carry out and have provided me with a hoard of memories that writing this book has allowed me to revisit and share. I hope what you find in its pages adds to your own enjoyment of playing and listening to one of the greatest instruments on earth.

*David Mead*
*www.davidmead.net*
*Summer 2004*

# the ROCK PLAYERS

# FRANK ZAPPA

As far as I know, this was the penultimate interview Frank Zappa gave before his death in December 1993. The album The Yellow Shark, featuring the Ensemble Modern playing classical arrangements of some of Zappa's music, was due for release within weeks and I had been chasing the interview for several months, hoping to tie the two together. But owing to Frank's poor health and busy work schedule, it ended up being a last-minute affair.

Returning home from the office on 24 March 1993, I found a message from Guitarist's deputy editor, Rick Batey, asking me to ring the office urgently. On doing so, he told me that he had some good news and some bad news.

'OK, good news first,' I said.

'You've got the Zappa interview...'

'And there's bad news?' I asked.

'The interview's in two hours' time...'

It was the only way it could be done, I found out later. Frank had to pick a day when he felt well enough to talk to the press – a thing he generally didn't enjoy in any case – and I definitely wasn't going to pass on this one, whatever the circumstances.

So I phoned Zappa's studio at his home in LA at the appointed time – 9pm – and was greeted first of all by someone telling me that we had a bad line and would I phone back? This didn't do anything for my nerves particularly, but I complied.

'Is that better?' I asked when my call was once again answered on the sunnier side of the world.

'Hang on,' I was told.

*I waited for a couple of minutes before I heard the phone being picked up at the other end.*

*'Can I help you?' said a voice.*

*'Yes, hi. My name's David Mead, I'm interviewing Frank for a British guitar magazine...' I began.*

*'This is Frank,' said the voice. 'We're right in the middle of a session here and so I'm taking time off to do this,' he said. I got the impression that he really didn't want to be talking to me at all, but I was genuinely a fan of his music and didn't want him to think that I was just another career journalist and he was just a notch on my CV.*

*I told him that I had heard an excerpt from the new album on BBC2's Late Show – a track called 'The Be-Bop Tango', which originally featured on Zappa's Roxy & Elsewhere, adding that it wouldn't be the same without the girl from the audience on the original track who says on mic, 'I'll do anything you say, Frank...'*

*'Heh heh – what was her name? Lana!'*

*After this, Frank relaxed a little. At least he knew I'd listened to one of his albums. I told him I was going to ask some guitar-related questions...*

*'Well, there's not anything guitar-related [on The Yellow Shark] although there's a guitar player and a mandolin player in the Ensemble Modern.'*

*What follows is a far more complete transcription of the call that followed than has previously been published.*

**What attracted you to the instrument in the first place?**

I liked the way it sounded.

**You've cited Johnny 'Guitar' Watson as an influence before.**

I used to listen to him all the time and I used to listen to Clarence 'Gatemouth' Brown.

**So it was the latter end of the '50s blues period that first got you interested?**

Yeah.

**You've spoken too of an interest in '50s doo-wop records.**

Yes, I like that music.

**Mixed together with your interest in classical music as well – it's a fairly bizarre combination.**

I just listened to it and liked what I heard. It became my musical world.

**The first piece by Edgard Varese you heard was...**

'Ionisations'.

**You've always been interested in percussion?**

Yeah, in fact the piece I'm working on now is all percussion. It has some synthesiser sustaining things in it, but 99 per cent of what's being heard in this piece that we're working on today is all different kinds of percussion instruments.

**I remember you talking in a radio interview once about writing 'percussive harmony'.**

Oh sure. You can write rhythmic dissonance or you can write the equivalent of rhythmic consonance, too. What I would describe as a dissonant rhythm is 23/24, where things would rub up against each other in a dissonant way, in just the same way that notes that are a half-step apart have a certain tendency to twinge your ear. Rhythms that are fractionally off from each other create another kind of linear dissonance. A consonant kind of rhythm would be like march or disco music where everything is 'boom, boom, boom...'

**Common time like 4/4 or simple 2/4, you mean?**

Yeah.

**What did you learn from Johnny 'Guitar' Watson records? Was it the pentatonic approach?**

Well, you know, what Watson was doing was not just pentatonic scales. One of the things I admired about him was his tone – this wiry, kind of nasty, aggressive and penetrating tone – and another was the fact that the things that he would play would often come out as rhythmic outbursts over the constant beat of the accompaniment.

**Is that something you tried to incorporate into your own playing?**

Yes. It seemed to me that was the correct way to approach it, because it was like talking or singing over a background. There was a speech influence to the rhythm.

**What was the first guitar that you had?**

It didn't have a make on it – it had been kinda sandblasted. My brother got it for $1.50 at an auction and it was an archtop, f-hole, ugly motherfucker with the strings about a half-inch off the fingerboard.

**That's usually a good sort of guitar to start with...**

It builds your wrist up...

**Everything you play afterwards feels like going downhill after one of those.**

Heh heh, yeah. My father had a guitar which he kept in a closet, but I never played that. I didn't really decide to mess around with the thing until we got this god-awful thing at the auction. That's why I liked it – because it was so tinny-sounding. It was just an acoustic guitar, but for an acoustic instrument it was moving closer to the direction of that wiry tone I liked with Johnny 'Guitar' Watson, especially if you picked it right next to the bridge.

**Did it have one of those moveable wooden bridges that wrecks the intonation?**

I had no idea what intonation was! I didn't find out for maybe five or six years that you even had to think about things like intonation. It was bad enough just tuning the damn thing up with the pegs, let alone worrying about whether you're going to be in tune at the octave.

**When did you make the move to electric?**

The guitar my father had was a round-holed guitar of anonymous make and I stuck one of those DeArmond sound hole pickups in that. So it would be one of those bad-sounding magnetic pickups that you stick in the sound hole of a normal acoustic guitar. It would merely amplify the acoustic sound – so it wasn't a real electric guitar. I guess it was around four or five years later that I actually got an electric guitar. There was a music store not far from my house, and I rented this Telecaster for $15 a month. Eventually I had to give it back, because I couldn't make the payments on it any more.

**Were you ever in high-school bands?**

I had a band when I was either a sophomore or a junior in high school. I actually started off as a drummer, playing in a band in San Diego, but that didn't last very long.

**A lot of guitarists started out playing drums – like Eddie Van Halen or Nuno Bettencourt, both of whom seem to have developed solid right-hand techniques as a result.**

Well, I don't know whether I could vouch for that because I wasn't a very good drummer. My main drawback was that I didn't have good hand-to-foot co-ordination. I could play a lot of stuff on the snare and the tom-toms and the cymbal and everything, but I couldn't keep an even beat on the kick drum while I was doing all this, which was one of the reasons why I was no longer employed as a drummer – nobody could dance to it.

**This is something that obviously didn't translate into guitar, with hand-to-hand co-ordination.**

Yeah, hand-to-hand I'm fine. The only thing I had to co-ordinate with my feet was the wah-wah pedal and turning little stomp boxes on and off.

**How would you sum up your guitar style on the early Mothers recordings?**

It was OK, but back then the guitar wasn't a featured instrument in the way it was on the later albums. As far as a precedent for it... I don't think there was anything you could compare it to; it was the only way I knew how to do it. There was no reason to do it another way and, anyway, everybody else was doing it the other way.

**The rock guitar influences that are the most common are the '60s icons, players like Clapton and Hendrix...**

When *Freak Out* and *Absolutely Free* were done, there wasn't any Hendrix. We met Hendrix in the summer of '67; he sat in with us at the Garrick Theater, so we'd already made those albums before I even knew that he existed. But Mike Bloomfield was a popular guitar player, he was in The Butterfield Blues Band. I saw Butterfield when they came to Los Angeles, but I don't own any of their records. Actually, I think my playing is probably more derived from the folk music records that I heard: Middle Eastern music, Indian music, stuff like that.

**What specifically?**

For years I had something called *Music On The Desert Road*, which was a recording of all kinds of different ethnic musics from different places in the Middle East. I used to listen to that all the time – I liked that kind of melodic feel. I listened to Indian music – Ravi Shankar and so forth – before we did the *Freak Out* album. The idea of creating melody from scratch based on an *ostinato* or single chord that doesn't change – that was the world that I felt most comfortable with.

**You prefer to improvise over a single chord vamp.**

If you listen to Indian classical music, it's not just pentatonic. Some of the ragas that they use are very chromatic, all sustained over a root and a fifth that doesn't change, and by using these chromatic scales they can imply all these other kinds of harmonies. The chords don't change; it's just the listener's aspect that gets to change, based on how the melody notes are driven against the ground bass.

**That sounds like a parallel with your own guitar improvisations, where the band plays a fairly straightforward rhythmic vamp, and you insert dissonance via the solo – you use a lot of chromatic tones and whole tone scales in your solos.**

Well, you stick them in where you think they belong *when* you think they belong. Sometimes you guess right, sometimes you guess wrong. The most dangerous thing is improvising with a band and thinking 'OK, now's the time to play that diminished scale', and somebody in the band is thinking, 'Now's the time to play a major chord.' Those kinds of accidents do happen...

**Your guitar style underwent a marked change around the time of *Overnite Sensation*.**

That was partly because of the rhythm section, and partly because of the equipment I was using. I imagine that anybody's guitar playing would change if one day your keyboard player was Don Preston, and suddenly the next day it's George Duke – know what I mean? Or the difference between [drummers] Jimmy Carl Black and Chester Thompson – that certainly made a difference. Or the difference between Roy Estrada and Tom Fowler. When you have a completely different rhythm section with a different musical perspective, you'd be a fool not to take advantage of it.

**So things became tighter?**

Much tighter and harmonically much more interesting, because George is a more interesting keyboard player.

**It was you who got George Duke into playing synthesiser, wasn't it?**

I had to almost strangle him to make him do it! Up to that point, the closest he would get to a synthesiser would be to use an Oberheim ring modulator that he'd plug his Fender Rhodes into and every once in a while he'd jerk the handle on it and get some sort of a metallic sound out of his Rhodes. It took quite a bit of persuasion to get him to pick up an ARP Odyssey. Also, I knew he had a really nice voice, but it was hard to get him to sing, and now he sings all the time.

**There have been many musicians that have gone through the various manifestations of the Mothers and your later bands who have since come to prominence. There's a parallel there perhaps with the Miles Davis bands – almost like a music college or finishing school.**

Well, if you come to it with that attitude, then it's true – you can derive a lot of information from doing the job. However, most of the musicians look at it as just a way to earn an income. It takes an exceptional musician to work in the band and to really appreciate the type of training and information that is being delivered during rehearsals for the show. So you can either learn a lot of different things in the band, or you can just learn your part, play the gig and pick up your paycheck. I've had both kinds.

**You've had some remarkable musicians in the band, Steve Vai being a fairly obvious example. But Chester Thompson, Adrian Belew, Scott Thunes, Arthur Barrow...**

Terry Bozio – he was here yesterday for a visit...

**Now you always cite his playing on 'Hands With A Hammer' from Vol. 3 of *You Can't Do That On Stage Anymore* as a near-perfect drum sound.**

That's true, and you know it was recorded with just one of those AKG Dummy Head microphones and a C24 – there's no close mic'ing on the set at all. It's all just ambient mic'ing. It's really a fat-sounding kit.

**If we can move back to that radical change in your guitar sound...**

It also changed because I started playing an SG.

**Was this your custom-built one?**

The first one I had was stock, I got it second-hand. At a gig in Phoenix, Arizona this guy came up to me after the show with this handmade SG and he said he would like to sell it to me and I played it and liked it and bought it for $500. As a matter of fact, Dweezil's guitar roadie was just here and he's taken it down to get it strung up with really light strings.

**So you could put the difference in your guitar sound down, at least in part, to a new instrument?**

Not just a different instrument, but also different amplification, because prior to that time I'd been playing either a Gold Top Les Paul or a Gibson ES-5 Switchmaster, which was a large, fat, three-pickup jazz guitar, which really had uncontrollable feedback. I was playing through a Fender amp or an Acoustic amp with a fairly nondescript tone – I just didn't have enough money to invest in new equipment. But by the early '70s I was playing this SG, and I switched over to Marshalls, and started playing through a device that a friend built for me, which had compression, phase shifting and some other little specialities.

**Wasn't there a control you had fitted to one of your guitars that acted as a sort of parametric EQ?**

That came later.

**In the past, you've quoted *One Size Fits All* as being your favourite album.**

Well, I think it was probably a good example of what the band with George Duke and Ruth Underwood could do. I think it's a good-sounding album, representing that group.

**Volume 2 of *You Can't Do That On Stage Anymore* features that band live in Helsinki...**

Yep.

**...and the full version of the solo from 'Inca Roads' shows just how dramatic your editing was on the *One Size Fits All* version. Where did you pick up your editing technique?**

I started around '62, before the Mothers, when I was working in Cucamunga.

**Those were all razor edits – literally cutting up the tape?**

That's right.

**But everything's right on the beat. You'd never know that you're not hearing the complete story.**

I'm a pretty good editor.

**What about your technique of editing together a song from completely different performances, even different bands?**

They come in on the beat!

**I was thinking of the 'Drowning Witch' section of 'Ship Arriving Too Late...', from the *You Can't Do That On Stage Anymore* series.**

Oh yeah, where it goes from the '84 to the '82 band?

**How much time does an edit like that take?**

Well, it took years. I worked on it for five or six years.

**You're also a fearsome archivist of your own material...**

I do have a large vault with material in it.

**Any idea how many hours of material it represents in total?**

[Laughs] No. There's mountains of stuff in every format from little five-inch reels of quarter-inch tape, a 1 7/8 IPS, all the way up to digital video and all stops in between.

**You've also taken live backing tracks and superimposed studio performances on top – for instance, the *Sheik Yerbouti* album...**

Yes, but I've gone in the other direction, too. For example, 90 per cent of the guitar solos on the *Joe's Garage* album were from live shows, pasted on studio tracks. In the studio, they called it the 'Ampex Guitar'. I had all these quarter-inch tapes of guitar solos that I liked from the '79 tour, and when we went into the studio to do *Joe's Garage*, I would just go through my files to see what key a certain solo was in, and just experimentally hit the start button on the playback machine and lay it on to the multi-track.

**Didn't you have trouble with tuning variation?**

Well, we did that with a VSO. We did have to wiggle the pitch around to make sure it sounded like it was in the right key.

**At one time, the live band used to tune to the vibes as a source of fairly constant pitch, didn't they?**

Yeah, when we had vibes in the band. Remember, we were on the road long before there were Peterson strobe tuners. If you tuned up to a piano that happened to be somewhere on the stage, there wasn't any guarantee that the piano itself was in tune. So, for the first five or six years of touring, it was really a crap shoot as to whether you'd be in tune with anything.

**You overdubbed the guitar solo on 'The Purple Lagoon' from *Live In New York*, because you recorded it on *Saturday Night Live* and had to fill the gap where John Belushi did an act as a Samurai be-bop musician.**

Yes, that's right, although he didn't do that act in the regular live show. I overdubbed it with the guitar through a Pignose amp and an Eventide Harmoniser set at 99.

**Can you remember which guitar you used?**

Yeah, it was the handmade SG.

**How did you come to own the fire-damaged ex-Jimi Hendrix Strat?**

Well, there was this guy named Howard Parker – they called him 'H' – who was Hendrix's roadie, gofer and general assistant. He stayed at our house for a couple of months in the late '60s, and he had this guitar which Hendrix had given to him – I thought it was from the Miami concert. He gave it to me and we had it hanging on the wall as a decoration for years and years, and then I met some guys who were capable of putting guitars back together, so I had it done.

**When I spoke to Dweezil he said that you still have the original neck.**

Yeah, somewhere around here...

**Does it have an individual sound?**

Yes, it did have a sound all its own, especially after it was reconstructed, but that sound was not what you would expect from the Hendrix guitar. It didn't sound like all the Hendrix guitar solos you've ever heard. It was a different kind of sound.

**It's gone through various pickup transformations as well, hasn't it?**

Yeah, it used to have a chrome scratchplate and it had, I think, at that time a Barcus Berry in the neck, and also a pre-amp...

**Didn't you use that guitar on a couple of tracks from the *Shut Up 'N Play Yer Guitar* set?**

If it's in the liner notes, it's true, but I can't remember off-hand. I didn't play it that often because one of the characteristics of that guitar was it liked to feed back unless you were in exactly the right environment where you could stand in exactly the right relationship to the amplifier.

**What was the story behind the 1988 band? It seemed to start off large, get smaller and then stop altogether...**
Actually, it didn't start off large and get smaller – it started medium and got large. It was a 12-piece band, and an argument broke out between Scott Thunes and just about everyone else in the band apart from me and Mike Keneally. The others all decided that they hated Scott's guts; it was very weird. We were almost at the end of the European portion of the tour in the early summer of '88, and we had other dates booked in the United States – big, outdoor, high-paying gigs. But because most of them refused to go on stage with this guy, I had to cancel them all. There was no time to replace anybody at all, no breaks in the tour to rehearse anybody new, so I just had to break it up.

**Was that one of the formats of the band that you were most happy with?**

Well, I was very happy with it and also the audiences really liked it too, and the reviewers thought it was a great band. It was unique because it combined a very strong five-piece horn section with all kinds of electronic stuff, with effects on the percussion section, on the drums, multiple keyboards – a very interesting blend of this horn harmony and very strange sound-effects.

**I missed seeing the band on that tour. I was on the way to Scotland the day you played Wembley...**

Wembley was the only concert on the tour that got a bad review! Someone wrote that we were all too old to play rock 'n' roll. But all the rest of the reviews, even *Rolling Stone* writing about our performance in New York City, surprisingly gave a good review.

**The resulting live CD of that tour – *The Best Band You Never Heard In Your Life* – is testimony to the fact that it was a great-sounding band.**

Think about it: there are no overdubs on that, either. All those little effects and things coming in, that's just the way it was on the live show.

**You've got sampled dog barks and stuff on that – was that the Synclavier?**
Yep.

**Were you generating that from a keyboard?**

There were three stations generating samples: there was Ed Mann, who had this whole vocabulary of dog barks and bubbles and weird shit, then there was Chad Wackerman, who had all these strange percussion things hooked up to a big rig, and then there was the Synclavier, which I could play when I wasn't playing the guitar. There was a MIDI link between the other two stations and the Synclavier, so that they could trigger Synclavier samples while something else was going on.

**So you played your parts on keyboard?**

Yes, I sat down and played the keyboard.

**Did you ever try using a MIDI guitar to control the Synclavier?**

Yes, but I couldn't make it work...

**Was that to do with your playing style?**

Well, I think in order to make it work, the detector only wants to hear the vibrations of a single string, and if you're not constantly damping and muting and doing all sorts of gyrations, then the detector can't really read accurate pitch. So if you're playing on the top E string and you've got an A string ringing or something like that, it tends to fuck things up. So you have to worry about damping the other strings while you're playing and it's just a technique that I'm not very good at.

**You pick with a lot of upstrokes...**

It's just the way I learned.

**A lot of people will pick 'downstrokes heavy', but using a lot of upstrokes is fairly unique.**

It's just the way I learned...

**What's your attitude towards the guitar now?**

I seldom touch it. I was doing a little overdubbing here in the studio, but I don't have calluses any more. In a way, I think I used to be a guitarist, but not any more.

**How do you feel guitar playing is going at the moment?**

I don't think there's much on the street that interests me. I mean, there are certain guys that I admire because they play well and they play musically: I like Jeff Beck and I like Allan Holdsworth and Michael Hedges. These people are all real geniuses at what they do. And I can't remember the guy's name – one of the heavy metal groups – I heard him play a solo that was just wonderful, really interesting stuff. But I can never remember the name of the group or the name of the guitar player! I just saw it whizzing past the channels on MTV.

**What interested you about it?**

Well, it was the whole approach to the solo. The tone was great, the intervals were great and it wasn't the usual thing where a guy will just weedle away on any kind of scale that he thinks he can get away with in the middle of some fast, fuzztone background. This really had some thought to it.

The Steve Vai-transcribed *Frank Zappa Guitar Book* is amazingly complex-looking stuff...

It's even more amazing when you get him to tell you how he did it!

**He said he didn't slow it down.**

He couldn't slow it down. He was taking it off a cassette machine.

**He must have an incredible ear...**

Yup. [Laughs]

**There's a song you did called 'The Jazz Discharge Party Hats'. I heard that when Vai was playing with you, he wrote out your skat-singing vocal part, and then overdubbed it on acoustic guitar.**

That's right.

**That's frightening!**

That's right!

**And was it 100 per cent accurate?**

It's not 100 per cent accurate, as a matter of fact, because if you play the pitches of his transcription without the vocal, there are certain things that just sound a little bit weird. I'd give it 99 per cent, though. I don't think there is anybody wandering around that knew they could do something like 'The Jazz Discharge Party Hats' unless some other lunatic said, 'Do it.' When you're transcribing something to publish in a magazine, that's one thing. But when you're transcribing it and you know that within a day or so you're going to be overdubbing on the track, and you're going to be sight-reading your own transcription, and it's got to sync up exactly with what's on the track – that's when you'll really know whether you're a good transcriber or not. But that's how he did it: he wrote it out, he came in, we turned on the tape, he read it and he did it in two or three takes. He even put in a string-scratch for when I laughed! I went 'Huh, huh, huh' and he's got that little 'scrape, scrape, scrape' in there. He nailed *everything*.

**He got a lot of criticism for doing the big rock thing with Dave Lee Roth and Whitesnake.**

He should be able to do whatever he wants. If he wanted to go country and western he should do that, y'know?

**It's interesting that not all the members of your bands have been able to read music...**

That's right; maybe 10 per cent have been readers, but the rest of them all had to learn it like a parrot.

**There seems to be a free exchange between your 'orchestral' pieces and your 'rock band' pieces. The transfer of 'The Be-Bop Tango' on *The Yellow Shark* from band to orchestra is one example...**

Well, look at it this way: they're pieces. Pieces of music that have harmony, melody and rhythm and some sort of an idea that makes them go, and the rest is just a matter of orchestration.

**How did you acquire your skills as an arranger?**

Trial and error.

**Did you have any formal training in harmony?**

Uh, I had a couple of classes early on. When I was a senior in high school I was an incorrigible student and one of the people in the office decided that maybe I would be socially better adjusted if I was given the opportunity to study something that I was actually interested in. So they arranged for me to go to the junior college to take a harmony course, one hour a week; that lasted for two or three months. I was studying out of the Walter Piston harmony book and I found it really boring. I probably finished up with a D grade, or something like that. There wasn't anything there that I thought was going to be useful for what I wanted to do. I didn't like the sound of the musical examples, I didn't like all this fucking roman numeral horseshit that you have to deal with. Still, I guess it was better than putting up with the stupid classes they had at the high school.

**Is there a way to teach music in a constructive and 'student friendly' way?**

I think that it's kinda useless to teach it, because what are you going to do? A person gets out of school, how's he going to earn a living? In order to make money doing something that you call music, what you wind up doing to earn a living is not music – it's shit! So why bother to teach them anything? It just seems so redundant to teach composition or harmony, when the people who will make the most money will come out of a metal shop or something like that, do something sub-mongoloid and make a fortune out of it!

**So you still stand by your quote of a few years back when you said that the average American wouldn't know good music if it came up and bit them on the ass?**

That's right. But I mean, it's not their fault, because they haven't been exposed to anything other than the commercial stuff that is the non-stop stream of shit that comes out of the media.

**No ready solution, then?**

Well, how can you draw a conclusion about music unless you've heard a wide range of it? I think that the most useful thing that could be done in school is to put more emphasis on music appreciation and make sure that people, whether they're going to become musicians or not, get to hear music from different cultures, music from different eras, different periods of classical music – something so that they have some kind of a home base of knowledge from which they can make personal decisions. The cost of the music education course is so small compared to what it costs to buy new uniforms for the football team and the rest of the shit, and yet most schools in the United States don't even teach it any more.

**Really?**

That's right. I mean, I was lucky that I was in school at a time in American history where they not only had music appreciation courses, but had record libraries at the school. Even in the little towns where I lived you could go in and have access to a large portion of the Folkways library. If you wanted to listen to music from Tibet, or wherever, just go in there and find out what it is. Not any more.

**There was a story about you finding something in a harmony book that conventional wisdom said should never be done and you tried it and liked what you heard...**

It wasn't a harmony textbook, it was a counterpoint book. It was on the first page and what it said was, 'You may not write the following intervals.' The intervals were F and A, a major third, expanding to E and B, a fifth. It also said you could not write G and B, a major third, expanding to F and C, a fifth. So I played these things on the piano and said 'Why? Why can't we do this? This sounds great!'

**And so you closed the book?**

Yeah. I mean, I figured that if on the first page they were telling me that I would have to be going against something my ear immediately liked, then why should I learn the rest of that stuff?

# MARK KNOPFLER

## MAY 1995

*This particular conversation took place just as Mark Knopfler was putting the finishing touches to his Golden Heart solo album. It was the only interview he did that year and I got it totally by chance. There was an album issued called Dire Straits Live At The BBC and I asked the PR company concerned if there was any chance of an interview. I think I must have got through to someone who was either new or very inexperienced, because they actually asked Mark direct and he said yes. This very rarely happens...*

*The girl at the PR company went on to tell me that Knopfler was in Ayr in Scotland and asked if I would be prepared to go there to do the interview. I was puzzled by this, but made the necessary enquiries and was indeed ready to jump on a plane in the name of some Strait talking, when something made me check Knopfler's whereabouts. It turned out, of course, that I was involved in a game of Chinese whispers with the PR company concerned, and Knopfler was in fact at Air Studios in Hampstead!*

*At the time, Mark hadn't yet heard the new live album and, what's more, he didn't seem unduly interested. To him, it was a slice of history from early on in the story of Dire Straits, captured by the BBC in 1978. One thing's for certain: it's certainly the only time you'll hear Knopfler introduce 'Sultans Of Swing' to absolutely no response from an audience. When I mentioned this to him, he shrugged, saying, 'Oh, really? I can't even remember the session...well, hardly.'*

**So tell us about *Golden Heart.***

I'm just finishing up the last session which I did in Nashville. I went over there and did a few sessions and recorded some songs in London and some more in Dublin. So basically it's been Ireland, Tennessee and London...and that's about it.

**How long's it been going on?**

A couple of years, I suppose, because I've spaced it all out and done it easily over a period. The actual studio time hasn't been that much; I'll just take a while off and then go back in, because it's not like I only have four or five weeks to do the whole thing.

**So this is a solo project outside of Dire Straits, like The Notting Hillbillies?**

The Hillbillies was never a solo thing. It started off with me doing a thing for Steve and Brendan, then somehow I ended up recording it, and Guy and I had such a lot of fun doing it that we just carried on. That's how that was. This thing's quite different...

**Well, is it material that wouldn't fit into the Straits jacket or what exactly?**

Just songs that had to be recorded – that's all it is. Nothing any more complicated than that. A couple of the songs I wanted to do in Ireland and a couple I wanted to do here, but most of them I wanted to do with players from Nashville, even though they aren't country songs. I think there's maybe one country-style song on the record, but I love playing with these guys. They rock 'n' roll like nobody's business.

**So what's the delineating factor between a 'solo' song and a Dire Straits song?**

I've never thought that way. Never have. The song to me dictates the way you treat it; that's really it. I mean, there are a couple of songs that I could have done in Ireland and didn't, but that was just a time thing. So I ended up doing them in Tennessee. They would have been different, but they would still have been OK.

**Why Ireland? Does some of the material lean towards traditional Irish music?**

Yes, there was a couple where I wanted to have Uilleann pipes, the fiddle and whistle, so Paul Brady put together a wonderful group of people over there and we managed to get a couple of good things recorded. Paul Franklin fixed things in Nashville earlier on and I'm really grateful to them for that assistance. Even when Paul Franklin is not involved in a session – he wasn't involved in this last one – he would still take an interest and come by and all the rest of it. I did want him for this Shadows thing and the thing I did with Waylon Jennings for the Buddy Holly album. The last time in Nashville, I wanted to do about six songs, but I wanted to do this thing with Waylon for the Buddy Holly tribute and that took a day, and then I had to do this Shadows thing for Miles Copeland and that took a morning. Then Clive James came down doing *Clive James Goes Country* and I ended up helping Clive out with this demo and a whole bunch of other stuff, and so it was quite a busy time. So there wasn't a great amount of time left for socialising.

[*When I visited the studios, a whole history of Knopfler's guitar playing lay on the floor in open cases: the 'Sultans Of Swing' Strat, the 'Money For Nothing' Les Paul, the 'Romeo And Juliet' National – star players amidst a cast of thousands... 'They're not here because I'm trying to be flash,' said Knopfler emphatically, refusing to be photographed with his treasured hoard. 'I'm not into that... In fact, I kinda find that sort of thing offensive – it's as if you're saying, "Look at all my guitars," y'know. They're here because I'm obviously using some of them, but it's very rarely that we can get them all together to allow [guitar tech] Ron to work on them.' He still can't resist showing off his pride and joy, a mid-'50s Gibson Super 400CES in near-mint condition.*]

**So much for guitars; what about amps?**

Well, this new Crate amp just turned up the other day and so that only just got in on the end. I did the backing track to 'Atlantis' when I was in Nashville and brought it back over here and the Crate turned up, and I plugged into it on the clean setting and with this Jurassic Strat – a '54, second or third month of production – and it was just instant Hank Marvin. Obviously not as good, but it just makes me smile to be playing it and hearing it. It's kinda funny for me too, because I had to use the tremolo and I decided to play it with my fingers – I could have played it with a pick – just to make it something else. And I had this idea to use a bit of pedal steel for the voice parts and I think it's worked pretty well. Instead of having this choir thing happening, you have the steel swooping around and it's worked – I think.

**Was the choice of track for the Shads tribute album imposed?**

No, it was my call as it was on the Buddy Holly album where I did 'Learning The Game'. There are thrills involved with both these things, and the thrill with the Buddy Holly thing was that Waylon said to me, 'You know I always felt that Buddy never finished that song – but you did.' That was nice, and then the Shads thing – it was just a thrill to be playing that song. When I was a kid at school the teachers would say, 'Knopfler, stop making that metallic noise at the back of your throat, boy!' because I'd be banging on the top of my desk and singing 'FBI' or something. I had a Shads book when I was 15 and that was where I learned my first chord shapes, and a couple of years ago Hank asked me to write the foreword for his new guitar tutor system...so it's funny the way the wheels go round.

**It's a pretty familiar story that your first Strat was bought as a direct result of seeing Hank B playing one.**

Yeah, that's what I said in the foreword; it had to be red and so on. But my dad, bless him, couldn't afford a Strat so I got this Hofner V2, with the two pickups and the curly bit of metal for the tremolo. It cost 50, quid which was a big stretch for dad then, and this old bloke in the shop said as I walked out with it, 'Stick at it.' I didn't have the nerve to ask for an amplifier, so there I was with this guitar and no amp, and so I just blew up the radio and everything. I had to get a jack with a double end to plug it into the back of the radio and it didn't amplify at all. Hardly at all... A lot of times I just used to put my ear on the guitar and put the head on the arm of a chair and use the reverberations through the chair.

**What sort of songs did you first tackle? Presumably Hank Marvin called the tune for a while.**

Yeah, but obviously it all changed very quickly when I heard the Stones and The Kinks and all of that. But very, very soon after then I was listening to the compilation records of blues and R&B that were coming over, and then full-blown albums by Howlin' Wolf, Muddy Waters, Buddy Guy and BB King, so I was listening to John Lee Hooker and all of that. So that's really what I wanted to do more than anything. That's what it was then; it was a serious love affair. It was a kind of a multi-faceted thing: it was Radio Luxemburg-based pop and all that, but with this real interest in blues and folk music. I got involved in folk music because I couldn't afford an amplifier, so I couldn't be in a beat group, even though I desperately wanted to be. Bob Dylan told me that he was in the same boat: he really wanted to be Little Richard, but he couldn't do that. I used to borrow acoustic guitars and ended up learning fingerstyle, and when I met Steve Philips in Leeds when I was 19, I started going much further back into the blues then, as well as playing West Coast rock 'n' roll style. I was listening to everything from Buffalo Springfield and all that kind of stuff, as well as playing stuff from the '20s and '30s. So it was always pretty wide like that.

**So you went back to Robert Johnson and the other Delta players, too?**

Yeah, absolutely. And Blind Willie McTell and Blind Blake and early jug band stuff. Me and Steve had a duo, and then I went and found my first National; it was 85 quid. I had to borrow the money, borrow somebody's car and drive to Wales in the rain, I remember – that was the triple. I got my first Gibson for 80 quid: it was a Les Paul Special, a cherry one – although it was black then and I started stripping it, and Steve finished the job and got it back to the cherry... God, I loved that guitar.

**So when was the first Strat?**

That was in '77.

**That late? That would have been around the start of Dire Straits, then?**

Yeah, I really wanted to have a Strat. In fact, my first 'Sultans Of Swing' I wrote on a National in open tuning and it was a completely different tune, and when I got the Strat, the sound was so different that it just became another song, another arrangement. That may be an example to readers: I don't know if it's of any use, but sometimes if you take your lyric and change the tuning or the instrument that you try the song on, pick up something else and do it a different way, very often it will dictate something else to you. It's the difference between sitting down with a piano or sitting down with a guitar, or sitting down with a Spanish guitar as opposed to an electric. I often find that what you've written can yield something else. A capo is an amazing thing; just a simple little capo... I mean, maybe it's just totally bleedin' obvious to you, but it very often happens that way. Even a different string gauge can create something completely different: very often I've found that if I'm playing something with very heavy strings, you're not bending them and so something else happens.

**Listening to the first Dire Straits album, it's difficult to see exactly from where the sound of the music drew its influence. It's not blues, it's not folk and yet both those elements play a part.**

I dunno. I suppose that's when I cut my teeth arranging. I didn't know anything about it. I remember thinking very differently when keyboards came into it. I started to think much more seriously then about bass lines, chord inversions and voicings. I think I learned it the hard way. It helped doing a lot of folk stuff and solo acoustic stuff and then having a duo, then a four-piece, then a five- and then a six-piece, and so on; your ability to feel at home with a lot of instruments develops from time spent in the driving seat. Arranging doesn't faze me at all now, but then I was an illiterate – still am in a lot of ways. I think it's just from time spent doing it, really.

**Dire Straits was one of the few bands that managed to fly in the face of punk, successfully finding a foothold in a music industry that had apparently turned its back on anything other than angry young men with an indifferent musical aptitude.**

There were a lot of little kids with bands, but there were two other things, don't forget: there was the *Saturday Night Fever* syndrome, which was huge, in that everyone was buying disco records and making disco records. And then there were these big, pompous bands like Boston and Kansas and The Doobies doing things like, it seemed to me, a big rock disco thing in some ways. I wasn't really interested in any of that. I liked the idea of little beat groups and a stripped-down sound. That's just what interested me at the time, just having this little group. I wanted a vehicle for the songs, but I wanted it to be stripped down. You just go all the way around the houses sometimes, and you just come to where you started in some ways. It's amazing really, but sometimes that audacity just works somehow. I can't listen to that stuff. I just won't. Can't.

**The early stuff?**

Yeah, I can't listen to any of it, ever; I never do. I listen to a bit of it when it's made, but...

[*So that explains why he hadn't heard* Live At The BBC. *Things fall into place.*]

Continuing the train of thought about the 'little group' manifesto that Dire Straits professed in the early days, things had become a lot more orchestrated and BIG sounding by the time *Love Over Gold* was on the shelves.

I suppose so, yeah.

That album was scorned by some critics for being over-produced.

Yeah, I think it was. I think that there are far too many moves on it. You just have to go through it and learn. I mean, what you're doing is doing a lot of your learning in public, artistically and technically. I remember doing things on *Local Hero* I wouldn't dream of doing now: playing Ovations and putting them in the board – just ridiculous things.

So it was an evolutionary process for you as a musician and as a songwriter?

Yeah... And also I started to discover that the more you put on a record, in many ways the less you're getting out of it. I've told this one before, but I was sitting in a bar once and unfortunately 'Telegraph Road' was playing, and I was sitting there thinking, 'Fuck, it sounds like this big lifeless thing.' All this work has gone into it and it doesn't feel like it's got any life in it somehow. And then straight after that came 'Rave On' by Buddy Holly; it sounded four times louder, 20 times bigger and with 100 times more life. Just to really make my day.

Is that what led you to go on and produce 'Twisting By The Pool'?

No, I don't think so. It was after that, the bar story. 'Twisting By The Pool' was just another bad idea. I didn't know anything about making rock 'n' roll records, really. You have to learn the hard way and that's all I can tell you, really.

All of the above was contrasted greatly with the infamous and enormously successful *Brothers In Arms*. There must have been a point where you realised that the album was growing legs and about to run marathons.

No, no, not at all. I think it just happened to coincide with compact discs and it was a sheer fluke. If it hadn't been that album it would have been something else. It was just an accident of timing – it got connected. 'Brothers In Arms' was the first CD single, or so I'm told, and I suppose it was one of the first CD albums. That's all it was, I think. Plus we had a couple of hits in America – 'Money For Nothing' and 'Walk Of Life' – so it got connected with this American success. People always want to make something into something else, but that's really all it was.

**It must have been strange to stand back and watch that album go like it did?**

When you're involved in something, you're so in the middle of it, you don't share the perceptions that go on outside. I don't like being part of that vibe, I'm just happier to be on the inside, working. I don't go around saying, 'I've got a number one record all over the world, aren't I fabulous?' That's never interested me. I like success very much because it lets me come into a studio like this and it lets me play 'Atlantis', but having said 'I like success', it's a completely different thing from saying that you like *fame*. Fame has got no redeeming features whatsoever; in fact, if you wanted to make an equation, you could say that the price of success is fame.

**Clearly, you find fame a hassle.**

It can be, but I try not to let it get to me because I've never wanted to be babied. I go around the world on my own, go to the airport by myself and check into hotels, pay my own bills – I live like anybody else, in other words. I go down to my own motorcycle and go backwards and forwards by myself. I don't like to be nannied, but I suppose that is because I was 28 years old when the band hit. A lot of other people have to face it when they're 17, and they don't get the chance to get involved in the responsibilities of an ordinary life.

**So you have your hands firmly on the controls of your own career?**

In terms of making deals, I leave that to management, but in terms of day-to-day living and fixing light bulbs, I get on with that myself. What I'm saying is, having my motorcycle serviced is not a problem for my management company. Some of the problems in terms of being a writer are that you get used to looking at the world and writing about it, and it comes as a bit of a shock when you're on the front cover of *NME* and you suddenly feel that the world is looking at you. It's a question of getting used to that reversal, and it messed me up for a while; it's just a question of time I think. It's like everything else, you just get used to it.

**Returning to the Dire Straits story, *Brothers In Arms*, Live Aid and the Prince's Trust all helped establish you as a gold card-carrying member of rock's elite. The day you find Eric Clapton playing rhythm guitar in your band, you can be sure things are looking up!**

It's just enjoyment, y'know? Talking about Buddy Holly and the Shads and stuff, well, part of my growing up musically was John Mayall, too. Playing those albums and Paul Butterfield records, Jimi Hendrix and Eric – wishing you were Bob Dylan! So the whole thing is connected with that. It's like a fan's enjoyment, y'know? It's enjoyment because of making those circles with your childhood, and there's more than that. I mean, one morning, Chet Atkins took me round to see Scotty Moore, and they were talking about all sorts of things, and it's very interesting to be a part of that because you find out so much stuff that the journalists never do and the book writers never do. People who feel that they've got the whole history of the thing down; it's never the way it is, the way it's written in books, and you learn so much more by getting a lot of this stuff at first hand. With country music, for example, I've learnt an awful lot from Chet. He was making hundreds of rock 'n' roll records in the 1950s:

Cajun, everything, all sorts of records. About three weeks ago I said to him, 'When did you first meet Merle Travers?' He said, '45... You learn a lot about the history of the music. Sitting around one night with Waylon and Chet, Don Gibson and Roger Miller, Chet and I were playing 'Just One Time' and Waylon grabs this guitar and plays the solo that Chet played on the record. So you learn what sort of a fan he was and how hard he'd worked to get that solo. That was a great moment for me.

**Over the years you've played with so many of your heroes, there can't be many that you'd still like to pluck the strings with?**

It was great playing with the Everlys and the Shads and everybody. It goes on, I suppose. I remember the lad in the studio; we were making a cup of coffee in the studio in Dublin before the session started, and he said, 'You know, that's the finest bunch of musicians in Ireland down there...' I said, 'I know, I know...' But I did think about it, and it's quite thrilling, really.

**You seem to be a man who constantly employs a great deal of self-evaluation. After the first wave of fame struck, I've heard that you decided you needed to improve as both a guitarist and musician, and sought help through the pages of the Mickey Baker jazz guitar tutor.**

After I'd been in it quite a while, it struck me rather forcibly that I knew sod all about music and what I would have to do really would be to learn a little bit about it, seeing as I was doing it; going into these sessions and different things. So I thought I'd try and figure out a little more about it, that's all. So I just sat down and made myself stick at it, just like the man said in the shop. It wasn't easy, but then it just started becoming easier and easier, and I realised that even if I couldn't always remember the name of something, then I would recognise the sound. It's like learning a language where you don't know the long words, but after a while you recognise them, like a child. So now I say, 'That's a 13th with a flattened ninth,' because I know the sound of it.

**Did all this hard graft pay noticeable dividends in such a way that the average man on the street would be able to detect a change in the Knopfler style?**

Yeah, straight away. Voicings and so on, it's all just theft. If I learn something, I have this nasty habit of employing it. I'll use some of the simple – or supposedly simple – stuff, but another thing it's done for me is it's taken a lot of the mystique away from jazz. Not that I particularly like jazz – I never have – but in fact what it did in many ways is reinforce the fact that I don't really care for jazz, that I'm far more emotionally attached to another form of music. Somewhere where the Delta meets the Tyne, I suppose.

**I heard that story about you going through the Mickey Baker book and it struck me that it could have been around the time you wrote 'Your Latest Trick' that you started to employ some of the more jazzy chord voicings in your songwriting. Would you say that was true?**

No, I don't think so. That song seems to me to be very simple, very simple. I think it just becomes employed in different corners and turns and different things here and there. I suppose people these days learn from videos more, don't they?

**Yes – and CD-ROM and things like that.**

Really? I'll have to get some stuff...

*Brothers In Arms*, like many other mega-platinum rock indispensibles, must have proved a tough act to follow. In fact, the world had to wait until 1991 for *On Every Street*, an understated sequel, received with mixed critical acclaim, and that had an almost 'thief in the night' relationship with the world's charts.

I never worry about stuff like that. People talk about pressure and all of that, and I don't feel it, because I'm inside and not outside and it doesn't worry me.

**How do you think *On Every Street* was received, in general?**

I haven't got a clue. I haven't got the faintest idea… The other thing is that it varies all over the world and you tend to think, because you're travelling around the world, you have a relationship with the whole world. You don't have the same relationship with your home town as you used to, you don't think of it that way. You're actually marking the difference in France over the years, or marking the difference in Canada or Australia – it's a big world.

**The subsequent tour certainly covered most of the globe. In a world that is well used to rock tours of mammoth proportions, the Dire Straits tour lasted a year and a half and yielded the live album *On The Night*.**

Well, it's a given that you've got to love it. If you don't love it, you might as well go and do something else. If you can't handle it, get out. It's like a lot of things. I'm very lucky, in the sense that I like to get to the studio quickly; I'm actually in a hurry to get here and I like to rehearse. I love to record and I love to perform and I love to play music at home. So I'm very lucky because I like the whole deal. There are bits about the road that are awful, but it's made up for on stage, and if you don't love it, then do something else. You've got to be a round peg in a round hole, otherwise it's just going to end in tears.

**So do you still enjoy playing 'Sultans Of Swing', 'Money For Nothing' and all the other Straits anthems?**

Oh yes, I do. It's always fantastic fun. I don't like to hear them, but I like to play them…

# DAVID GILMOUR
MAY 1995

In September 1994 I was invited to join Pink Floyd in Strasbourg to witness all the pomp and circumstance of the band's The Division Bell tour. Not only did I witness the spectacle from the perspective of being in the audience (VIP seats behind the mixing desk, no less), I also got to witness the numerous wheels in motion behind the scenes. It was a huge affair with sound men, stage crew, caterers and various sundry support staff all working together to put on one of the biggest shows on earth.

I had been after an interview with David Gilmour since the album's release earlier that year, but he was playing hard to get, and my 48 hours on the French/German border saw me come away with a quick 'Hi' and a handshake and nothing more. I did manage to grab a quick chat with Tim Renwick, but otherwise – zilch.

It took me another five months to nail the interview, which was done when the live album and video of the tour was released the following year. The interview was carried out at a private club in London's Soho, where the new video was to be screened in full for we gentlemen of the press. In actual fact, my erstwhile colleagues on the dailies failed to put in much of an appearance and I ended up viewing the film virtually by myself. I say 'virtually', because I was joined by David after a while, who fussed about the sound reproduction in the screening room...

Pink Floyd have a reputation for excellence in all things. Their original '60s commitment to provide an audio-visual experience for their audiences – which was second to none – was still very much in place nearly 30 years later. Always keen to take advantage of new technology, they had reground acknowledged *cutting edges in both the recording studio and on stage with every album release and subsequent tour. In 1994, with another chart triumph under their collective belts, they undertook a tour that went above and beyond anything seen, heard or done on a rock stage before. What's more, some audiences got to hear a contemporary reading of* Dark Side Of The Moon. *But far from being a masterstroke of strategic planning, the decision to perform the piece, which had not been heard in its entirety since 1975, was almost off the cuff. For, although plans were afoot to resurrect the Floyd magnum opus well in advance, it wasn't actually performed whole until the band were three months into the US leg of the tour. 'It was just one of those ideas that gradually fermented in our minds,' Gilmour told me as we started. 'We realised that we were actually doing two-thirds of it and thought it would be really good fun to do it as a whole. We'd been intending to change the show; in fact, we were changing the show every night, doing slightly different versions of the songs. Gradually it got to the point where we could do the whole thing when we got to Detroit, towards the end of the American part of the tour.*

*'We initially didn't want to announce it or have people knowing about it. We thought it would be a really nice surprise to do it without anybody knowing about it. We only did it about four times in America, because it was into the last three weeks of the American leg of the tour before we did it, but then I suppose we were doing it once every five or six shows around Europe just on a purely arbitrary basis, usually when we were playing the same place twice or something like that – we would just throw it in...'*

**Was the performance of *Dark Side Of The Moon* ever announced at the beginning of the concert or was it left as a complete surprise?**

No, it was never announced. The most work was getting all the stuff together, the necessary bits of quad tape and bits of film – some we had to reshoot – and remembering how and where some of them went. That took a while, and of course rehearsing on the road is not easy, because we would usually go along in the early afternoon for a bit of a sound check, but at those stadium shows in America they like to let people in at two or three in the afternoon, and we don't have rehearsal rooms or anything. We just used to go on and rehearse one song and run it through a couple of times. I don't know if we ever played the whole thing through before we did it! I think we played all the changeovers, you know. We did a shortened version, like you'd start a song then finish that song and do the tapes and changeovers and things like that and move on to the next. It was quite frightening, the first time we did it in Detroit – we weren't at all certain how it would go.

**One would think the audiences tended to see things Floyd's way.**

Well, in America it was received with stunned, shocked silence quite often! I think by the time we got going in Europe, through the fan base and the Internet and all that sort of stuff, people were aware that this was a possibility, so it was maybe less of a surprise. So that would bolster them up a bit and they'd start cheering quicker and earlier at the beginning, as soon as the heartbeats and stuff started.

**At the beginning of the live album, the crowd are chanting. Was this with expectation or is this just something common with audiences on the continent?**

It's just that some places in Europe love chanting. Every country has its different song in Europe...

**Can you remember which gig that was?**

No, I'm not sure.

**The album was taken from many different locations, wasn't it?**

The live album is recorded from 20 different concerts all over Europe, but the video is just the one night. So I can't remember, I'd have to check...

**The decision to revitalise *Dark Side* could be awarded the same significance as, say, The Who performing *Tommy* or The Beatles deciding to dust off *Sgt Pepper*.**

I don't know. I don't know about significance, it was just really good fun. On the *A Momentary Lapse Of Reason* tour we'd done 'On The Run', and we'd done 'Money', 'Us And Them' and 'Time', so there was not that much more to rehearse, just 'Breathe', 'Any Colour You Like', 'Brain Damage' and 'Eclipse'. We've never really thought that much of doing 'Brain Damage' and 'Eclipse' before because those were the two songs on *Dark Side* that Roger actually sang. I thought I might feel a little uncomfortable singing them, but it was fine.

**But in general the piece was welcomed back with tumultuous applause.**

Yeah, it was brilliant.

**One of several staples of Pink Floyd's live performances is the famous crash sequence during 'On The Run', featuring either a bed or plane flown over the heads of the audience from the back of the stadium to a fiery, explosive end behind the PA.**

On the last tour we played 'On The Run' with the flying bed, because we made a film for it and we thought it would be good. And it gives us a little break as well, to pop off stage for a fag or something.

**But you resurrected the plane for this tour?**

There was always a plane, initially, but the bed seemed appropriate on the *A Momentary Lapse Of Reason* tour, but seemed obsolete again for this one.

**Was the plane crash always part of the live *Dark Side* performance, even in the early days?**

Yes, there was always a plane crash. We had a plane down a wire way back then, back in '73.

It's probably an impossible question to answer, but musicians responsible for other acknowledged indelible rock masterpieces have often been asked whether, at any stage in the preparation of the work in question, it had occurred to them that it was beginning to take on a life of its own. Literally that they were present at the birth of a 'masterpiece'.

An impossible question to answer! [Laughs] We knew it was good, probably the best we had ever done as we were making it. But no, you can't possibly know that it's going to reach the sort of significance that it has.

**It had been performed prior to the recording, hadn't it?**

Yep. We performed *Dark Side* quite a bit before we recorded it. We actually did it for five nights at the Rainbow in London in '72.

**And that was in a slightly different form to what appeared on the record?**

Yes. The 'On The Run' section was a sort of instrumental jam back in those days, and many of the other tracks were slightly different.

**Can you remember back to the original recording sessions for the album?**

I can remember them fairly well, yes.

**The film *Pink Floyd Live At Pompeii* includes historic footage of the band recording the album at Abbey Road.**

An awful lot of time went into writing it in rehearsal rooms, and when we first got it together, took it out and did it in shows, it changed all the time. I can't remember when the specific changes happened and cemented it into being. We had finished the *Live At Pompeii* film a year and a half before and, as they had taken so long to get it ready for release, they wanted to modernise it a little bit because it was already out of date before it was releasable. So they came along to the studio to record us doing a bit of *Dark Side Of The Moon*, to show a bit of our latest album being made in the process and to try and cut it into the film to update it a little.

**Were any of the recording sequences in the film staged for the cameras?**

No, they were as it happened, as far as I remember.

**There was a line you played in the film on the track 'Us And Them', which went [sings the tune] that didn't turn up on the album.**

No, can't remember. You sang it beautifully, though...

**Thank you! It must have been difficult to follow an album like *Dark Side*, and yet you managed to release another classic album with *Wish You Were Here*.**

I'm very fond of *Wish You Were Here*. I think it's better in some ways than *Dark Side Of The Moon*.

**Certainly the beginning of 'Shine On You Crazy Diamond' has been taken as a textbook example of sparse, bluesy guitar.**

Good. My problem with *Dark Side* – and I've said it before and I'll no doubt say it again – was that I thought that Roger's emergence on that album as a great lyric writer was such that he came to overshadow the music in places, and there were moments when we didn't concentrate as hard on the music side of it as we should have done – which is what I voiced to all the band after the making of *Dark Side*. That was absorbed into an effort to try and make the balance between music and the words a better one on *Wish You Were Here*.

**The recording of *Wish You Were Here* was not without upset. At one point concert favourite 'Shine On You Crazy Diamond' had to be rerecorded owing to a slight mishap in the studio.**

It was a new desk and no one was certain how to work it, and the engineer had actually recorded the reverb from the whole of a track on to the drum mics, so it meant that we had spill from things we no longer wanted and reverb all over the drums, and there was no way we could get rid of it. We didn't notice it for a while, we carried on working on it because we always thought, well, that's just the reverb... But then we tried to get rid of it, tried to kill the reverb one day and we couldn't.

**So you had to go back and redo a lot of it?**

I think we ended up redoing the whole of the basic track of drums, bass and all the guitar for 'Shine On You Crazy Diamond'.

**Was it recorded as one piece – both parts of 'Shine On', which book-end the album?**

Yes, then cut in half...I think, if my memory serves me well.

**Is it true that the whole of that song was inspired by the four guitar notes that occur a little way into the piece?**

All that opening stuff came from that guitar phrase. We were rehearsing in a room in King's Cross and that sort of fell out of my guitar somehow and fell out several more times because I liked it, and Roger sort of went, 'Hmm...yes' and it sort of kicked us off. Roger said it was a highly evocative little motif, if you like, and maybe that's what got him thinking about Syd.

**And the story goes that Syd was actually at some of the recording sessions...**

Well, he came in one day, yeah.

**A lot has been talked about over the years regarding Pink Floyd the band, but the individual members have always fought shy of too much personal media**

attention. Not much, for instance, is known about your initial influences as a guitarist.

Blues players, folk players, all sorts of players... Hank Marvin.

**Seriously?**

Yep.

**Anybody significant from the blues point of view?**

Not really that significant, no. Blues a bit later, I suppose.

**Chicago blues as opposed to the original Delta stuff?**

Yep. Yeah, I would think so. My initial early guitar-playing stuff came out of folk music, actually: Pete Seeger and all sorts of other people. I spent a lot of time with friends, and Bob Close, who was in the very early incarnation of Pink Floyd and was one of my childhood friends, he played a lot of blues music and stuff to me. My scale of interest was incredibly broad: folk music through blues and through to straight pop music. I wouldn't say blues was the dominant one.

**What age were you when you started playing?**

I was about 14, probably.

**And what was the first guitar?**

The first guitar I got was a Spanish guitar, I think it was a Tatay. My next door neighbour's mother gave it to him and he was not terribly interested, and so I borrowed it from him and never gave it back. I think.

**What were the first things you played on it – was it folk, or whatever?**

I wanted to be able to play along to Elvis Presley records on it, but I was given by my parents a record called *The Pete Seeger Guitar Tutor Record* and the first band of that record is how to tune the thing, then it teaches you a few chords, and I never got beyond the third lesson. But that got me started, and thereafter I would sit up and listen to Radio Luxemburg on headphones late at night, trying to work out the bass, the rhythm and the lead guitar parts of every record that came on.

**And when did your lifelong association with the Strat begin?**

Hank Marvin had a Strat and it was all I always wanted, but I couldn't afford one. When I was young I had a Hofner Club 60, which was a very nice guitar, and my parents gave me a Telecaster for my 21st birthday, which was when I was living and working in France. That got stolen while it was in transit on a flight to America, and I took that opportunity on the first American tour I went on with Pink Floyd in 1968 to go and buy a Stratocaster. I've played other guitars, but the Strat's my number one choice for versatility.

**When somebody thinks of the archetypal Strat sound, yours is never far from their mind, and yet some of your more famous solos were in fact recorded on other instruments. Take, for instance, the solo to 'Another Brick In The Wall Pt 2': Strat? Nope – played on a Les Paul.**

That was a strange sound, because that solo on 'Another Brick In The Wall' was done through the desk; it was direct-injected straight on to tape from the neck pickup of an old Les Paul with P90s. But then I didn't think it was quite biting enough, and so we then ran the tape out through a bit of wire and plugged it into an amplifier and put a mic in front of it, then I fiddled around with the amp and turned it up a little bit, got some volume on it, and then we mixed that sound and the direct-inject sound back together.

**So, although it's a Les Paul, it's gone through many processes?**

Well, two processes: one direct-inject on to tape and then chugged up after on an amp, and then the two sounds mixed back together.

**That would probably go a long way to explaining the mighty bend in that solo where the B string is bent from a C up a major third to an E – easier on a Les Paul where the string tension is less, but on a Strat it can spell doom for your B string...**

I do it on a Strat live. It's easy enough...

**You don't slide your finger along the string, then?**

No.

**It's all bent from a single fret location?**

Yep, yep... If I need a bit of help, I sometimes pull up on the wang bar at the same time, and I always expect the string to go, but luckily it doesn't too often.

**Have you experimented with other guitars?**

Well, I've tried them all; I just don't like the other guitars as much as a Strat. The third loudish guitar solo on the original record of 'Money' isn't a Strat, it's a guitar called a Lewis, made by a guy called Bill Lewis in Vancouver, Canada. When I was trying that solo out I wanted to get higher than a Strat goes; you can't get up to high E on a Strat, you're three frets short. I do it on tour sometimes, but it takes a lot of bending and it hurts your fingers. This guitar had two full octaves on it, so I did the third solo on this other guitar, which I've still got somewhere. There were also some different guitars used on *A Momentary Lapse Of Reason*; I used a Steinberger on some of it. I had one of those funny little white Steinbergers with three pickups, quite similar to a Strat in some ways with three single-coil pickups. I think all of 'Sorrow' was done originally on that, but you couldn't tell the difference – you'd never know. I could do all those strange bend hits because it's not that whammy in tune and that's one of the sounds on the record which I now have to fake a little bit live on a Strat, because the Strat strings go down completely different – they don't go down anywhere near in tune.

**Was it the Steinberger with the oblong body?**

Yep. One of the little-bodied things, yeah.

*The Final Cut* **is often overlooked as a Floyd album, despite the fact that it has some excellent guitar playing on it. However, due to the well-documented internal problems within the band, it remains your least favourite album.**

Very much to do with the problems within the band. I think there are three great tracks on it. I don't think it's completely a pile of shit, but I think some of the weaker moments on it are filler. I didn't approve of them; I don't think enough went into it. But a lot has been said about that moment in time. I don't think anyone's particularly proud of it. But there are three very good tracks on it: 'The Final Cut', 'The Gunner's Dream' and 'Fletcher Memorial Home' are all really good.

**There's some pretty aggressive guitar playing on that album.**

We went and did some guitar overdubs for that album in Wax studios – Mickie Most's – and we took the big guitar gear. Sometimes I use big stuff, sometimes I use little stuff. We just put the big stuff in and Phil Taylor [Floyd's head of backline] wasn't around. I had someone else who wasn't a roadie or anything take it in. I told him more or less what to plug in and we just turned it on and it instantly sounded great! We did most of the guitar stuff just there and it was so easy. I don't know why, that room for some reason at that particular time just worked so great.

There are moments where you've overdubbed the guitar parts to produce harmony lines.

Well, there's some of that on *Animals*, as well.

**I was thinking about one track in particular on *Final Cut*...**

Well, I don't know. I can't remember; I haven't listened to that album for 13 years!

**Apart from the four central players in the band, Floyd have occasionally called on other musicians to lend a hand.**

If I remember correctly, we actually used Lee Ritenour on one part of *The Wall*, on a rhythm part for 'One Of My Turns'. Mike Landau, I think, played on 'One Slip'; there are these funny little notes [he sings them] which originally came out of a thing I was doing with Mike Manzanera. My timing is not that precise and sometimes those things get tough, and when they do I'll get someone else in to play them. If I can think of a part but I can't actually do it as well as I'd like to hear it done, then I'll get someone else who can.

**Coming as it did after a very public split within the band, the *Momentary Lapse* album and tour must have proved that many still had faith in the band's durability.**

It wasn't really something I needed particularly proven to myself. I know that through our early years, through *Dark Side Of The Moon*, *Wish You Were Here*, I was the lead singer and I was the lead guitar – I mean I was a large part of the sound, and a large part of the writing force in the band – it wasn't something that I particularly needed to prove. Obviously how the audiences would react to it was something that one didn't know, but I didn't need to prove it to myself.

Throughout the band's career, it's possible to find references to previous works nestled within contemporary songs. Recently, for instance, the Strat-enhanced 'whale song' from 'Echoes' turns up once again on *The Division Bell*. Is there a conscious plan to insert these 'bookmarks' occasionally?

Not really. I mean finding the old whale noise out of 'Echoes' and sticking it in whatever it was in more recently is just a little joke. It's nice to jog people's memories. You can jog people like that in the way that you can jog your own mind and emotions with a smell you haven't smelled for years – going into your parents' house when you haven't been there for a long time or one of those things – and to do that with one of our little things, I thoroughly enjoy.

There seem to be certain lyrical references, too...

Obviously you'd have to talk to Roger about most of that, most of the lyrical theme throughout the years. But it's not a conscious thing to try to follow; it's just the areas that one's mind tends to move towards when you get into a contemplative mood when writing.

Are aware of the so-called Publius Enigma?

No, I don't know about that. What's that?

As soon as *The Division Bell* was released, the Internet was awash with rumours that the album's cover and musical content were encoded with clues that would lead the crafty cryptographers among Floyd's fans to a 'tangible prize'. The rumours were started by an anonymous character calling himself 'Publius'. So, for the last year, theories have abounded – some faintly plausible, some frankly ridiculous.

I think some people have got over-active imaginations, myself.

Even the site of the cover photographs, our very own Ely, is allegedly at risk from hordes of American Floyd fans, intent, it would seem, on excavation.

Poor farmer!

**So there are no hidden clues musically, lyrically, photographically or otherwise on *The Division Bell*?**

No.

**There was meant to be a date on the tour last year when the word 'Publius' appeared in lights at the foot of the stage, and on the Earls Court video someone scrawls 'Enigma' on the rear screen, which would seem to imply that someone's up to something.**

Not to my knowledge. I don't know, maybe Marc Brickman, who's keen on the Internet and stuff, was playing along. I haven't seen it – I hadn't noticed really.

**What about *Pulse*: it's an analogue recording, which would seem to contradict the Floyd's hi-tech stance.**

Does it? I disagree.

**Well, the world's gone digital...**

The drums and bass and stuff on *Momentary Lapse Of Reason* – we did all the backing tracks analogue, then we synced up to a Mitsubishi 32-track and did vocals and lots of the overdubs digitally. I mean, the technology, the progress in analogue equipment hasn't stopped because digital equipment has come along. The reason for using digital is because of ease of use and because there's no tape hiss and stuff, but I defy you to hear any bloody tape hiss on modern tape machines. And whether one is persuading oneself or whether it's a reality that there's a warmth and a presence to analogue recording, I'm not a 100 per cent certain. I know one time we did quite a hard test in the difference between recording a drum kit digitally and recording it analogue, and we could all notice that the sense of space and the sense of air that surrounded the drum kit was significantly better on analogue, because taking to pieces the incredibly complicated sound wave forms of reverbs and echoes and sibilance and transients, and translating that all down through an analogue to digital converter into little numbers, and then converting them all back again... Some people think that 44,000 of them a second is quite enough.

**When the masters of the live album had been pressed, Floyd rejected them and held out for better quality – putting the album's release a month behind.**

Yep, that's right. James Guthrie rejected them, they came back and then he sent me the ones when he thought they were good. I never listened to the difference. I did try to listen to the difference between some of them at home, but by the time you've got up, opened your CD drawer and put another one in and got to the same place and played it again, I couldn't honestly tell the difference. You really have to have two of them running more or less in sync and just be able to flick A/B between the two and I never did that. James and Doug Sax at the Mastering Lab in Los Angeles are two people whose ears I trust better than anyone else's in the world; they're both agreed that more could and should be done, and we tracked something down to some clocking problems and we believe that these ones now are as good as we can get.

**The album benefits from having been mixed in Q Sound, too.**

Yeah, it's quite an interesting thing. It's not the same as being in a hall obviously; it's something you have to handle with a great deal of care and be very careful what you put into it and what you use it for. For most applications it doesn't suit, I mean most actual instruments, most percussive things – drums and stuff – it really doesn't work for. But for some of that audience sound, some of the sound effects and the quad tapes, where it doesn't matter if these quad voices sound a bit faint and strange, there it's great. You can add a little ambience, a whole sound around the stereo. It means you've got your stereo picture in front of you, six feet wide or whatever it is on your stereo system, and we are getting some effects and things that come right out to here in quite ordinary home speakers, and that's great.

**I noticed that the explosion at the end of 'On The Run' seems to travel right over your head.**

Yeah...

***Pulse*, of course, has a winking red light on its spine with liner notes ascribing some sort of significance. Really?**

It's a winking red light! Someone came up with the idea – Storm Thorgerson, I think – of having this little LED flashing. It's good fun, it's sort of a visual representation of the heartbeat at the beginning of *Dark Side Of The Moon*, if you like. It helps you find it when you're staggering around your living room late at night, with the lights dimmed down a little bit and your tired old eyes can't pick out one CD from another on the shelf...and it's a gimmick!

**And, according to those liner notes, a bogus car alarm.**

You can leave it in your car and try it...

**But as far as the music on *Pulse* is concerned, it has to be said that much of the music is very similar – as is the personnel – to that found on the last live Floyd epic, *Delicate Sound of Thunder*...**

We wouldn't have done a live album or released a live video if we hadn't been doing *Dark Side Of The Moon* at that stage. I think a lot of people would like to have *Dark Side Of The Moon* live and on video, but we wouldn't have put it out, we wouldn't have bothered with the live album on this tour, although there are significant amounts of people that would like to have a live record of the shows that they've been to see. But I don't think we would have justified it without the fact that we were doing *Dark Side Of The Moon*, so that was where we came from. At one point we nearly put out just the *Dark Side Of The Moon* thing but then it was too short, so we thought we might as well give them the whole lot again, and fought and fought with the record company to keep the price down to a nice reasonable price for a double CD.

**How involved were the members of the band in the planning stages for the live show?**

We're very involved, all through the process. I mean we couldn't do it all ourselves: one has to delegate, and we have other people in to make things, and we have other people in whose ideas we usually like. I mean, Storm has been doing work with us since I've been doing work with us, virtually. He was involved in the cover on the *Saucerful of Secrets* album, which was the first one I was on, and so he's part of our thinking team. Marc Brickman has been doing stuff with us since *The Wall* live, and Mark Fisher has been doing stuff with us and Roger since God knows when. So yes, we have a team of people, all of whom give us their views and their thoughts, and we take it on from there. We have lots of meetings where people suggest ideas, we put forth ideas and people go away and try to make them work. So we're involved all the way through in everything.

**When you talk to someone who attended last year's shows, they tend to refer to being almost spiritually moved by the whole thing. Is there a deliberate attempt to create that kind of feeling in people?**

It's entirely deliberate, yeah. We're trying to make people have an experience that is meaningful in their lives and we want to move them; we want them to come out thinking differently to when they went in. It's not just entertainment, not for me, anyway. One gets to the point where there's a very difficult line to be drawn in there, where some people start thinking that because we are trying to do that and succeeding to some degree, that we have some mysterious handle on matters of a much more deep meaning, and so the confusion between that and some sort of religious import comes about. Sometimes one finds oneself skirting a little close to the edge, but we don't have answers for anything; we're just musicians trying our very best.

**It must be hard taking some of the comments on board when you're on stage all the time and have never seen the show from the audience's point of view.**

No, I never have seen a show. I'd like to. I've tried being out at the front by the mixing desk and playing my parts there and watching it on stage, but you're so far out of sync that you can't actually do it.

**Supposedly the only problem for Pink Floyd now is how to follow the *Division Bell* live shows.**

That's something for you to worry about, not for me. You just do the next thing; the terms 'bigger' and 'better' don't really mean anything. You just do the best you can do at any given moment.

**Surely the show can't get any bigger or better?**

They said you couldn't get any better or any bigger when we did *Dark Side Of The Moon* in 1973, and 22 years later you're asking me the same question!

# BRIAN MAY

SEPTEMBER 1992

*This interview with Brian May took place shortly before the release of his solo album* Back To The Light. *Freddie Mercury's death was still comparatively recent, and so it was inevitable that, despite the official reasons for talking to me, we'd end up reminiscing about Queen. But first things first. Just about everybody knows that Brian built his famous 'Red Special' guitar himself, before Queen were even princesses...*

**So how's the guitar actually wearing? It must be going on 23 years old.**

It's amazing how it's holding up. The only thing we've ever replaced are the machineheads. Everything else is original. The frets are very worn down but they still work, and I wouldn't like to touch them until I have to. It does have a good feel.

**What about the frets?**

The frets were one of the few things I actually bought for the guitar. Everything else was junk. I bought the fretwire from Clifford Essex in Cambridge Circus. They used to publish a magazine called *BMG* – banjo, mandolin and guitar – which was rooted in old acoustic instruments and older players, bluegrass players, really fascinating stuff. You could get anything in that shop, though; it was one of the only places that you could get banjo strings to put on the top, because in the old days you couldn't get thin guitar strings. So we used to go up there and get our .008" banjo strings and put them on the top, and it really transformed what you could do.

**You've always used a combination of very light-gauge strings with a very heavy pick – the notorious sixpence.**

It is heavy, but I hold it lightly to compensate. What I like is that I can feel the movement and it all gets transmitted to the fingers. To me, it's a very sensitive way of playing.

**How's the stock of sixpences holding up?**

Fine, we've got thousands! Bags full, anyway…

**Do you get them sent in by fans?**

Some people send them in, for which we're really grateful. But Jobby [Brian's guitar tech] gets the occasional bag from the bank – well, he used to. I don't know if that still goes on – maybe they've all gone by now.

**What do you think of the new five-pence pieces – any good for a plectrum?**

They'd be all right. I've played with just about everything: dimes, pfennigs and all sorts of things. It doesn't bother me that much. The sixpence is nice because it has that serrated edge, and it can give you a bit of extra 'rasp' if you turn it sideways.

**The trem on your guitar is still holding up, too?**

Yeah. I'm very proud of that because my dad and I designed that from scratch, and in those days there was not a tremolo that really worked and had little enough friction to stay in tune.

**How close in design is it to some of the more modern trem designs – like the Floyd Rose, for example?**

What they have in common is the knife-edge system. The Kahler works on ball bearings, which I rejected because I didn't think it was reproducible enough, but Kahler did very well with that idea. But Floyd Rose went the other way with the knife edge, which I'd already gone with. The difference is that I had a separate bridge section, and whereas I designed the whole guitar to be low friction, they designed theirs to be maximum friction, which is two ways of solving the same problem. So with mine, the strings slip through the nut with very little friction, so that's the way it stays in tune, whereas the Kahler people clamp them at the nut, so you don't get any movement at all. The same with the bridge: the bridge is a part of the Kahler and works with it, but mine is separate and has low friction because it's on rollers.

**What with the AC30s and the guitar and so on, you must have got your gear sorted out pretty early on...**

I was lucky. I knew the sound that I wanted, in my head, and I just happened to find this old AC30. I played one which belonged to a friend of mine first of all. I played through it and thought, 'That's it, that's what I want', because of the warmth. And with the treble boost you can push it hard, smoothly into distortion. And it has this lovely articulation on the top...

**On the album sleeve of *Back To The Light* you say that you use both old and new AC30s. Are these the vintage reissues?**

Yeah, that's right. There was a period in the middle which wasn't too good. I don't like any of the transistor stuff and some of the modifications didn't work, but nowadays they're making them just like the old ones and they're brilliant.

**Your live setup was twelve AC30s, split into four banks of three, each group with a different effect. Were they all on at once?**

Not all of the time. Really, I played off the monitors. The bigger the venue, the less you can hear your own amps anyway. So I just played off the monitors. I'd have them all on if I needed a confidence boost, or just for the sheer enjoyment of the sound, but it was fundamentally one AC30 that made that noise, which I liked. And then I used a delay, which in the beginning was an old, modified Echoplex, to produce a single repeat with the regeneration turned down. That came back through a separate AC30 so they could both distort to their hearts' content and not interfere with each other. You wouldn't get this intermodulation distortion; they would both have this full-blown, distorted sound, which blended together really nicely. It was always a dream of mine to do that. Eventually I had the other repeat to make the three parts, so then I could make harmonies by playing along with the tape.

**Have you ever been tempted away from your tried and tested gear by anything that you've seen?**

I've tried out a lot of things on the way. I've tried most of the guitar synths and stuff, but I just prefer my instrument: it's very human and it makes the right noise. I do play through Zoom boxes these days, which I enjoy; I think they're a good little piece of apparatus. They're great for each end of the spectrum: for the full-blown solo or for clean rhythm. The only thing that perhaps they don't handle is that intermediate area, which the AC30 is very good at – where you can strike a chord and it's distorted, but you can still hear what the chord is.

**I've always maintained that there are very few guitarists who have an instantly recognisable sound – ones who would pass the 'traffic light test', where you're in a car at the lights and someone has a tape or the radio on in the next car, and you only hear a short excerpt, but you just know who it is – and you're definitely in that category...**

That's a very nice compliment! Thank you, that's great.

I can still remember the first time I heard your playing. It was on the *Old Grey Whistle Test* on BBC2, where Bob Harris played 'Keep Yourself Alive' and added that the bit in the middle wasn't a synthesiser. In fact, the early Queen albums had the line 'and nobody played synth' in amongst the liner notes.

My god, yes – I remember.

**You established some elements of your sound very early on: the stacked harmonies and so on. Was that a fixed idea from the word go?**

It was a dream to do that from way, way back. I was always fascinated with harmony, anyway, from the '60s records that I grew up with: The Everly Brothers, Buddy Holly And The Crickets. But I also felt that the guitar became a different instrument when it was turned up to maximum and fully distorted – it was no longer a polyphonic instrument, really. So it seemed to be crying out to be orchestrated, and I could hear just what it would be like in my head. This is long before Queen and even before Smile, which was the group before that. Then there were a few things that reinforced that feeling. For instance, Jeff Beck's hit 'Hi Ho Silver Lining' had a bit in the middle where he double-tracked the guitar and, just for a moment, it breaks into harmony. I don't know if it was by accident – I should ask him one day – but I used to play that over and over again and just revel in that sound, and I thought if you could get hold of that sound and make a feature of it, and if it were not just two guitars but as many as you needed to make a proper arrangement, the possibilities would be endless. So, as soon as we got in the studio, I was on the trail.

**You must have an established formula for achieving your harmony sound. So where do you start?**

I try not to get into any ruts. If it sounds like anything that's gone before I try to get rid of it and step out somewhere else. But it does sound like me. There's a certain thing that happens with the guitar...but where do I start? I think it starts in the head. I find the best ideas come from when you're not actually touching the guitar, otherwise your fingers fall into the same positions and you get stuck in ruts. Also, the best solos often come from the best songs, because there's something in the song to feed off – a chord structure, a feeling or an atmosphere. That's why it was so great working with Freddie and the band; there was always something unusual to work guitar into, and usually it was in some weird key as well. And that helped, because then you have no preconceived ideas. So if you do come up with something, it's going to be something unusual.

**Do you think of it in terms of a melody and then harmonise it, or does the whole thing come as a block concept?**

I've always thought of the guitar as another voice, so I start with a voice, which is answering or singing along with the vocal, and from time to time you can hear a place where other voices would come in, like backing harmonies, which then become part of it.

**A sort of choral thing?**

Yes. It's just a question of realising what is in your head, because I find I can usually hear roughly what I'm trying to get to. Occasionally, there's a happy accident that leads me in a nice direction.

**How many tracks do you use for one of your multi-track guitar lines?**

It varies. It's been anything from three to, on this album, I think the maximum was about 30. On 'The Dark', I wanted this real frightening wall of sound coming out of nowhere to contrast this very small voice – the kid in the cot. You can get a long way with three parts, and with four you can conquer the world, I think! And after that, it's a case of either bringing in separate whole blocks to answer the first block, or working on the tone colour of the whole thing. You can put octaves in and you can do different things in one octave from those in another, or you can have a single line and different blocks answering it. In the case of 'Killer Queen', which I still like, it was just three separate voices, and they go in and out of harmony, but they play their own tune. I enjoy things like that, where they have a life of their own.

**The Queen harmony vocal idea was pretty much fully developed even on your first album, and it seems like the most significant developments since have been on the part of technology catching up. But it must have been very difficult to start with...**

True, you had to bounce things as you went along. It's a bit of a shame, really, because when we go back to those old multi-tracks, there's nothing you can do in some cases. Somebody remixed 'You're My Best Friend' the other day, and I always thought it would be nice to rebalance that stuff, but when we got the tape out, it was all on one track, so that's it.

**I was thinking recently that if anything was a prime candidate for digital remastering, it would be the early Queen albums...**

Well, we've been working on digitally remastering them all. There is a lot you can do when you get back to the original mix tape, but for us the mix was all part of the creative process, and I don't really want to remix stuff. We have let a few people remix a few things, just for fun, but normally that was all part of the creative process and I wouldn't want to change it; it had a certain magic at the time.

**It's a little like the difference between mono and stereo Beatles mixes.**

Yeah, you lose something...

**I guess you'd upset the purists, even if it meant an upgrade in overall sound quality.**

Mmmm, well I like most of those original mixes, but they were incredibly complex to do, and without any automation. We all used to be at the desk – four of us, plus Roy Thomas-Baker and Mike Stone – all six of us with fingers on the faders, and sometimes we'd work 30-hour mixes. At the end, you were totally blind and deaf to it. You'd go to sleep and wake up the next morning, and the mix was still going on! Weird…very intense. But they definitely have a special quality, those early mixes.

**The pioneer spirit. But that's what I meant about technology having caught you up. For instance, have you seen the Digitech Vocalist? Instant Queen vocals!**

Oh yeah, I've used one. The beginning of 'Driven By You' is just one voice, put through the Vocalist. I did it live, but it's only one take – great machines!

**Going into the studio now, you must know exactly what you want.**

Well, I try not to stay with the same methods. Certainly when I was setting up my studio in the country, which Jobby put together for me, the nice thing was that we didn't do anything standard. We didn't take anything for granted, whether it was mics, positions of drums or anything. We started everything from scratch, which is nice because people get so stuck in their ways: you walk into a professional studio and things are always done in a certain way. The guy says 'The drums go over there…', and it's nice to get out of that and just find your own sounds with no preconceived ideas.

**What are your favourite studios? You must have seen inside most of them over the years.**

You name it. We've been in most London studios, and I sort of lapped up whatever was around – they all had their advantages and disadvantages. All rooms sound different. There was one little overdubbing room in Air Studios which was tiny – it was about as big as an armchair – but we used to put the

AC30 in there, and put the mic facing the window and get this amazing sound. A sort of 'bottle-y' sound – amazing. You can use all those different colours. There was a very nice room in Wessex – I don't know whether it's still there – but it was the main room, where we recorded 'We Will Rock You', and that was all acoustic stuff. It's just us stamping on boards and clapping over and over again, and that had a particularly nice sound, I thought.

**There wasn't a bass drum on that?**

No, no drums whatsoever – just feet on the boards and handclaps.

**The new album starts with an entirely different version of 'We Will Rock You', that is to say, the traditional Christmas carol. Was that kind of polarisation with the Queen song intentional?**

Er, yes. [Laughs] I'm a bit wary of explaining things, but the theme of the album is 'back to the light', and I think throughout the whole album you can hear this person who is very small and very confused, confronted by different situations as they roll past him. That's what it's meant to be. So I started off with the idea that there's this little baby in the cradle, he's completely in the dark and the dark is something really frightening. The album, in a very chaotic way, is all different glimpses and visions of roads on the way to try and find the light. So you hear this child at the beginning and at the end, and you hear him struggling in various forms throughout the album. It was convenient that it was 'We Will Rock You', because here was this nursery rhyme and the version Queen did was very big and macho. Total opposites.

**It must have been very strange making an album containing many familiar Queen attributes, but without Freddie.**

Very strange. It was always a project that was in parallel with Queen, because we always had a positive attitude to people doing stuff outside the band, getting new experiences and bringing them back into the band. But it did become something very different at the end, when Freddie went. I started to realise that this was a kind of bridge toward the next part of life, whatever that may be. I always felt close to Freddie in the studio, whether he was there or not, because we worked together so intensively over the years. So I can still hear him talking to me when I'm doing some of this stuff, especially when I'm trying to sing – which has not been that easy. But I wanted to do it, because I didn't want anyone else to be speaking my ideas on this album when it was such a personal statement. So it was good for me to imagine Freddie sitting there. In the beginning, Freddie didn't have all the powers that he wanted to have as a vocalist; he worked to achieve those and improved as he worked over the years. So I just took that as a good example. I thought, 'If I'm going to sing this album, and I am – there's no going back – I'm going to have to work at it', and I treated it rather like a weight-training programme. I went in there every day and sung my guts out, and tried to reach further every day. It's amazing what you can do if you really try. I was quite stunned, because in the beginning I was struggling with it – all those regions around top A – and in the end, in 'Resurrection', I got up to a D above that, without going into falsetto, which was quite a little crusade for me. I was amazed that I could actually do that. It's another question as to whether I can do it on stage, but at least it happened; at least I know I can get there if I really try hard enough.

**When you first performed 'Too Much Love Will Kill You' at Freddie's tribute concert at Wembley, you played it solo, and there was a point where you paused and the audience went a little wild. You seemed to register surprise...**

Relief, more than anything else! It was a big step to do it and I knew I had to do it, and I wanted to do it for Freddie. It wasn't that the song had a particular relevance – it wasn't about AIDS – but it was a song that I felt was the best way of expressing myself, and also the best thing I had to offer at the time. It was terrifying, I've got to tell you. It was the first time I'd sat at a piano in public and did that. It was in front of 72,000 people in the stadium, half a billion people around the world, and so it took an incredible amount of getting hold of myself to do it. As I was walking over to the piano I was still thinking,

'Should I really be doing this?' So it was difficult, it really was. It's so easy to do in rehearsal and yet, when that moment comes, something happens to your throat. Plus it really brought me back into touch with what was going on; suddenly there wasn't a big show happening, there was only me doing my personal little bit.

**At the tribute and subsequently in Seville, it must have been great to be surrounded by so many people who openly acknowledge Queen as a huge influence. I'm thinking of Extreme in particular.**

It's fantastic, a great compliment and I think Extreme are great. If they're going to carry the banner, they're very worthy. They're all incredible musicians and they have this feeling that they can cross all the boundaries, which we had, too. The new album is unbelievable. They're so adventurous and they have a habit of pulling it all off, whichever area they go into.

**I remember the medley of Queen songs they did at Wembley…**

That took a lot of courage, more than people realise. In front of our audience, to do our songs, it could have gone awfully wrong. If they hadn't hit the right note it would have worked against them, and they must have known that.

**The minute they got into it, the audience were with them because they were doing it right.**

Yeah, incredible. They're excellent musicians, no doubt about it.

**What was the 'Guitar Legends' concert in Seville like for you?**

Fun. Really great fun. I had the opportunity to get all my favourite people together. What made it fun on the night was the fact that we knew what we were doing. We put enough rehearsal in to know we were going to be OK; it wasn't people just going up there and jamming. I was particularly keen on the idea that, for instance, Joe Satriani should play with Steve Vai. This is an opportunity for interaction; it's a one-off and a chance to do something special. They both played on my stuff and we all played with Joe Walsh, which was really a great buzz, pounding out 'Rocky Mountain Way'...

**Although the riff went wrong...**

Ahhh... You noticed that!

**Only because it's one of my all-time favourite riffs.**

It was very funny. I guess Joe Walsh started it, but the two drummers heard it in opposite senses – you can see we're all laughing.

**At one point, you can see Nuno turn to someone and shrug, like, 'What's going on?'**

Hmmm, strange...

**And you all got to play with Paul Rodgers.**

I know. What a great thrill. I've got this attitude that if you're going to show guitarists off in their best light, you don't just put them on stage and let them weedle around all night. It needed structure, and some of the greatest guitar songs have been the riff songs – it's not just about being techno-flash – so I immediately thought of Paul Rodgers. Sadly, [Paul] Kossoff isn't there, but I knew every guitarist in the world would enjoy playing 'All Right Now'.

**It must have been some challenge to oversee that. You had to learn some of Steve Vai's stuff too.**

Yeah! My God! What a fool to even try!

**But you played 'Liberty' from Steve's album, and that brings it right back to your influence – the tightly arranged, harmony guitar thing...**

He said that 'God Save The Queen' was an inspiration for that.

**You can hear that, certainly...**

It was very interesting to see the different things happening on the different nights.

**You were there for all of them?**

Not all of it; I saw the last three and saw the rest on video afterwards. I always thought that the best things were the things that were the most prepared. I believe that more and more. It's great to improvise, but you should have a structure. You get much more out of each other that way, rather than all hanging around in the dark waiting to see which chord comes next.

**How did the Ford advert come about?**

I had some time off while I was working in Los Angeles, and I was down by the hotel pool. There were these two outrageous guys, splashing about in the pool, and they just came up and asked if I'd ever considered doing anything in the advertising world, and I said no. They said, 'Do you want to?' and I said, 'Not particularly', but they suggested running a few things by me to see if I was interested. Anyway, they came up with this slogan, which in the beginning was 'Everything We Do, We Do For You', which was uncannily similar to the Bryan Adams song which came out a little while afterwards. I thought it sounded a bit slushy and didn't really relate to it. But then they came back and said it was changed to 'Everything We Do Is Driven By You' and my initial thought was 'Yuk, I don't think I can do anything with that either', because it just sounded like motor cars and I'm not interested in singing songs about motor cars. But then I thought 'Driven By You...' and ping! The lights went on. I thought of it as the power struggle that goes on in relationships, which is very much what my album is about anyway. So this song sort of sprang to mind in my brain, and I went to the bathroom with a little cassette recorder and sang the song into it, and it was virtually done at that point. Things do happen quickly sometimes. I could hear it as I wanted it to be and I could also hear a few little modifications that would suit their purposes, too.

**So you didn't see any footage from the ad before you wrote the music?**

No... Or did I? [Long pause]

**I was thinking about a comparison to when Queen did the music for *Flash Gordon*.**

I think I might have seen a rough demo. It wasn't actual footage, it was more of a mock-up of what it might be.

**So in a way it was similar to the *Flash* and *Highlander* projects?**

In a way. I thought that I've spent most of my life thinking of advertising as a sort of dirty business, but in fact, the same mechanisms work: you get input from someone, you get inspired and you give back. So I enjoyed it, and they were great to work with. Very quick, very efficient, and that appeals to me because I'm a person who doesn't naturally do that – I tend to pore over things and get too involved and too perfectionist. I produced a first version of that track in a week and they had it on the TV the next night! They really don't mess about. I was impressed, and it also gave me a lot of momentum for the album. And it also gave me a hit, which I never expected.

**They cut the guitar solo from the TV version.**

There were various versions, I think...

**The guitar solo is in the version showing at cinemas...**

Oh yeah, that's right.

**...which is where you want to hear it because of the sound system!**

The original 90-second TV version had the guitar solo in it, but it wasn't shown very often. They showed the 60-second version a lot more. Then there was a 10-second and a 5-second version – I did all the edits for them. I did most of them, anyway. Occasionally they would come back with, 'Do you think we can get away with this?' and I'd go, 'Hmmm...'

**Have you done anything else in the TV or radio commercial vein?**

No, I wouldn't want to become a jingle writer as such. It was just a single venture.

**Presumably, the next step is to tour with the new material...**

Yes. I'd like to start somewhere not too much in the public eye, because it takes the pressure off, so I'll probably go to Argentina or somewhere like that, do some rehearsals and some gigs, and see what transpires.

**But you're used to doing challenging material on stage. I mean, 'Bohemian Rhapsody' can't have been a picnic...**

I think we copped out with 'Bohemian Rhapsody'. We never really played it all the way through. But we never played to a tape, either. I mean, with the middle bit, we'd put the record on and get off stage, so there was never any doubt that we were playing live while we were on stage.

**The middle section was time for a costume change.**

That's right; change the frocks! But you're right, we did bluff our way through everything. It's a nice way to be. I don't think you need all the backing tapes and samples. A live show is something separate and you do different things in a live show to what you do on a record. Personally I don't get any joy from seeing people reproduce their records exactly on stage; I want to see something which is special for the night. It can sound different and I don't mind, as long as it all makes sense in context.

**Queen certainly had a reputation as one of rock's most impressive live acts... Are you going to try and follow that tradition?**

I'm not going to try and be Queen in any sense. I want to do my own thing. Stage shows become a little formulaic, and a lot of the things we brought in are now very commonplace. But I don't really want to compete in that world; I want to do it a bit differently, something a bit more personal. I say this now, of course; we'll see how it goes.

**For Queen the stage show was never a prop, though.**

No, that's right...

**For some acts it's a question of, 'This is a slow dull song, let's have some lasers...'**

[Laughs] Yeah. But I'd like to do it a little different in the future, more in line with the album, which has a different slant to it. I do want it to be an exciting show, though. I want people to come out feeling like they got their money's worth and got a little shocked as well. I think a good stage show should be a little frightening.

**So, if you could look back at Queen's official reign, what, for you, were literally 'the days of our lives'?**

Well, there were lots of them, really. We were lucky enough to have a broad base, you know? We were never just in one country and so we moved around, and we went where the action was sometimes; we went where it was hot. So there were lots of moments where we were able to kind of crystallise, like the first moments in South America, which were incredible because the time was exactly right. The material had actually got there and people knew it, and it was a shock to see people actually singing all our songs in English, in this place called Argentina, which is such a long way away and has a totally different language. So that was incredible: Argentina, Brazil, all those frontiers. We were a very good working unit, and we discovered that we could actually play stadiums and pull it off, and make an event out of it. So they were great times, you know: the last *Magic* tour in which we went to Budapest, and that was another great step into the new world because you couldn't play behind the Iron Curtain up until that point. You couldn't get people from those countries to see you. It's all changed very rapidly now, but at that time people from Poland and East Berlin, Czechoslovakia were able to get to that concert, and it was an incredible meeting point. I think the band was a very good, functioning unit.

**How did Czechoslovakia take to Queen?**

Amazing, with open arms. We could have sold out so many nights in those stadiums if we'd been allowed to stay there longer. It was amazing – I'll never forget that. The final tour was pretty hot, too: the final gig at Knebworth, which is the one that, unfortunately, we didn't capture on video, except a few documentary clips.

**The Wembley concert certainly stands as a testament to how good a live band Queen was.**

It was a good band. I'm very proud of what we did. I'm not always proud of what I did. There are moments where I'm glad that I've moved on, even now. I can look at it and I don't mind it so much – I can see all the mistakes and inadequacies – but I don't mind so much because this is history now... [Sits reflectively for a few moments] On the whole, Queen was a good old band, really.

# PETER FRAMPTON

OCTOBER 1998

*To those who think that Peter Frampton really did 'come alive' in 1975, it will probably come as quite a shock to learn that he enjoyed considerable celebrity for many years beforehand. His band The Herd, for instance, were to be found giving Orpheus a good run for his money as long ago as 1967 with their hit 'From The Underworld' and, after that, Peter could be spotted playing awe-inspiring guitar with the amazing Humble Pie. Many will have fond memories of the free Hyde Park concert in 1971, for example, where the Pie won game, set and match in a head-to-head rockathon with Grand Funk Railroad.*

*'We blew them away,' Peter told me emphatically, and he's not wrong. I know; I was there.*

*Humble Pie's live album from the same period,* Rockin' The Fillmore, *stands as one of the most definitive live statements from any band. Ever. To this point Frampton happily concurred.*

**A few reminiscences, then, about Humble Pie.**

I grew up a lot in that band. Steve Marriott and I were musically incredibly compatible; the music was really fiery, but so was our relationship. We were going to call the band 'Chalk And Cheese'! We had a good sense of humour about it, and when we met up later on we had a great time, and it was a privilege working with him again. I think Humble Pie was a natural thing for me to do, though our direction had really narrowed. I enioyed what we were doing, but the original Pie played everything from acoustic stuff to balls-to-the-wall boogie, y'know? I continued to love all those sorts of things, but then we were sort of narrowed into one tiny area, which became kinda monotonous to me. The material I was writing at the time was suitable for the first few Humble Pie records, but there was just no outlet for it in the end, and I felt that my kind of creativity was going nowhere, even though the last thing I did with them was *Rockin' The Fillmore*, and it was pretty evident that it was a great band.

**Even before Humble Pie, you had revealed yourself as a prodigious talent on guitar, fronting The Herd with fresh-faced enthusiasm at the tender age of 16.**

Throughout that period I was very much into Kenny Burrell, Wes Montgomery, Joe Pass, Django, very much into the jazz side. Everybody seemed to have locked into the blues thing and Eric Clapton, who of course I listened to as well, and would not miss a concert with him and The Bluesbreakers, naturally. It seemed that everyone was going that way, but I wanted to be a little more original. My style had always lent itself in its formative years very early to more of a melodic approach, y'know. Hank Marvin was my hero; he's the reason why I'm playing guitar today. The jazzy, more melodic side of it seemed to appeal to me instantly, but since then I've broadened to take in everything. I think that's what made Humble Pie so interesting, and I'm told that it was one of the first bands to have the sort of R&B backtrack with a more jazzy, bluesy guitar over the top.

**Indeed. Check out the *Rockin' The Fillmore* album today, and despite its 'vintage' status, most of the music sounds as fresh and vibrant as ever. But it was after you left that band that your career stood on the launchpad ready for megastardom.**

I left Humble Pie before the *Fillmore* album was released – in fact, I left as we were looking at the album cover. I told the guys I was leaving and they thought I was crazy, and then when the album was released and went zooming up the charts, I agreed with them. But it was just something I had to do, and I felt much better being in control of my own material and stuff like that. So I set about starting again – not exactly at the bottom, but the first two albums didn't sell 100,000 copies between them, which is pretty much starting again, y'know? It took another four or five years before we recorded *Frampton Comes Alive*.

**Talking of which, the kind of success which followed that album was enough to turn a young man's head.**

It was very exciting, yeah. It wasn't new to me exactly – success, I mean – having been in The Herd and having been very successful with them in Europe, and with Humble Pie, which had spilled over into the States pretty big time. This was bigger than all of them put together, and so it was just on a much bigger scale. Everybody says it must be terrible, but it's not; it's so exciting. You are in the profession to be, hopefully, in everyone's record collection – that's the dream, isn't it? So therefore you take what comes with it. You are going to lose your privacy, your life is going to be an open book to everybody, and you're not going to be able to go to the local record store and hang out without being bugged by people. It gets annoying, sure, but that's what you wanted – put up with it, don't complain about it. The hysteria and the screaming and fans chasing the car is all very exciting. It's not that bad. People would give their eye teeth for a week in that situation!

**According to *Wayne's World*, *Frampton Comes Alive* was issued to every American suburban kid at birth during the late '70s. But the fact that it was a live album makes the 20 million seller that bit more of a phenomenon – it's one hell of a lot of albums, after all.**

It's a lot, yeah. [Looks wistful] It changed the record industry, especially in the United States. It was explained to me a few years ago that music is a business, but at that point, the record industry woke up and thought, 'We can sell multi-multi-millions here…' and that's when it really became much more of a business. I mean, my album was first, but then there was *Rumours* by

Fleetwood Mac, which did another 20-something million, and it goes on and on. Then Michael Jackson came along...

**Another project you were involved with a few years back found you playing with your old school chum David Bowie on the *Glass Spider* tour.**

In '86 I was out promoting the *Premonition* record, and I was in Chicago when I got a call from David, and he said that he just wanted to tell me how much he enjoyed my record and that he enjoyed my playing on it. I said thanks very much, me old mate! And he said, 'What do you think about coming over to Switzerland and doing some guitar on my new record?' I said, 'What flight?' [Laughs] We'd been to school together, we'd played guitar together on the school steps, and I would go to his concerts and he would come to mine. He'd supported Humble Pie in '69 and our careers had gone off in different directions, but I'd never even thought that we'd play together on the same stage. So it was a terrific honour to do that, and he gave me virtually free rein to play whatever I wanted; I didn't have to stick to the record and it was a thrill. I mean, there was me out front playing the intro to 'Rebel Rebel' and 'Jean Genie' – c'mon, it was great. I'm a huge Bowie fan as well as his friend, and so I have a lot of respect for him.

**Playing guitar for Bowie involves dipping into a great many styles; first there was Mick Ronson, then there was the Fripp and Adrian Belew eras...**

Basically I just listened to all the stuff to refresh my memory, and stayed within the guidelines of what all the different guitarists had done, but played it in my own style. But it was a long show at two and a quarter hours, with me playing solos all night.

**You were also a member of The Ringo All-Stars, a band made up from the considerable talents of Ringo himself, plus Jack Bruce on bass, Simon Kirke on drums and Gary Brooker on keyboards...**

We started off in the States doing an early summer tour of about a month, and that went so well that Ringo asked us back to go to Europe. The set list is quite impressive: I do 'Show Me The Way', 'Baby I Love Your Way' and 'Do You Feel'; and then Simon does 'Shooting Star' and 'All Right Now'; Jack does 'White Room', 'I Feel Free' and 'Sunshine Of Your Love'; and Gary does 'Conquistador', 'Whiter Shade Of Pale' and 'Whisky Train'. Ringo does about eight numbers, too... So every night I get to be Robin Trower, Paul Kossoff, Eric Clapton or George Harrison.

**Sounds like a dream gig.**

Yeah. I started out just being the guitarist in a band, I was never the centre figure – that came later – and I always enjoyed that spot, being just the guitarist. I wanted to be the Hank Marvin of my time! This is what I enjoy the most, it's fantastic. I enjoy doing my own stuff, but I enjoy playing other people's stuff more.

**If you could pick an album from each stage of your career that you feel best represents you as a player, which would they be?**

The Herd only made one album, called *Paradise Lost,* and so I guess it's got to be that one. [Laughs] We did actually make another album, but it was never released. Someone has the tapes and so maybe one day – if anyone's interested – I'd love to mix it. Then there's *The Fillmore...* In fact, can I be allowed two from then? Because Rock On, the one with the police demonstration team on motorcycles on the front, that is my favourite studio album that I did with Humble Pie. But it was *The Fillmore* that broke us through in America, because it really did capture the band at its best. I think, from the early solo stuff that I did, *Frampton's Camel* is probably my favourite, because I think the songs are really strong. But then there's *Frampton Comes Alive* has to be in there. All the songs had been done before; it was my live 'best of' in a way, representing six years of my career. But it's the biggest-selling live album of all time still, and so it really means a lot to me for many reasons. It'll probably be the record that I'm remembered for. I'm not saying that I wouldn't want something like that to happen again, obviously.

What else? *Breaking All The Rules* which was 1981, that was the last record that I liked that I did with A&M. Then, I think if you move along to 1994's *Peter Frampton*, that's probably my favourite from the recent stuff.

**How did 'Show Me The Way' come to be?**

In 1974, I'd been touring and I had three weeks off to go and write the next record. I went to Nassau and stayed in Steve Marriott's cottage, and nothing happened for a week. The second week, things started happening, and in the last eight days I wrote the complete album. In fact, I wrote 'Show Me The Way' in the morning and 'Baby I Love Your Way' just as the sun was setting the same day. I'm still trying to work out what I had for breakfast...

# WALTER BECKER
# AND
# DONALD FAGEN

## MAY 2003

*Steely Dan have run the gamut of musical styles over the years, at least as far as the media are concerned. They've been tagged as being techno pop and progressive rock, and have even been accused of playing jazz on occasion. Each successive album places new demands on the listener – 'We find this one takes about two weeks for people to get into...' says keyboard player and vocalist Donald Fagen of the new 2003 album,* Everything Must Go. *But the crowds continue to turn out in stadium-sized proportions to witness the phenomenon that is the Steelies live.*

*Of course, I'd been warned about interviewing these two. Both Becker and Fagen enjoy a reputation for giving journalists on the prowl a hard time. They're a formidable double act, the musical equivalent of Monty Python's Doug and Dinsdale, or a thinking man's Bjorn and Benny, prone to finishing each other's sentences and with a sense of humour drier than a desert noon. In short, sometimes it's difficult to get a straight answer from either of them. Take, for instance, the standard music journo gambit of asking for their individual favourite bits from the new CD:*

> WB: *The cheque for the advance, I thought that was pretty good. Then there were the cheques when we finished the album. Those were highlights. True artists like ourselves love money above anything else, I think. Would you agree, Donald?*
> DF: *For sure...*
> WB: *Darling big money, darling small money, was the way Nabokov put it.*

*Even interviews with the Steelies call for space-age technology. On the evening*

*I spoke to them by phone, Walter was in Hawaii and Donald was in New York. Walter was first to join the conference call, and while we waited for Donald to join us, we chatted amiably about the weather.*

*Eventually, Donald joined the conversation by announcing 'I don't know anything about guitars...' but we managed to reassure him that we would be discussing the new album and would only just occasionally dip into the subject of actual guitar playing.*

**So no favourite tracks on *Everything Must Go?***

DF: No, forget it. I've heard them too many times. I can't bear to hear any of it.

**So what happens when you come to play it live?**

DF: Ah, that's different...
WB: We'll play it different every time.
DF: Yeah, different every time.

**With only a year since *Two Against Nature*, does *Everything Must Go* represent you being on something of a roll?**

WB: Well, in the process of making the *Two Against Nature* album, we discovered that we virtually had a band, and that it was a band of players we wanted to continue to work with, and so we were tooled up to do things. We realised that during the '70s, when you were making one album after another, you were essentially building each time from what you learned the last time. If you go off and do a bunch of other things in the meantime, you lose the perspective that you had that could be very helpful.

**Steely Dan albums are renowned for containing a multitude of overdubs, which was taxing for the old multi-track tape system for recording. So how do you look on the recording technology available to you today when compared to the past?**

WB: Digital technology is very advantageous for certain things: for editing, manipulation, for overdubs, being able to punch in precisely, being able to play the tape over and over again without degrading the sound, and so on. Having more tracks to work with is helpful, and tape handling is better because it's faster, and so on. So there are a lot of advantages to the digital storage medium for certain parts of the process. However, we did use two-inch analogue tape to track this album with. The band recordings were analogue and so were the mixes.

**So the album was kept in the analogue domain right up to the mastering?**

WB: The overdubs were digital.
DF: We wanted to capture the band playing live on analogue, and then the next time we played those tapes was when we mixed, and so we integrated the digital overdubs with the analogue recordings of the live tracks.

**Why the decision to record live in the studio?**

WB: Well, we just felt that it would give a unity to the material on the album, to have it all done with a single band.
DF: Although we've always done a lot of overdubbing, it's usually been restricted to vocals and 'sweetening', as they say…
WB: Guitar solos, vocals and sweetening…
DF: Generally speaking, we've pretty much tried to do live tracks all through the years.
WB: When you create a track with five or six people at once, they're all contributing to the feel. They're all helping to define the feel in a very complex and texturally rich way…
DF: They have a curve of drama to them if everyone's playing together…
WB: Yeah, that's right. If you do it the other way, you can only approximate that; you can't get it any other way.

**Do you look at the stage and the studio as being two very different mediums?**

DF: Pretty much, wouldn't you say?

WB: Yeah, I think they are.

DF: You can't really hear very well when you're on stage playing live. Everything's all jumbled together, but at the same time your adrenaline is very high. It's really like being on some hideous drug.

**Do you enjoy playing live?**

DF: Tremendously!

**Steely lore has it that this wasn't always the case. Check out some of the fables from touring on the Steely Dan website, for instance.**

DF: That mainly had to do with bad touring conditions. I think in the '70s our touring band was very energetic and tried really hard, but I don't know that we ever really achieved what we were trying to do sonically.

WB: The bands that we have now are much more true to our intentions, I think. At the same time, there was a sort of exciting train wreck quality to our '70s band that we don't have the absolute moral courage to even approximate any more.

DF: Once music is in the air…

WB: It's gone…

DF: You never capture it again.

**A lot of it could be that the musicians who play with you now have had 30 years to catch up, in certain respects.**

DF: Yeah, actually some of them said they are young enough to have grown up figuring out the chords on our records. In fact John Herrington, our guitarist, sometimes helps us remember chords that we've forgotten and have been playing wrong for some time.

WB: He corrects us…

**There's been talk over the years about how jazz has influenced the overall flavour of Steely Dan's output. Would it be true to say that this is mainly from Donald?**

DF: Walter also has a jazz background. Neither of us, I think, are jazz quality musicians in that modern sense. Especially these days, jazz musicians are real virtuosos, and both of our techniques have improved over the years so that both of us can kinda get along playing jazz at this point. But because I play the piano, chords are my business in a way, so that may have something to do with it. I think that almost all rock bands, especially white bands, followed the branch of rock 'n' roll music that most people associate with Elvis Presley or Carl Perkins, or perhaps the sort of Dick Dale kind of surf playing. It's really nothing whatsoever to do with jazz; it's more to do with country music and simpler kinds of folk music. I think that Walter and I, because we were jazz fans, were more attracted by the be-bop wing of rhythm and blues, which is mostly black and has a lot more to do with Ray Charles or Bobby Blue Bland than Elvis Presley or Carl Perkins. Very few people have followed that branch, although at one time it seemed to be pretty much equal with the other branch.
WB: Black music and white music in the contemporary scene have diverged again.
DF: That's true, yeah.

**Was there an actual jazz guitar influence on Walter?**

WB: No... nah...
DF: What about all those Grant Green records?
WB: What Grant Green records?
DF: [Laughs] Never mind...

**So who were Walter's guitar influences?**

WB: Oh, well... BB King, Hubert Sumlin, older-type blues guitar playing like Delta-style blues, Lightning Hopkins, Eric Clapton, guys who were derivative from that style also...

DF: I remember when I first saw Walter playing the guitar, I didn't know a lot about blues, but I knew what Hubert Sumlin sounded like from listening to Muddy Waters records and I thought, hey that sounds like Hubert Sumlin.

WB: He was the greatest.

DF: You know I met Hubert Sumlin? Oh, I told you that...

WB: Yeah.

DF: He was having some surgery or something in hospital here in New York and I went to visit him.

**Eric Clapton is on record as saying that Sumlin's style was the weirdest he'd ever seen.**

DF: Yeah, for sure.

WB: Well, there are a couple of guys who are really great guitar players, like Otis Rush, who play the guitar strung upside down and have the high string up at the top of the neck...

**Like Albert King...**

WB: Albert King also, yeah. When I first started playing, I tried to simulate that; you can only really do it on the G string. But instead of bending by pushing the string up the neck, I used to bend it by pulling it down and that gives you an incredible control over the string, and it's a cool way to do it.

DF: One of Walter's bandmates was Randy California; didn't he teach you some stuff on the guitar?

WB: Oh, definitely. I would say that he was the first guy I met who knew how to do that stuff, and so I could sort of see how it was actually being done. He also knew, for example, that the guitar had to be set up with pretty light strings, which I didn't know yet, and that the amp had to be turned up pretty loud to get some of those sounds.

DF: We're going back aways here.

WB: Yeah, we're talking about high school here...

**While we're talking about guitar tone, can we run through the gear you used to record the new album, Walter?**

WB: Sure. I used a Sadowsky guitar and a Mesa Boogie Maverick amp and a couple of stomp boxes once in a while.

**What sort of effects?**

WB: Oh, on one song there was an analogue delay – you know, the MXR green box? And I used a chorus pedal of some kind, I can't remember...
DF: I keep trying to get Walter to throw away those effects boxes, but...
WB: But we only ever used them that one time, and I think that's it for the whole album.

**The guitar signal on the new album sounds quite pure, from what I've heard...**

WB: Yeah, just the amp with a little reverb. I usually spend about half an hour tweaking the amp and getting to the point where it feels right for that particular tune on that particular day, and then we're ready to go. I like to get it going as quickly as possible. I'm basically always trying for roughly the same basic thing, y'know?

**Do you stick to the same basic rig when you play live?**

WB: Yeah, plus a second amp, usually. It just gives you another part of the tone, so you can have one amp set a little cleaner and the other set a little hairier, and that's sometimes useful for the guy who's mixing the house or for me.

**Do you switch between the amps or are they both in the mix at the same time?**

WB: They're both on at the same, or they have been in the past.

**Are they both Mesa Boogies?**

WB: No, the other one is a Bogner.

**You've employed some great guitar players on albums in the past. Why has it taken Walter so long to take over six-string duties, as you have done for the last two albums?**

WB: [Laughs.] Well, in the '70s we were trying to do something a little bit different. We were more concerned with more fiery virtuoso blowing, and the intervening musical history has persuaded us to use solos as more structural elements in the music, rather than showcases, wouldn't you say, Donald?
DF: Yeah, but also Walter used to be the bass player, for one thing.
WB: But the guitar has those extra two strings on it, and that can be very tricky.

**I remember Larry Carlton talking about playing with you guys, and saying that the approach to soloing over the somewhat rarefied harmonic backdrops you provided him with was to treat everything as a blues and shrink to fit.**

DF: That's pretty close...
WB: It's definitely true for me. It's probably more true for me than it is for Larry, if you know what I mean.
DF: We figure that we're just some kind of a blues band with frills, really.
WB: Blues band deluxe...

# STEVE VAI

MAY AND JUNE 1993, AND APRIL 1994

*Steve Vai enjoys something of a reputation in guitar circles. Undoubtedly a virtuoso on his instrument, his somewhat patchy recorded output has seen him dubbed both wonderkid and crown prince of weird. But one thing remains certain: an interview with Steve is always as much fun as it is informative. His enthusiasm for his music boils over infectiously as he talks about his experiences with Frank Zappa and touring under his own name – as I found out when we first spoke in 1993...*

**First, let's talk about the bane of every guitar student's life: practice.**

When I first started to practise, I used to do scales and exercises. But now what I do is to create a vamp – a tape with music on it – and I play along to it. I think the most important thing is that when you practise, you focus on your instrument. When I want to learn something new, I just focus on that one thing. When I want to practise vibrato I'll just do vibrato, and if I start to do other things I have to bring my mind back to that.

**What about influences?**

As I was growing up I listened to Jimmy Page and Jimi Hendrix, and a lot of other great guitar players like Van Halen were inspirational too. I took lessons when I was very young with Joe Satriani, and he was always fantastic...and still is. When I was practising I always tried to steer away from playing things that were on records. I learned a lot about individuality from Joe... But today, as a rule, if I come up with something on the guitar that I know somebody else is doing, I either try to elaborate on it or I don't do it at all. And I'd recommend that to everybody, because everybody is unique and individual, and everybody is capable of developing their own style.

**After lessons with Satriani, you continued your studies at Berklee...**

When I was at college I did practise a lot, but I also studied, so I was using what I was learning instead of just playing it, and that was important. The best thing I did was to go to Berklee when I did, and the best thing I did was to leave when I did.

**What do you feel about the value of guitar schools in general?**

I'd recommend a guitar school if you felt that you needed it, but if you do go then you have to have the right attitude. You have to know that you're an individual. What you learn you have to interpret in a way that is right for you; to simply copy the people around you is anti-productive.

**Did you ever want to do anything else outside music?**

When I was young I had no thought in my mind other than to be a musician – it wasn't even a question. I never reached a point in my life where I had to decide to be a musician or a carpenter. When I was young I was never concerned with being famous or making money; it was all just alien to me. The most important thing for me was being alone and playing my guitar.

**From where do you draw your inspiration?**

Inspiration comes from a place that's hard to identify, but I think it's a combination of everything that you hear. True inspiration, in its raw form, is very beautiful. But how you take it to the world via your instrument or your poetry or your art, that has to do with all the influences that you have. When inspiration does hit us, we just have to do something. Sometimes we're inspired but we don't know it, or we don't think our inspiration is real, and so we let it go. That's a real waste. Sometimes people are intimidated or insecure, and their beautiful inspiration is lost because of their insecurity. Unfortunately, I can't demand inspiration to come to me. Some people can – but they're geniuses.

**There are common traps guitarists fall into when they begin to play – an obsession with speed is quite common, for instance.**

When you start playing and practising you begin to build your technique, and it's like a trap; it really enthrals you like a drug. It's like working out with weights to get muscles: all you want is more muscles, and all you want is more technique and going faster and faster!

**The turbo mentality?**

Yeah. It's like going for a ride through Vermont: if you're going too fast, you won't enjoy the scenery. But, you know, it's really amazing: I've met a lot of guitar players at seminars who all felt proud of the fact that they didn't know music, and that they learnt my stuff by ear. But even if you know music and you learn a song, you have to learn it by ear unless you're going to read it from a page. The big rap when I was coming up through the ranks was if you know music then you can't play from the heart, which is really pretty preposterous. There's nothing wrong with learning music; it's like learning a language. If you're going to be a musician, then you might as well learn the language. Believe me, it can help you a lot. Some of the kids need it; they need that little push to drive them into a uniqueness. Not knowing about music can be fine, but you can enrich your playing and your whole outlook so much more by just knowing… The thing is, you need educated musicians to make a mark on the world, and it's those musicians that give students the incentive to learn what they're learning. But for me as a composer, when I compose something without using my guitar, just sitting there with score paper, it's such freedom, such a liberation. You're not bound by the parameters of your own personal playing.

**Would you agree that your first solo album, *Flex-able*, was very Zappa-influenced in parts?**

Are you kidding? I thought I was Frank. I wanted to be Frank. He represented everything I love in music: a sense of humour, funny fast notes... When I first heard him, tears of joy filled my eyes. There was 'Electric Aunt Jemima', and then there was 'Carolina Hard Core Ecstasy' from *Bongo Fury*. I died right there. It was everything I wanted to hear in music!

**It must have been a real thrill to work with Zappa...**

I was very young and naive, but Frank was like a mother hen. He was great, he really brought me along nicely. Frank's concern wasn't how old you were – I was 18 when I started working for him – it was that you played the notes right; you had to do your best. I just concentrated all my energy on his music, and that's what he needs, because all his stuff is so intense.

**What was the most challenging piece in Zappa's repertoire for you?**

I was thinking about that the other day. There's this thing called 'Moggio', which was released on *You Can't Do That On Stage Anymore*, Volume 6 or 5. The fingerings in it were really awkward, and at that time my technique was such that it didn't allow me to do a lot of the things I can do now. Frank would write on the piano, and that melody was so awkward on the guitar. On the record he mixed me really loud, and I hear some of those parts and I can remember every night thinking, 'Oh, God. Relax. Concentrate. Think about it.' It was really tough – sometimes I screwed it up, but most of the time I made it through.

**Eighteen is very young to tackle such a high-profile role in a big touring band. How did you deal with nerves?**

Well, I was always very nervous before I went on stage with Frank, but I'd practised the music so much and I knew it so well that once I got up there I played it fairly correctly. Sure, there were times when I screwed up. I'd get all the way through 'Rdzl', and then on the last riff I'd always have a little problem with something – it always burned me up. I was very nervous, but I wasn't tense. I never really got tense; my nervousness used to come out in different ways. Now I just get excited.

*Passion And Warfare* **was a major leap forward from the style you had previously established with** *Flex-able.*

Well, I wanted to do something different. After I'd done 'The Attitude Song' and 'Call It Sleep', I wanted to do a record of balls-to-the-wall, rock guitar instrumental stuff. Joe was doing it and I didn't want to copy him, but I still wanted to do an instrumental record, so I kind of brought it to a different area. I love Joe's records and what he does, but I knew I didn't want to do a record of rock instrumentals with just guitar. So I ended up with some very peculiar things, like 'The Riddle' and 'Answers'.

**The album** *Sex & Religion* **was a departure for you. Fans were disappointed with the album because they were expecting either** *Passion And Warfare II* **or at least** *Son Of Flex-able* **and what they got didn't even come close. For some, the eccentricity bill was too high; they were demanding 'The Attitude Song' and what they got was an attitude problem...**

I kinda felt that *Sex & Religion* was, saleswise, gonna do very well or not very well. It kinda did in between, but it did a lot of things for me personally; I made a record that was different to what I'd done before and it put together some pieces for my puzzles. I was exploring, y'know? I could make instrumental records forever, it's not a problem for me, but I always wanted to have a band and I like vocal music and whatnot, and so I took a chance on making that kind of record. It was more to fill a certain void in me. It got some miserable, horrible reviews, but what are you gonna do, y'know? I think *Alien Love Secrets* was what people mostly expect from me.

The reaction to the live show was incredible; it was received a lot better than the record. It was a very energetic show and it was the first time I had ever toured on my own, under my own name, and it was a lot of fun. It was a lot of work, but it had great rewards. One of my favourite things is touring. I feel like I'm a touring machine in a sense. I'm built for playing live – I really enjoy doing it.

**Your sense of fun is often misunderstood and mistaken for pure, 24-carat weirdness.**

Sure it is. [Laughs] Are you kidding? I get criticised pretty heavily, especially in this day and age where wearing anything other than a pair of dirty jeans and a T-shirt is considered tragically unhip. But what do I care?

**Do you enjoy being in the studio?**

When I've been in the studio for a long period of time, I'm really eager to go out and play live. Then, once I'm out on tour for a long time, I ache to get back in the studio. So they kind of balance each other out.

**One thing that is always transmitted successfully on any of your albums is the amount of fun you have making them.**

Yeah I do. I mean, it's a real fun process for me. Sometimes it's agonising; when you get the idea for something like the 'Fire Garden Suite', it takes literally minutes to have the whole idea conceptually, but then it takes weeks and weeks of torture to get it on tape. But listening back, though, it's like the woman after she's had a baby – she forgets the pain she went through.

**There must have been a few changes to your signature Ibanez guitar since its inception.**

The foundation of the Ibanez guitar remains the same. The things that change are the kind of wood, the pickups and the finish, and those things have a lot to do with the way the guitar sounds. A guitar is so temperamental, anything you change on it will change the sound. You change the pick guard and it makes a difference.

**At one point, you famously took a blowtorch to one of your signature instruments...**

We wanted to try something a little different with this guitar, so we burned the body with a blowtorch and stained it – we didn't put a hard finish on it – and it actually changed the characteristics of the sound, gave it more of a whooshier, warmer tone. But I just can't seem to break away from the white Jem.

**Nevertheless, changes are being made even there.**

Well, I'm changing it a bit: I'm going to put a 250k volume pot in, instead of a 500, so it will take some of the brightness out and warm it up a bit.

**You benefit not only from a signature guitar, but a signature pickup, too – the Dimarzio Evolution...**

Yeah, they're pretty hi-fi pickups.

**What's the difference between the Evolutions and, say, a Dimarzio PAF Pro?**

Well, the Evolutions have a little more at 3 to 4k – they're brighter and there's more of a tight bottom end. The PAFs are sort of a balanced pickup; their frequency response is a little more generic, whereas the Evolution might be a little more animated.

**What about amps?**

On *Alien Love Secrets* I had the opportunity to use a lot of different amps because I had this device made which is a real splitter box. It allows you to plug your guitar into it and have six outputs that aren't loaded down or moulded in a strange way; no DC hum or ground noise, either. So I was able to go into a Marshall, a Bogner and a SansAmp direct, and bring these up on the console and mix them in at any ratio I wanted. I also had a Fender Performer and a Fender DeLuxe, and I used DigiTech equipment, pre-amps and speaker simulators, and so on. I tried to get as much room sound as I could; the room sound in my studio has a nice warm sound to it.

**The mix certainly makes the guitars sound enormous...**

Well, we aims to please... I wanted 'em big. Even in 'Boy From Seattle', where it's clean, it's encompassing.

**How did that track come about?**

That was a riff that I just played backstage on to a cassette someplace, listened back a few years later and decided I would make a song out of it. It's very Hendrix – in fact I was probably trying to play 'Wait 'til Tomorrow'! But it's his type of chord approach, a technique I thought was really brilliant. People are not really aware of that style of his playing; I mean they hear it but they don't realise how unique and wonderful it is for a guitar player. When I was a kid I inundated myself with Hendrix chord playing at one point and figured out all that really great stuff like 'Electric Ladyland', and it became a real staple in the way I played. So that song pays tribute to that style of playing. The 'Boy From Seattle' was Jimi Hendrix, so it's somewhat of a tribute song.

**Which guitar did you use for the original track?**

It's a Fender Strat. I had not owned a Strat and I wanted to get one, and I wanted to spend a lot of money and get an old one. I played about 30 or 40 and I bought two, and the one that I bought and used on that record was a $500 brand-new Japanese Fender, and I'm telling you it was the best sounding one of the ones that I played. It was the sound that I wanted, and I hated having to buy it because I wanted to buy a really expensive one to make myself feel better. Like a dope I ended up buying an older one, which I use more now, but it's not even that old – I think it's '70s...

**After completing *Alien Love Secrets*, you went to India. Rock highways and byways are littered with other artists who have made that pilgrimage in the name of self-discovery. Is the same true in your case, or was it just a holiday?**

Both, probably. I'd never been there and I was researching some eastern philosophies, which I went to investigate. And I got what I went for.

**'Fire Garden Suite' sounds as though it could have been inspired, at least in part, by your Indian trip.**

Actually, yeah. One movement, 'Pusa Road', was inspired by the road in India I was staying on.

**The suite itself sounds very exotic...**

Well, the original impetus was to create a musical performance that would have a visual, musical but eclectic impact in the live performance of the show. I'm bouncing from guitar to guitar to guitar, you know; starting with the electric, I go to the sitar, then the acoustic, then back to the electric and it's all done in one piece.

**What sort of acoustic guitars do you favour?**

The pure acoustic that I use the most is my Taylor.

**What are the highlights on *Fire Garden*, from your point of view?**

Well, there are ones that give me different feelings, different emotions. I like the aggression of 'Fire In The House'; but the 'Angel Food' movement of the 'Fire Garden Suite', which has the piano and the guitar, I really enjoy listening to that; and 'Brother' touches some pretty deep button in me too.

**Not being able to tour often enough must be hell for an artist who obviously loves playing live so much.**

You have no idea how much I miss it! I'm built for touring and I love performing live – I'm a touring machine, I really am. I can do 30 shows in a row, two shows a night, but it's frustrating for me sometimes because I don't get a chance to perform. I think my live performance with the band is my highest card, the funnest, I mean – that's what it's about. Man, I go crazy in the studio.

**Isn't there the opportunity to play small one-off gigs more in the States?**

Not really, because to do one gig takes a lot of rehearsal. You've got to get a band together and that costs a lot of money. It's not like I'm in a band where we all live and die by the sword. I have to call people and pay them, lose their day jobs and come and play for one show. But I've been fortunate, things have been going real good. Last year I toured Russia twice, one time to do the White Knights festival, and it turned out so good that they asked me back. I went to South America and that was some of the best gigs I ever did in my life – it was unbelievable! It was the first time I went out as a solo artist and I wasn't really sure what to expect because on the *Sex & Religion* tour I had a wild man singing, shaking his bald head around, but for this I was just totally on my own. I wanted to kick myself in the ass and say, 'Why didn't you do this when you were 21?' instead of all the other stuff I did, because it felt totally natural. And the audiences were some of the best I've ever played to – I mean they really got it. I thought to myself, 'What are they going to do? Sit and listen to instrumental guitar music?' and, bam, they were out of control, and I had seven bodyguards stand in front of the stage! It was wonderful.

**You often read about guitar players using amps with serious gain capabilities who still feel the need to supplement their distortion with a humble stomp box. Maybe you can shed some light...**

Well, I like doing rhythm and stuff, and I don't necessarily want it to be too distorted – I have to keep it a dull roar. But when you want to kick into a solo or something you need that extra edge, so that's when I hit the distortion box.

**Couldn't someone achieve the same result with a multi-channel amp?**

If the amp can handle it. The [Bogner] Ecstasy can do it between channel two and channel three; but channel two is not quite grungy enough and channel three is too grungy, so I've got to find the happy medium. In any case, there's something about the sound of that distortion box that I like – it squashes everything and makes it really fat.

**Finally, any words of wisdom and encouragement for all the struggling guitar virtuosos out there?**

Stick to your guns! If you want to be a virtuoso by all means don't be embarrassed, and if you want to just plug into your amp and slam out distorted untuned chords don't be embarrassed about that either.

# JOE SATRIANI
## JULY 1992 AND SEPTEMBER 1993

*The aftermath of the instrumental guitar outburst of the '80s and '90s has seen few players survive with their credibility intact. One very notable exception, though, is Joe Satriani. Maybe not everyone is aware of the fact that before Joe took his place in the hallowed halls of plank-spanking celebrity, he taught guitar. Having existed in the twilight world of private guitar tuition myself for a considerable amount of time during the '80s and early '90s, it was easy to establish some common ground. In fact, when we sat down to talk in 1992, we became so absorbed in relating our relative rites of passage, the interview was almost forgotten. I finally flicked the tape machine on at the point where I'd suggested to Joe that he had swapped sides, from the analytical guitar teacher to being the very subject of such analysis himself...*

**What's it like being the one who is taught in classes now?**

Well, the funny thing is that I don't know really what it's like because I'm not in that little room any more. It certainly was a challenge to have to teach people stuff by Steve Vai or Yngwie Malmsteen, but the most difficult was Allan Holdsworth. Even when you could figure it out, the student generally couldn't play it anyway. And writing it out in a half-hour or hour lesson was almost impossible because it took too many sheets of paper. You couldn't just use repeats and codas because he doesn't really use them.

**Did you slow them down?**

No, I just listened to it. I developed a pretty good ear, although I started out as a complete idiot. But I had a really good music teacher in high school and he taught me relative pitch. I guess he taught me the right way, because after a couple of years, when I heard something, I knew what it was before any intellectual wheels were turning in my head.

**Did you write things out in standard notation or tab?**

It depended. Some of them didn't read music or tablature and they just needed chord symbols and little expressions that made sense to them. We'd agree on a symbol for, say, anticipation. Other times, though, if it was a student who stuck with me for a couple of years, eventually they would get interested in reading in some form. They would begin to know that the next bar meant anticipation and that made things easier because, if you have a half-hour lesson and they want to learn something by Iron Maiden, and you want to show them a Dorian mode in three octaves, and they've got to show you their chords in four or five positions, you've got to work fast. Generally, it was a trade-off. I'd play for them or write out any song they wanted to learn as long as they gave me 10 or 15 minutes' worth of scales and exercises first.

**Did you find that there is an obsession with speed?**

Oh yeah. [Laughs.] But there are students that come in who don't want to learn lead – they want to learn chords and rhythm. They would come in with different agendas. Maybe they're songwriters – they don't really care about really good guitar players, they just want to know, 'Are there any other chords?','How come Lennon and McCartney used all these chords for these simple pop songs?' and 'What's Allan Holdsworth using?'

**You must have been familiar then with the books containing transcribed guitar parts from albums – and now you see your own work presented that way. Have you ever picked one up and said to yourself, 'That's wrong... It's not what I played'?**

Yeah, they send me the stuff before it's published, and I try to proofread it as well as I can. For some of the stuff, they use symbols that go beyond me, because I never learned to read guitar book music. I learned to read for drums first, and then to sight-sing choral music, and then I learned to read music in general. I had to write string quartets and little symphonies, and I had to write jazz melodies over chords and, eventually, I had to write down my own music. But I never developed symbols for whammy bars and screaming dive bombs or scraping the strings. I just figured, well what's the point? I didn't need it for myself and none of my students could read it anyway. Everyone was more interested in playing than reading – with the exception of Steve Vai, that is. He really took to reading at a very early age. So when I look at the books now and I see all the symbols and all the stuff they do, I think, 'Well, I've already played this, and I'm not really interested in reading it.' In my mind, the notes are the most important thing, and not all the little directions about how exactly Joe was holding his pick when he made this note. To me, that was one fragment of a moment in the studio that got to tape. I played it probably a million different ways during the days leading up to the recording, and what's on tape is some form of an improvisation on a somewhat generalised idea. So it's funny to see it written in stone, as it were, something that I did off the top of my head.

**I've seen many of those books and the moan I've had is that sometimes they try to be too accurate. There's maybe a little 16th note at the top of five or six ledger lines, and the text says 'feedback' – like I really need to know that.**

Yeah, that's right! There was one thing where a guy was writing 'The Bells Of Lal Pt 2' from the *Flying* record, and he had done the entire song an eighth note off. He didn't understand that it was in four, and that the snare drum was on beats two and four. It's a very simple rhythm, but he had written the whole thing shifted over, and I got the manuscript and I'm looking at it and going, 'Man, I know it's been a while since I read a lot of solo guitar, but this doesn't look right.' And I kept thinking, 'What's wrong with this thing?' I picked out notes where he had just screwed up totally, but then I went back to the beginning again and realised that the whole song was just shifted. Some of them figured that I played 'Headless Horseman' on bass, y'know…the weirdest concepts. I think the first time I saw 'Day At The Beach', they had it written on the wrong strings. It was note perfect, but everything was one string over.

**Have you ever been tempted to put a couple of booby-trap techniques in there on purpose, just to screw up the poor guy transcribing it?**

That's funny. [Chuckles.] I can see that, but I don't think there was ever anything that was obviously not playable by a human. We never used speeded-up tapes, except on vocals.

**I was thinking about certain techniques, like the single-handed arpeggios on 'Mystical Potato Head Groove Thing'. When you played Hammersmith a couple of years back and it got to that point in the song, I looked around and a lot of people were craning their necks, checking out how that was done. It's obviously a hell of a technique to master, and somebody told me that, just to make things worse, you grinned when you did it!**

I used to laugh at myself because that's a particularly difficult song to pull off. I have to make decisions every second about when I leave the rhythm guitar part to play the melody and how I balance between switching the pickup selection, reach over, mute the strings and play. I would laugh at myself because sometimes I would pull it off and other times I'd go to reach over real fast and I'd just go, 'Aaaaaargh.' I'd create an extra note, and I'd just laugh at myself and think, 'I never should have written this song!'

**You have to get back really fast for that E chord in the rhythm part…**

Yeah, and that E chord should really be on the bridge pickup, but I could never get it, and every once in a while I'd be thinking, 'I'm gonna try it… Nooo!' Up until the solo I just had to think constantly as I was playing. It was very difficult to do the rhythm and play the melody and then go back to doing little bits of rhythm.

**Why do you sometimes use a stop tailpiece guitar?**

Well, when you use a vibrato bar guitar and you hit the strings really hard, a lot of the vibration gets transferred to the springs and back into the bar in a sort of flutter, and I really don't like that sound at all. I've never used it as a technique like Steve Vai does. But I hate that sound. To me it just sounds horrible or like there's something wrong with your tape. So I've always tried to eliminate it, and Ibanez worked with me to try to get as little flutter in that vibrato bar as possible by using certain springs or arrangements of springs. One day I had one of the prototype JS1s; it was an ash body and that didn't work out too well when we were looking for woods. So I brought it to Gary Brawer, the San Francisco luthier who does a lot of my setup work, and he filled it up – took out the springs and the bar and filled it all up with ash, and we put in a regular DiMarzio stop tailpiece, with through-the-body strings. And it was perfect for me because a lot of the vibrato that I had developed over the years suddenly sounded more like me, because the vibrato bar wasn't there taking up the slack and giving way every time I applied vibrato. And when I hit those chords really hard, there was none of that fluttering noise, and so the rhythm parts became a little spankier sounding. All sorts of different tunings suddenly became really easy for me, and we wound up using that guitar for 'Friends', 'The Extremist', 'War' and 'Motorcycle Driver'.

**There are a couple of tracks from *The Extremist* where it sounds like you could have been using a Les Paul, and that could have been the influence of the stop tailpiece...**

Yeah, the sound in front of the amp is sort of a cross between a Les Paul and a Telecaster. It's big, but it's not fat. It's round, but it has a clarity to it that you might associate with a Telecaster and not with a Les Paul.

**The Les Paul/Telecaster idea is a very Jimmy Page thing. Was he an influence on you?**

Oh yeah, certainly. Hendrix was my number one influence, but I spent years playing Led Zeppelin covers in a band; Black Sabbath, Cream, Beatles and Stones, and stuff like that. A lot of that stuff is in my head, but Jimmy Page is one of my all-time favourite guitar players. Amazing producer, composer and he can play great stuff. The solo on 'Since I've Been Loving You' is amazing. It's one of those solos that's got so much personality all over it that, even when you learn it and play it perfectly, it will never sound as good as Jimmy Page doing it. That's what happens when people play Hendrix songs: they just pale.

**My first impression on hearing *The Extremist* was that it is a very positive sounding record. Lots of strong, major harmony...**

Yeah, it's a collection of tunes that I've been working on for a while. 'Friends' I think I started writing in 1988, and I just worked and worked on it. A lot of the tunes represent not only musical goals, but more down-to-earth events of recent times with my life – unlike the other records, which were more fantasising about other-worldly situations or remembering dreams and make-believe world material.

**The title track on *Extremist* has a very Zeppelin feel to it – the harmonica solo sounds very much in the mood of 'When The Levee Breaks'...**

Well, I said to Andy Johns, the producer, that I would really like the harmonica to sound like 'Levee Breaks'. [Andy was involved in the production of *Led Zeppelin IV*.] He didn't know that there was a harmonica solo on *The Extremist* until the day we got to it and he said, 'Well, I guess we're done...' and I said, 'No, there are two harmonica solos.' And he went, 'Really? So what you gonna do?' And I said, 'What did you do on 'When The Levee Breaks'?' And he said, 'Well, we put this Tremolux amp up and I put it through this compressor.' So we called up Andy Brauer and rented one, and in about ten minutes, there it was.

**Is that E-flat tuning on there?**

Yes it is. The first three songs on the album are tuned down a half step.

**'War' is firmly Phrygian based. Was this to suggest a sort of Middle East flavour to the song?**

The whole song is about the thousands of years of war in that particular part of the world: North Africa, Arabia, the Orient and Middle East. Amazing cultures have sprung up out of that area. And the present conflict between presidents Hussein and Bush dragged the rest of us into it, causing even more ridiculous carnage over what, I still don't know. I was writing a lot of tunes around my studies of that culture and then the Gulf War broke out, and so there was more stuff to influence me.

**'Cryin'' is the album's big ballad. You've pitched the melody very high…**

Very high, very difficult to play. It was difficult to settle on the right key. When you're doing a melody like 'Rubina' or 'Always With Me, Always With You' they sit in a nice register, but the chorus, second verse of 'Cryin'' is right up there, 'War' is up there, 'Friends' is up there. But I knew it would work, I knew it was the perfect register for it: it was just a question of the right tonality and the right feeling.

'Cryin'' was a one-take, reference guitar track. I plugged into a Zoom and everyone said, 'It's just a reference track, so let's focus on the drums.' Earlier, I had put down a keyboard part to a click track and so Gregg and Matt [aka the Bisonette brothers – bass and drums] and myself went and did 'Cryin''. When we got to the end of it, Andy Johns had goosebumps on his arm and he said, 'Man, that was the track.' So I felt really good about it until I remembered, 'Damn, I was only plugged into a Zoom. I wish we had set up the amp.' But Andy worked with the tone on tape to get it so it really came out.'

**Where did the bagpipe idea at the end of 'Rubina's Blue Sky Happiness' come from?**

That was completely improvised by Phil Ashley. We had gotten to that section of the tune where it was obvious that we had played enough for the outro and I decided, off the top of my head, to start playing a song that I had started writing earlier in the week. And so I just started playing it and the other guys started improvising around me. Doug Wimbish started playing harmonics on that funny Guild bass (a rubber-stringed Ashbory model) and I got down to a really quiet moment, and suddenly Phil just surprised the hell out of us with this keyboard patch! I think if you listen hard, you can probably hear some laughing. And Simon Phillips, when he heard the bagpipes, started in on this Highland drumming thing!

**There's hardly any dissonance on this album. You haven't gone for the 'Enigmatic' or 'Hordes Of Locusts' style of material.**

Well, I used a form of editing here to create the proper mood. Getting into certain scales and saying, 'What happens if I don't play a third? How can I suspend the mystery of the scale?' Specifically, that worked best on the song 'War', where the melody is played over an E riff, and then it's played over a B riff and then over an A, but the melody of the verse never uses a third, and so you don't know whether it's Phrygian or Phrygian dominant. The chords are D minor, D min sus2 to A flat major 7th, 6th and sharp 11th and then to the E again – that sort of ambiguous E Phrygian riff thing. Those are the three chords for the chorus, but the melody and harmony represent fourths on the first two strings at the fifth fret, third fret and then open. So there is this simplicity going in one direction while we've got this sort of tritone bass line going in another. The bass line is the one that is saying, 'Major third before we go to E', but the melody stays out of it. And the chords don't express that either. That's the kind of concept that interests me. After I wrote and recorded songs like 'The Enigmatic' or 'Mystical Potato Head Groove Thing', I started to zero in on just being careful. 'The Bells Of Lal Pt 2', it's absolutely pure minor scale; I didn't throw in harmonic minor or other stuff to make it sound exotic. I kept the thought and the intent very pure on that. As a result, when I did 'Friends' or 'War' I had to make sure there was a distance between them, because they are about completely different subjects. So I didn't say, 'OK, I'm Joe and I can play anything, and I'm going to make sure that everyone knows on every song that I'm Master Shredder!' To me that's really annoying, because all you do is destroy your song and you turn it into a guitarist's track, and I've never really been interested in that. I've always thought that you get a bunch of songs together and, if they're good songs, you're really lucky. And if they all fit together and make a great album, you're really, really lucky. And the worst thing you can do is to screw it all up by putting a lot of technique all over it.

**Your recording career began with a self-financed EP, some tracks of which turned up on the retrospective CD *Time Machine*.**

There were originally five songs on the EP, but one of them didn't survive ten years being stored in the box, and we didn't have the time or the technology to restore it. But the other four pieces were absolutely beautiful sounding and, luckily enough, they were the better compositions on the record. The EP was originally titled 'Joe Satriani' on my label called Rubina Records – which was just my living room. I tried getting the EP distributed but I couldn't. That was when I first realised that to be in the record business meant that you had to go through channels – there was just no way you could start your own record company and think that you were going to get something done. I couldn't get any alternative record distribution company to distribute it; nobody wanted this record, absolutely nobody. I think I sold maybe 17 copies or something, and the rest of the 500 copies were sitting in my living room. So I bought record mailers that held two or three copies, and I got a copy of these alternative magazines, and I just sent them to record stores, college radio stations, anyone. I only got a review in *Sonic Options* – a bad review – and I got a good review in *Guitar Player* magazine, and that's about it.

**After the EP experience, what spurred you on to making an album?**

Well, a year later I decided to do a real record, but I couldn't find financing for it. I knew it was going to take more than $1,000, which is what the first record cost, because I was going to be playing it all myself, which takes more time in the studio. So lo and behold, in the mail a couple of days later came a credit card, a pre-approved credit card with a $5,000 credit limit. So basically I went to the studio and said I'd pay for 200 hours in advance and they gave me a break on the costs. The studio was dying for money as well, so I paid everybody in advance and immediately wound up with a $4,999 debt on my credit card!

**So what happened between *Not Of This Earth* and *Surfing With The Alien*?**

In early 1985 I went into the studio and started recording, a night here and a night there. By about June of that year, I finished the record and had it mastered. I met with guys from Relativity and they got excited about it and wanted to sign me to a record deal, but nothing happened until Christmas of that year, by which time I'd joined Greg Kihn. So we finished Greg's record and did some touring, and I signed the contract on December 31st '85. They waited an additional 11 months of '86 before they released *Not Of This Earth*, so I stayed with Greg until September '86, just touring around the States. The record was finally released around a year and a half after its creation, after I'd left Greg's band and picked up a tour with [bass player] Jonas Hellborg. We did about three weeks or a month's tour of Scandinavia and I got back around Christmas '86, and Relativity wanted me to do a little party at the China Club. But before I did that they gave me some bucks to go into the studio to record demos for a new record, and so I recorded 'Crushing Day', 'Echo', 'Dweller On The Threshold' and 'Midnight', and I brought that to New York and did a performance. At the performance I did a version of 'Satch Boogie' as well, and they were very excited about the whole thing and worked out a budget for me – I think it was supposed to be $13,000 – to go into the studio to record the album. $13,000 was not going to do the trick, so we wound up using 'Echo' and 'Crushing Day' mainly from the demos. We tidied things up a little bit, and ultimately we spent $29,000! It was finished by June of '87 and released that October. I started to tour with the material, but in January I auditioned for the Mick Jagger solo band, and so I spent two months with Mick – one in rehearsal in New York City and one spent in Japan doing a tour. I came back and *Surfing With The Alien* was sitting in the top 30 – it was a hit record – and so I resumed touring.

Eventually I took about a month off and went back in the studio in early '89 and started *Flying In A Blue Dream*, which was recorded in stages of, like, three weeks on, three weeks off, three weeks on, a month off. After it was finished in January '90, we started the *Flying In A Blue Dream* tour, which ended in November, and then took four weeks off, and then flew to Woodstock in New York and started *The Extremist*. We worked for a month, took two months off, worked for two months, took ten months off, worked for four months – all of which brings us to the summer of '92, which was when *Extremist* was released and I started to do press.

# STEVE HOWE

NOVEMBER, 1993

*For many of us, Yes seem to have been around for ever. The band's beginnings were in the post-psychedelic late '60s with a couple of prog-pop albums and a commitment to do things differently. But it was 1971's* The Yes Album *that proved to be the true overture to the band's progressive-rock passion play. Along with bands like King Crimson, Pink Floyd and Genesis, Yes introduced the world to a new age and style of rock composition.*

*Since then, there have been Yes masterpieces like* Close To The Edge *and critical low-spots:* Tales From Topographic Oceans, *which saw the genre collapse upon itself, only to recover slightly with* Relayer. *Fans have witnessed almost bi-annual personnel changes within the band, with maybe only bass player Chris Squire and drummer Alan White in line for long-service medals!*

*Steve Howe has been with the band since* The Yes Album, *leaving to form Asia and GTR, rejoining for the* Union *tour, leaving again and then returning... This interview took place in 1993, on the cusp of the release of Steve's solo album entitled* The Grand Scheme Of Things.

**So, back in the days when life was a lot more simple, what were you listening to?**

When I was a teenager, I was drawing my most important influences, which were the great jazz players of the '40s, '50s and '60s. I heard Duane and I heard Hank, but when I discovered Chet Atkins I knew that I had found my guy.

**What are your memories of your early experiences with Yes?**

Well, I had an audition with the band somewhere in Putney, I believe, in their manager's house, and the next thing we did was come to this house in Devon. First of all we had a house up near Barnstaple and we didn't like it very much, and so we advertised and the people on this farm answered and said, 'Yes, we'll have a rock band...' and so we moved in for two months.

**The first Yes album that you played on was *The Yes Album*, which formed part of the cutting edge of the UK prog-rock movement at the dawn of the '70s.**

The concept of both King Crimson and Yes was to be adventurous and a little way out in terms of time signatures and lots of playing. But when I heard *The Yes Album* for the first time after mixing it, I realised that, to me, it sounded totally crazy! It sounded like as quirky a record as I had ever heard in my life. It was a production attempt at everybody playing furiously at once; the complexity was there, the multi-layering was there – all the interesting bits to listen to – all jammed together. I almost felt a little bit paranoid that the sound was so meek and friendly that I wasn't sure if anyone was going to be bothered to listen to it!

**At the time, your guitar sound contradicted the popular choice of fairly heavy distortion in favour of a cleaner, more rounded variety.**

That was one of the features of my style, in that I never had an aggressive sound. I wanted to be fluid, but natural – as natural as an electric guitar sound can be.

**Added to that was the fact that your influences leant more towards jazz than rock or blues.**

I also had a very strong connection with rock 'n' roll, with people like James

Burton, Chuck Berry and particularly Jimmy Bryant, the early guitarist who pre-empted all of the great rock guitarists. He was playing mad be-bop country music with Speedy West, sometimes behind Tennessee Ernie Ford, and also on their own records. I was conscious of them because of their session work with Ernie Ford, and they made a great many hillbilly rock records. All those guys were the normal guys; the jazz and classical things were my own exploration, and I'm glad I did that, particularly that I saw Wes Montgomery when I was only 16. The main thing I was doing was not playing guitar style clichés; not so much rock but blues guitar clichés. That was something that was a mission. But I think that I may go back to playing blues in the near future...so watch out. But I certainly won't come on playing a load of blues clichés. What I understand about blues is that it is a music form, it's not about style.

**Let's consider your acoustic tour de force, 'Clap', which was in fact written for your son, Dylan.**

That's because he was born on the 4th of August 1969 and there I was on the 3rd of August, staying up all night expecting to get the phone call that my wife was going to deliver. I was miles away in North London and my wife was in Watford and, to cut a long story short, I was preparing a new home for the family to come back to, and that night I stayed up late and put that tune together. My tunes tend to evolve out of me practising, they don't really evolve out of me writing as such, because I write a bit, I record some things, I look back at them, I update them, I lengthen them, I fix them with other bits, but there is a time when it comes together and that was when 'Clap' came together. I could easily have called it 'Chet', because it was huge tribute to Chet Atkins. I didn't make that particularly public, but it was pretty obvious to other guitarists – despite the fact that I don't think Chet played flat body steel string guitar very often. But with 'Clap', instead of emulating his style on electric guitar, I took that inspiration and mixed it with blues and folk guitar. There was a bit of Merle Travis and a bit of Big Bill Broonzy, a little bit of Scotty Moore, too. A lot of the single lines that I put in between the phrases are very much my way of improvising. I had done so much work in D during the psychedelic era, that when I came to improvise in D, I had a huge array of things I could do – I'd spent so long droning away in Indian improvisation.

**You were responsible for bringing the Gibson ES 175 guitar into the rock arena – a guitar that was perhaps more at home in a jazz context.**

It's a very beautiful guitar. It has a certain charisma – a lot of guitars do, but that guitar had a special impact on me. It's fascinating the way that I just keep coming back to it. Every album I've made, it's on there somewhere. There's always something on every album I make that just won't work unless I use this guitar. Sometimes I look at it and it says, 'Don't play the others, just play me!' because that guitar represents everything I've tried to do. It's been a life's work just to look after it. When you care about something, it can be the subject of neglect, strangely enough, because you assume that it's always going to be there for you when you want it. And so I've guarded it, because even throughout the big, successful years, that guitar never left my side. I also cleaned it, which a lot of guitarists didn't do after a show. Ike Isaacs or Ivor Mairants might have cleaned their guitars after a show, but the rock guitarist didn't.

**With Yes, you seemed to use a particular guitar to represent each album in a way.**

Yes I did. For instance, after using the 175 on *The Yes Album*, on *Fragile* I used a Gibson Switchmaster, except for 'Heart Of The Sunrise'. On *Relayer* I used my Telecaster, *Close To The Edge* was my ES345 and a Les Paul Junior for *Topographic Oceans*. But by the time I got to *Drama*, I was using just about every guitar I'd ever used on all the albums. So from then on I started using different guitars for each track, particularly in Asia, although on stage I used the Artist all the time.

**There was a Strat and a Tele in there somewhere, too...**

I did Teles madly on *Relayer* and then eventually the Strat came in for *Going For The One*.

**What is your most treasured piece?**

Very hard to say, because I have quite a number of extremely rare guitars – the earliest guitar I have we dated at 1780. But I suppose the 175 is always going to be my greatest guitar: it's a '64 in mint condition and very exceptional to me. I have things like semi-acoustic twin-necks from the '50s, a six and twelve, and also a mandolin and six-string, I think they're unbelievably rare.

**Taking all of those guitars on the road must have been a severe headache.**

It expanded my workload. It took me about two hours to sound check whereas everyone else probably had about 20 minutes. But it pleased me… I don't know what else I would have done for those two hours. It gave me a very productive thing to do. If I could prepare all my guitars myself, which I have always done right from the '60s, then if they're right I can take a lot of pride in that, but if they're wrong, I haven't got somebody to lean on. Some of the guitar techs I had knew the songs pretty well. It was only around '85 that I became really adventurous and I played 'Roundabout' one night, changing guitars about seven times! I think I did the same thing on the *Union* tour with Yes. I enjoyed doing it. It gradually became more complex. I've seen pictures of me from one tour where I have two steel guitars linked together at the front of the stage. I had a lot of things to do; some of it was pedal steel, some of it was steel. Plus I had a huge pedal board and all these guitars. But it wasn't anything to me; it was a requirement. If I was going to stand there and play guitar then it was going to make the right sound, and if a song required a mandolin, then I was going to play a mandolin… There were some times when I bottled out of taking the 175 on the road. I don't know how I came to make that decision, but I did. But sometimes guitars would be flown over if something wasn't right. You know, 'Get Steve's Rickenbacker out of the cupboard and on a plane'… Life could have been easier.

**Things were a little different when you joined Asia.**

In Asia, I took a different approach of playing 335-style guitars all the time, and just filling in sitar bits or steel bits, but lightly. I enjoyed that streamlining, but I still had three of them! I was playing most of the night on one guitar and I liked that. The guitar gets hotted up and sweated up and you get hotted up playing it, and so it was a kind of, 'Let's stay on this guitar because it feels good...'

**Yes have been in and out, somewhat...**

Yes... God, that's an understatement!

**With a lot of line-up changes and alleged personal battles within the band, too.**

When somebody drops out of a band, the band can either fall apart or muster up a whole new kind of energy. This past year and a half has been, to me, a slow relinking with the band. I don't think we've done enough touring to justify our existence at the moment. We've done enough recording: between the two volumes of *Keys To Ascension*, there are about 65 minutes of new music. I really hope that we are going into a time when our plans do come to fruition, that we do stay on target. We're doing some dates in America towards the end of the year, and taking next year to go round everywhere and say, 'We're back with a new record...'

# ROBERT FRIPP

OCTOBER 1998

There's a distinct possibility that more people know Robert Fripp's guitar playing from his sustained intro on David Bowie's single 'Heroes' than for any of his other diverse projects. During a stellar 30-year career, he has played with the various incarnations of his own band, King Crimson, plus side projects like The League Of Gentlemen and The League of Crafty Guitarists, as well as making guest appearances with Talking Heads, Peter Gabriel, Blondie, Brian Eno and Daryl Hall, amongst others.

Back in the '70s, he could be found in small, irregular venues like record shops with a guitar, a battery of effects and two Revox tape recorders, from which he conjured mesmerising symphonic textures. To this side of his playing he gave the nickname 'Frippertronics'. Since then, and with the advent of new digital effects technology and advances in guitar synthesis, Frippertronics has evolved into its current form, dubbed 'Soundscapes'.

Apart from being one of the more amazing guitar players on the planet, Robert Fripp has also turned his hand to teaching by founding Guitar Craft, a series of intermittent residential workshops all over the world, which have been running since 1985. But just as you would expect from King Crimson's mainstay, Guitar Craft doesn't comprise days of ceaseless widdle with the occasional Nirvana riff thrown in for good measure – it's all far more esoteric than that. For a start, students are encouraged to bring only acoustic guitars – and very specifically Ovation acoustics, too. Then there is the 'new standard tuning' of C G D A E G, low to high, to cope with. In other words, preconceptions are left outside and only the open-minded survive. When we talked shop in 1998, these classes were the first topic of discussion...

**Have the courses been well attended?**

The quick answer is yes. How they develop now is that we tend to have on the introductory side of the course, or level one, an average of around two dozen people. In Chile it was more than that, I think it was around 33. But side by side we generally have a Kitchen Team, who are people who have been on several earlier courses and generally have an ongoing practice. For example there is a Seattle Guitar Circle, where a number of people have actually moved their families to Seattle to be together in an ongoing project. In Buenos Aires there is a guitar circle which has an ongoing residential base. In each of these two places are more experienced students. On a course now we would have generally 20–30 people in the Kitchen Team, maybe six or seven 'staff', and the Alexander Technique [a system for reducing stress in a musician's posture, thereby warding off problems associated with repetitive strain injury, or RSI] is present on all Guitar Craft courses and has been a feature since the very early days. On a seven-day course, an Alexander teacher will save me about three days. Then you have anything between 20–35 people on Level One, and so a Guitar Craft course today will generally have anywhere between 45 and 60 people on the premises for a week.

**What do you concentrate on in terms of technique? I have heard that cross-picking is one of the main features.**

That's a heavy metal wrist [indicates my cross-picking hand position mime: straight wristed, with thumb parallel to the imaginary strings].

**So it's more arch wristed?**

Arch wrist is more banjo, and you'll also find it a lot in mandolin picking, which is probably one of the very few codified approaches to a pick, funnily enough. Follow-through mandolin picking would now probably be considered quaint. My main guitar teacher was very much of the old school, 1920s/1930s Clifford Essex/BMG school; multi-instrumentalist, banjoist, mandolinist, guitarist. But when I began with him, it was fairly obvious to me, at age 12 or 13, that there was a gap: the right hand hadn't actually been addressed.

**So where do you begin?**

We begin by doing nothing. If anyone comes in with their guitar, they come in with a host of attitudes, opinions, expectations and judgements, and until the hold of our attitudes has been released to a degree, there's not much I can do to help. So in a Guitar Craft course, we might start by sitting on the floor and doing nothing for half an hour. Because until we can do nothing, until we can ask our body to do nothing for a short time, we can't really ask our body to do something quite specific for a short time. Then we would move to the operation of the left and right hands. If you're going to practise for four or eight hours a day, a fairly important factor is 'Can I sit on this chair for four hours?' Not, 'What do I do with my guitar on this chair for four hours?' but 'Can I sit on this chair for four hours?' So we begin by sitting on the chair or floor and doing nothing for half an hour, and then we move on to, 'Can I sit on a chair for three or four hours?' or whatever, because you're not going to stand and practise. So at this point the Alexander teacher on the course comes in – characters who come to me with problems with their hands find that it is often to do with tension. From there, we move back to doing nothing for half an hour. You have a problem playing that exercise for half an hour? Fine. Do nothing for half an hour. Working back purely from the tensions locked into the hands to the sense that, well, if I'm this tense in my hands is it possible that I am this tense somewhere else? Well, yes actually. But it's a surprise coming from me, but not so from an Alexander Technique teacher. We tried yoga, too, but that worked for some people and not for everyone. But Alexander Technique works for just about everyone. So you might say that this has virtually nothing whatsoever to do with the guitar, and I'd say yes, that's exactly right, and it has more to do with the person who is holding the guitar. But in Guitar Craft we begin with fundamentals. At this point, maybe three or four days into the course, something might begin to happen, but because the exercises take place within a context of music, the students are often invited to write, improvise, compose music and present it in performance, because you learn an instrument in the context of music, and music is only within the context of the performance of music. So we've moved from sitting on a chair and doing nothing to writing and performing music within six or seven days. Then, however well you are able to play your instrument in a relaxed and focused fashion, you may or may not be able to write music for it. But if you perform to other people, everything changes. To walk into any situation where music is being performed in front of an audience, it is impossible to control the situation. You might have a heckler, and if you don't have a heckler in the audience, then Robert might throw peanuts at you. Or maybe his shoes. I've thrown both my shoes at a Guitar Craft student performing in a rough red-neck bar in West Virginia. He was a Los Angeles attorney and it was so much performed in his sleep that I threw both of my shoes at him consecutively. So he looked up at me, took off his shoes and threw them back. You might say, 'So at Guitar Craft seminars you throw your shoes at students who perform?' and I say, 'Yes – and peanuts and soft fruit...' and sometimes I'm not the only one. Sometimes I even put out bowls of soft fruit out in case the audience wish to throw it. At a course in Buenos Aires a couple of years ago, the instruments and the performers were spattered with soft and overripe fruit. You could hear it splat on the instrument. Does this sound like a seminar you'd like to send your students to, David?

**Oh, I dunno; I think some of them probably deserve it...**

How we do one small thing, like hold a pick, is how we do all the small things that we do, because our approach to that small thing is the approach to another small thing. And all those small things taken together is how we live our life. If someone comes to you, or me, or someone else for guitar lessons and they say, 'Come on then, show me how to hold a pick', what they are actually saying is, 'Show me how to lead my life.' But, that's often not what they believe is the question that is being asked. Now some people come into Guitar Craft specifically with that intention. At our inaugural meeting we introduce ourselves and say who we are, where we've come from and what's our aim for the course. They might say, 'I have no interest in playing the guitar, but I have the sense that you have a way of living your life, or you have a discipline and I would like to have some sense of that.' And it's often people with a background in martial arts who understand what we're doing, rather than someone who is perhaps a professional guitar teacher. Because someone in the martial arts very quickly learns about having a centre of gravity. A guitarist sits on a chair for four hours, and he must have a centre of gravity, too. In martial arts, if you are slightly off in either direction, then you will have a bloody nose. In Aikido, you will be on the mat. So someone with a martial arts background understands when I put a lot of time and attention into holding the pick. They know why: it's not arbitrary, it's not anal retention, it's not being finicky, it's that if in the left hand there is no centre of gravity, if in the right hand there is no centre of gravity, if in the body there is no centre of gravity, you will not be playing that exercise for more than ten minutes, because the tension will be excruciating. If the right hand is out of balance, then you'll hear a horrible, nasty scraping sound as the pick scrapes across the wound strings.

So, getting back: Guitar Craft addresses the fundamentals to begin, and it's very rarely what you expect it to be. Before you do something, you do nothing. You establish a relationship with your body. Why? Because it is parts of your body that are playing the guitar. 'What's this got to do with music?' Well, write some then and please play it to us at lunchtime, and if it's crap people might throw food at you.

**Tell me more about Soundscapes.**

I must say that I find the concert tradition not appropriate for the music I want to play at the moment. The idea that, there in the audience, you sit and look up...there's a separation. So, from one point of view, Soundscapes as a music is looking for a connection, even a communion between the audience and the music. And it's a lot easier if people don't have to buy tickets. To put it another way, if the act of music is the music, the act of music in a commercial context is undermined and compromised to an alarming degree. So playing in

Salisbury Cathedral, where people come in and are invited to make a donation, you have an interesting situation where money does change hands, but it's on the basis of a voluntary contribution along the lines of the widow's mite, and an appeal to conscience. But it's not a commercial context and there's no concert tradition in Salisbury Cathedral, although concerts are given there; and freed up in this way, in the performance of music, everything can change.

**The concept really began through your work with Brian Eno, didn't it?**

Back in 1967, I had acquired a Burns fuzz unit. The sound of the guitar then was, for me, pretty limited, and Marshall stacks and Les Pauls were only just beginning to appear. And so you could begin to get, at the end of 1968, fairly savage guitar sounds that were meaty. But the guitar was still so limited. What I immediately heard in the droning and bleeping coming from Eno's Revoxes was comparable to a string quartet in terms of prolongation through time, which a guitar didn't normally have. So there was this wonderful 18 minutes of sustained texture and, on the second pass, the opportunity to solo over it. So in 40 minutes there was side one of *No Pussyfooting* done. We did a short tour of Spain, France and England in May 1975, and in the first venue in France we were booed off. When the booing reached a volume equal to that of the PA, we looked at each other, nodded and left the stage. Now, good ideas are often really good ideas 20 to 25 years later. At the time, if it's very new, it tends to create a radical division between the audience – half say 'yes', the other half 'no'. Stravinsky's *Rite Of Spring* is an obvious example. [When Stravinsky's ballet was first performed in the Théâtre des Champs-Elysées on 29 May 1913, it caused a riot.] The first performance of Fripp and Eno in Madrid, we had no idea what would happen. We walked on, we played, we walked off. Five minutes before we went on, we said to each other, 'What shall we play?' At the end, when the looping was continuing and we left, we went up into the balcony of the theatre to listen to it gradually die away over a 20- or 30-minute period with the audience. Five minutes after we left the stage, the lights came up, but the music kept going. So we sat there in the audience looking at their response, and some stayed and listened, while some left. But we were told afterwards that there were two Spanish audients sitting next to each other, and one turned to his friend and said, 'This is genius!' and the other turned to his friend and said, 'This is shit!' and, hearing each other's responses, turned to each other and apparently became quite argumentative.

Then, moving forward to 1977, I asked Eno to explain the two-Revox setup to me, which he did, and I said, 'You've done yourself out of a job, now.' Well, Eno was busy enough without that... So I began to work with it on my own in New York. Today you can do sampling, but then it was a question of recording each chord in, splicing it, putting it on the reel, and so if you needed chord changes, you had to record each chord on analogue tape, 30 seconds or a minute or whatever, and cut it in. I did all of this and used it as backgrounds for Daryl Hall. We used some loops for Peter Gabriel on *Exposure* in Holland, and then in '79 I went on the road with it for four months. Then, in 1983, the music system tour – about ten days in North America – and then nothing until new technology arrived at the end of '91. This brings us round to the 'Why?' As a guitarist, you can think symphonically in real time, rather than sitting down and working out the parts. It is improvised, and even if you begin and have a sense of where it might go, it's so complex. The mental process of thinking, 'This is repeating every 60 seconds and this one is repeating every 12 seconds and this other one is repeating every 18 seconds'...there actually comes a point where I can't follow the detail. You keep a broad view of what's going on, but when that becomes too complex, you simply respond. So you might go in there thinking you know what's going to happen, but the point comes where you can't hold on to it rationally – you have to let go and get in. I was listening to Soundscapes for a couple of projects the other night and I thought, 'How do I approach this?' It can be very frustrating if you approach it with the questions: 'What are we listening for? Are we listening for a tune, a chord, rhythm... Is it ambient?' The approach I adopted was that this is sculpture. It was more like I was listening to a sonic sculpture than I was the performance of music. It wasn't quite ambient, it wasn't quite new music or free music or improvised music – it was something else. As a listener to it, I have to give up my expectations and my demands of how I normally listen to music. And something can happen, and sometimes it doesn't. So it continues to be a wonderful and remarkable challenge as a player because it's always fresh and it's always rediscovery. Listening to it now, as we have been over a period of seven years, you can hear how it's changing and developing. But it's not a rational process; so because there is a development and there is a form and there is a process and it's not rational, there's something else going on. And I'm not sure I can tell you what it is... It's true to the moment in which it was created, but you can't quite make demands on it. What is its function? What does a concert do for the musicians or the audience? It's not like music on a slave gang, where you sing so that your work is in rhythm. Why do we listen to music? So then you do move into genuinely philosophical areas and the aesthetics of music. It's a process of ongoing discovery. It's always changing and inventing itself, as if it has a life apart from the person playing it. But it places a demand on the audience, and it's quite a considerable one. It assumes a measure of goodwill and commitment from the audience to make it possible. So it's better, from the standpoint of a working musician, that your audience don't pay any money to see this, so that they don't feel gypped if they don't get their jollies, or if they don't get their expectations met, or if they don't see flying fingers. It's better, too, if it's not performed in a place associated with the performance of music. So your expectations are, once again, side-stepped.

It's like a painting: you look at paintings, which technically can't move, but sometimes they do. Soundscapes seem to exist and move through time, whereas a piece of sculpture sits or stands there. But if you get involved in a certain way, the painting or the sculpture moves.

# EDDIE VAN HALEN

MARCH 1993

*I interviewed Ed during a break from the band's rehearsals for the European leg of their 1993 tour. Whereas most of us have to make do with the local scout hut or the bass player's front room to rehearse in, when you're Van Halen you hire Docklands Arena for the week. Previously, the band had made itself a stranger to the UK, not having toured here for several years, owing to what Ed called a 'terrible chain of events...' – the departure of David Lee Roth and the necessary re-invention of the band.*

**Van Halen has been through a lot since you were last here.**

Well, when Roth quit the band, it kinda left us going 'Hmmmm...' In the beginning, I was planning on doing a solo record, with Alex and Mike, but having a different singer on each track: Joe Cocker, Phil Collins, Pete Townshend. I was thinking of doing something strange. It wouldn't be Van Halen, but it would be Alex, Mike and me with all these different singers. But logistically, it would probably just be getting finished now, what with everyone's scheduling, y'know? So we nixed that idea and Alex said, 'Heck, let's continue with Van Halen. You write the music anyway.' So I called Sammy. That was on a Friday and he came down on Monday. We already had about five or six tracks. Sammy walked in, and I didn't tell him a thing to sing, I didn't tell him nothing to do. He just walked straight in; he just fitted in there like he'd been there all my life. And I just went, 'Where have you been all my life, you asshole?' On top of being a great singer and musician, he's one of the funniest guys I've met in my life! He's got such a twisted sense of humour, so we really get on like brothers. But, after that first record, we really had to establish ourselves on our home turf first. So what we ended up doing was touring for ten months in the US. That brought us to '87, and after that Sammy still owed Geffen a solo record. So I figured, to speed things up, I'd produce it and play bass on it. That took another six to eight months to do, and then of course he had to do a promotional tour, and after that, we had to do another record for Warner Brothers. So here comes *OU812* in '88. We had to go on tour behind that, starting in the States, because that's what everyone wanted – I'm talking powers that be: management, agents, record company and so on. OK, so we tour behind that for eight months and here it is, 1989 and Sammy and I are literally spanked! We're beat! Since '85, when we started recording *5150*, until the end of the tour of *OU812*, we had four years non-stop working. So we planned on taking a year off before we started recording *For Unlawful Carnal Knowledge*, but we owed Japan a long-form video! So we never got our year off, we had maybe six months, just enough time to start writing for the next record. I suggested to the guys that we hadn't been to Europe for too many years, but when we were starting the *For Unlawful Carnal Knowledge* tour, halls weren't available over here.

**Let's talk guitars. How important is the 'feel' of an instrument to you, as opposed to the sound?**

The feel and the sound is all. It's everything! I like it to be easy to play – why make it hard on yourself? It's like, why don't I put the action up to there [indicates an inch or two above fingerboard]? I remember reading an interview a few years ago – I won't mention the guy's name. He said, 'People who play Gibsons are pussies; a Fender is much harder to play.' But why make it hard to play? I ain't no macho guy. I like it to be easy and have fun. So that's what my amp and guitar are designed to do. It's buttery and easy; you don't even have to pick half the time.

**I notice from the live video that you don't play synth on stage any more...**

Well, here's the deal. I used to, and Sammy used to cover on guitar, but now he doesn't want to play guitar. He prefers that I play guitar. So I sequence the keyboards. We don't have someone sitting behind the curtains. It is me playing, but it's sequenced.

**You started off playing drums, didn't you?**

Yeah. I'm more of a rhythmic player than anything. I think it's just something you're born with, y'know? I mean, I've been making music since I was six years old. I think I got my melodic sense from playing piano. I got into The Dave Clark Five when they came to America, and I just loved drums, and so I started playing drums. But I don't think about what I do, I really don't. Put it this way: you've got this many notes… [he plays a chromatic scale] 12 notes. However you use them is up to you. None of this 'I'm playing Phrygian mode.' Fuck what mode you're playing in. You got 12 notes and how you want to play them is up to you.

**You must have favourite patterns…**

Sure, man – you got the 12 notes. Put it this way: you can do whatever you want that sounds good to you. There are standard licks that I do, but I really don't think about it that much. People always make fun of me because I can't pick the proper way. I have to use these two fingers [indicates thumb and middle finger]. Then when I do the hammer-ons, I just tuck the pick away. I don't know how I came up with that, but it just came natural. When I do the both-hands thing, I just stick it in my mouth.

**You record most of your songs live in the studio…**

Yeah. I think it's so funny… I won't mention the name of the band, but I walked into a studio and there's just a guitarist out there playing to a click, and then they add the drums later! And then the bass player comes in. I'm goin', 'What?!' Mike, Al, Sammy and I, we're blowin' live in the studio, we play. We try two or three takes of a song, and if we get a take, we go 'Good!' If not, we move on to another song. If that doesn't work, we call it a day and go, 'See ya tomorrow!'

**You've been in the position before of having to overdub your rhythm parts in the studio, rather than, as is usually the case, the lead...**

Yes, because we went in and did our first album the way we play live. I asked Ted Templeman and Don Landee, 'Can I just play the way I play live?' and they're goin', 'Sure. Do whatever you want.' Obviously, live, I don't play rhythm parts underneath the solo; I just solo. I didn't have any parts written for underneath the solo. It sounded fine, but a little empty, y'know. I've now learned how to do that, but back then I'd never been in the studio before.

**What about your recording setup. Do you scale down and use smaller amps?**

No, I've always used a 4 x 12 cabinet, with a Marshall or now a Peavey – one head with the cord fed into it, with a Shure SM57 mic on one speaker – pan it to the left with a harmoniser on the right. That's it.

**Are there any players around who you find yourself getting excited about?**

Beck, Steve Lukather... I don't know, I generally like everything, and at the same time nothing really inspires me, if that's what you mean. I think the last guitarist who moved me was Holdsworth, just because he was so out there, y'know? I wanted to work with him and try to bring him back to earth, so to speak, and make him more accessible, but it never quite materialised. The guy just has some insane technique; if he'd only make it a little more melodic. If you look back at Clapton, Hendrix, Page, these guys all played different. Nowadays it's all the same. I'm not saying that I'm the last one to be different, but I really don't think that anyone's done much different on the guitar since me. Nothing that blows my mind, anyway. I mean, Eric Johnson is a great player, so is Satriani and so is Vai. All these guys are great players, but back then, between Townshend, Hendrix, Clapton, Page and Beck, you had five unique mothers!

One of my favourite solos is in 'Cinnamon Girl' by Neil Young. It's a one-note solo and it just fits the song. Anyone else would have gone 'Woraaagh' and it wouldn't have made any sense. If I've changed over the years, it's that I've got more in tune with the song... You've gotta decide, are you making music for people or are you doing it for yourself? Anyone who says that they're not making music for people can kiss my ass. I dunno, maybe they should just sit home in their closets and make music. Why bother making records and trying to sell them, if you're trying to make music for yourself? These guys who claim, 'I'm an artist and I don't care if I make records or not...' well, why even bother making them? I want to sell records. I want people to enjoy what I'm doing as much as I do. And if that means I'm selling out, then I'm selling out...

# PAUL GILBERT

SEPTEMBER 1995

*I sat down with Gilbert in the late summer of 1995, just as his band, Mr Big, were putting the finishing touches to the* Hey Man *album. Earlier, during the day of our interview, Paul had cut the ribbon at the opening of the Academy of Contemporary Music in Guildford, but now, at the venue for an evening clinic, we were experiencing a power failure backstage. Despite planning to leave early the next morning for a four-day break before joining his Mr Big colleagues in the studio to mix the new album, the inimitable guitar wizard was unfazed. Anyone who has seen Paul's tuition videos will know the sort of thing to which the clinic audiences were treated: immaculate playing with a few surprises waiting in the wings. Who would have guessed, for instance, that he would choose to demonstrate his skills by playing tracks like 'All You Need Is Love' (including the horn and violin parts), Hendrix's 'Fire', the Prelude to Bach's Third Cello Suite in C Major, 'Fly Me To The Moon' (the Count Basie/Frank Sinatra big-band version), Emerson Lake and Palmer's 'Karn Evil 9' (the keyboard part!) and, during the afternoon soundcheck, Genesis's 'The Lamb Lies Down On Broadway' – a two-hand tour de force, during which he played Tony Banks' arpeggiated keyboard part whilst singing! But, as he explained when we began, it is the question-and-answer sections of the 90-minute show that tell their own tale.*

**Which queries crop up more than others?**

Let's see…People want to know about sweep picking, which is funny because it's not a technique that I use these days. I've found other ways of doing arpeggios, because sweep picking was always so difficult for me to do. I was very excited about it at first, because I'd never seen anyone do it, but it's always one of those areas where I'm walking the tightrope of my own technique, and I'm real close to messing up when I do it, and usually choose string skipping or something as an alternative. The best thing about a clinic is that I can then immediately play something to show what I mean. The other thing that people want me to do is play parts of Mr Big songs: the intro to 'Green-Tinted Sixties Mind' or 'Colorado Bulldog', those are the two common ones. Many people are curious as to whether there is any difference between my guitar and the one they see in the store. The only difference is that I have glow-in-the-dark tape stuck around my output jack so if the lights go out I can see where to put the plug.

**And that is the only difference?**

Well, that and the fact that mine has probably got wimpier strings on it.

**String gauges: that must crop up every night, surely?**

Oh yeah...[Chuckles.] I've been using everything. On the first Mr Big album I used .010s, the last one I used .008s and lately I've been using .009s, but I've got them tuned down to D because I do a lot of singing in the clinics, and I've got a low voice, and so it helps if I tune down. So .009s tuned down to D are real loose and real easy to play and I like that. I like having a guitar that's easy to play.

**Going from .010s to .008s must have needed some adjusting to in terms of technique?**

When I first put on a set of .008s it felt funny because it was almost like there was no physical effort, like I was playing guitar with my mind. I couldn't feel my fingers. I saw this TV show about the occult and some guy was bending spoons with his mind, just looking at the spoon and making faces, and the spoon was bending, and that's how .008s felt to me. I could play guitar just by looking at it funny and it would start playing. It was so much easier than .010s.

**What about playing action – high or low?**

Not low, not really. [He passes me his Ibanez for a quick look. It is, in truth, a medium to low action.] I just think of it as normal. With strings as light as these, you could get it a lot lower. I just get it as low as I can before it buzzes. There's maybe a little buzz in there, but it's not too bad.

**It's a big cliché that in order to play fast, you need a really low action.**

More than anything you need a lot of practice! All the other things help, but the main thing is putting in the time.

**On your PGM500, the volume control is much further from the playing area than normal.**

Yeah, I love that because most guitars have the volume control under the bridge pickup, which I guess is good if you're doing the fade-up thing, picking at the same time, but most of the time to me it just gets in the way, and I always end up knocking it. Also, on this guitar it just looks cool and that is important to me. Not only is it important that it looks cool on stage, but it's important when I'm practising. Believe it or not, I find that if my guitar looks good, I want to pick it up and practise, and I'm looking down thinking, 'This looks cool,' you know? Whereas if it's some ugly old guitar, I'll look down and think, 'Well I don't know…'

**Obviously you get asked a lot of questions about speed. What advice do you offer would-be speedsters?**

A lot of it is not playing fast until you have the co-ordination and making sure that the speed and co-ordination come together. I tell people that it took me eight years before I could do anything resembling fast picking, which I think is a long time. I could probably have learned to pick fast sooner, but there were no books or videos around when I was learning to pick, and so I just had to learn from records. I got a lot of my picking technique from listening to Yngwie, because I thought he was a great picker.

**So perhaps the only answer is to lock yourself away with a metronome?**

Well, that and listen to the way it sounds. Always use your ears – if something sounds bad, try to figure out what it is.

**One question you are asked a lot is why you use your left hand third finger so much when playing.**

It's not something I think about now, but it dates back to when I first had guitar lessons and my teacher showed me how to do half steps with my second finger, and whole steps with my third, and a minor third with my pinkie. My hands were big enough at the time and so it didn't pose any problem, and so it's just the way I always did it. But I don't think it matters. I've seen guitar players doing some really scary stuff with just three fingers, and then you start thinking about Django...

**Another FAQ must concern the learning of theory. Just how much theory do you need to know?**

An analogy that I always make is that it is like taking an English course in school for learning to speak. Before you go to school you can talk, you learn from imitating your parents, watching TV and from example. You do this without even opening a book or learning to read, but by the time you are three years old, you've learned a lot of the basics of speech and you can communicate pretty well. From then on you start learning grammar and begin to fine tune what you've learned with a set of specific rules; you learn spelling, how to write, how to read, and so on. Applied to music, I think the order that you learn those things is very important: the ears come first, and then after a certain number of years you can start labelling the things you've learned. For instance, you learn that this series of notes that you've been playing is now called a major scale. Otherwise it makes so little sense, because you're labelling something that you don't know how to use yet, and it's more confusing than anything.

**Billy Sheehan is on record as saying that he could name practically any tune and you could play it from memory.**

I know a lot of tunes, yeah, but not modern ones. From the late '50s until about 1984, I know a lot of tunes. I was in a lot of cover bands at one time and I just love playing music, and it comes from me just being a fan of music and saying, 'Here's something that I like, I wanna play along.' I'll go in phases, too; I'll go through a whole period where my favourite band of all time is The Hollies or The Beatles, or I'll go through a whole R&B thing. I just love some of that Michael Jackson stuff, like 'I Want You Back' [sings and plays guitar and bass parts all at once] – such a cool bass part.

**Obviously working out guitar, horn, piano or cello parts gets easier the more you do it.**

Oh sure. It was funny because after going to GIT and going through all the theory, I became a very diatonic player. I was so well versed in the modes of the major scale that I found my playing became very strict within whatever mode I was playing. It messed up my ability to play blues for a while. I remember I was playing with a friend of mine one time, and we were doing an A minor blues and he was playing the major sixth. And I said, 'How can you play the major sixth? It's a minor chord, it's meant to be natural minor.' And he said, 'No, it's blues. You always play the major sixth – it's Dorian.' I remember thinking that you could never play Dorian with blues because you must never have the major and minor together. Whereas, of course, in blues, major and minor are together all the time. You can play major pentatonic and go straight into a minor one, and it sounds great. So I had to go back and rediscover blues harmony...

**So there is a danger in being too well versed in theory, then?**

It's a temporary danger. There is so much to learn, that until you grasp all of it, you remain unaware of the flexibility within the music rule book. To me, the thing to start with is diatonic harmony – chords in the major scale – and soon after that you realise that there are other things, but you've got to start somewhere. Knowledge is good, but it can temporarily screw you up if you don't realise that you don't know it all. I think a lot of the best players probably don't know too much about it, they just got it by ear and they have all their shapes. They probably know a lot of theory, but they don't know what it's called.

**Is there some general advice that you would give to every struggling guitar student?**

I think the general thing is to practise as much as you can, play with other musicians as much as you can – especially drummers because it helps your timing – and use your ears. A lot of guys will do a lot of practice, but I'll hear them and think they're not listening to what they're doing; because if they were, they would have stopped and fixed some things along the way.

# ANDY SUMMERS

JANUARY 1994

*I interviewed Andy Summers long after The Police had hung up their collective handcuffs and ventured out into the world as individuals. He had just released an acoustic guitar album with jazz player John Etheridge. Our chat was a brief one, and, as usual, we started talking about the early days of learning to play.*

**What did you listen to growing up?**

As a teenager what I wanted to do was play jazz; rock came a bit later for me. I listened to all the American jazz players and played in a jazz club – that was the whole thing for me. Rock and R&B actually came much later.

**Who among the American players you mentioned were the major influences?**

People like Kenny Burrell, Wes Montgomery, Jimmy Raney, Barney Kessel – I guess most of them were out of the '50s, but were still the main guys. I'm naming the obvious ones, but there were probably a lot of others. I just started off by learning hundreds of standards. I tried to work out all the Barney Kessel Trio tunes when I was about 16... I bought a Django Reinhardt record when I was 17. There was one version of 'Nuages' with a clarinet which was a bit beyond me at the time, I think.

**People don't necessarily connect you with acoustic guitar. They probably see you as electric-guitar-through-effects man – mainly thanks to The Police – so an acoustic album from you may take a few people by surprise.**

I played classical guitar for six years in the States prior to joining The Police, barely touching an electric. So I spent years on an acoustic instrument prior to The Police. I've always had one. It probably will come as a surprise, but people don't know everything about you, do they?

**What about the guitars you used on the album?**

I have an Andrew Manson – an English guitar maker, a really nice one. Basically we had a few guitars that we felt at liberty to swap: a Martin D28, a couple of Lowdens, a Gibson B25, a Guild 12-string, a Guild fretless bass... We tried to make it really acoustic. The way we voiced the chords, we tried to get it big sounding. A lot of the compositions are modal because they work really well on the guitar – it sounds open. We now have this consciousness about sound: everyone is into it and it's very important to make a state-of-the-art record because it is a very sensual, ravishing, beautiful instrument. You don't want the music to be 'new age' – you want it to have content – but at the same time you must use this sparkling quality of the acoustic.

**What sort of gear do you use?**

Well it depends what I'm doing, but I've got a couple of racks. I use a PCM 70... I can't even remember, it's a long time since I looked in my rack! I was into electric guitar last year. I had this rock trio that I played with for about six months and I was totally electric. I've got two Bradshaw racks, one great big one which I've more or less abandoned, and I've got a much smaller one which contains various choruses... My big rack I had set up for looping. I had three or four looping devices. Doing this acoustic album with John meant that I turned my back on electric for about six months, and I think that's been very healthy for me as a guitar player, because now I look at all this rack gear and realise that I don't want to go back to it. I sort of want to go back to having two or three pedals on the floor. I remember that in The Police I felt like I had a lot more freedom: the Echoplex I could piss around with and I liked the 'hands-on playing' aspect of it. It's a lot more creative, a lot more artistic. With the digital gear, you set your thing and it does sound beautiful, but I feel like I'm locked into someone else's idea and not my own. I have found it frustrating. I've been doing about eight or nine years of this stuff, and I've kind of burned out on it. Going back to the acoustic has sort of freed me up.

**Are you still using your Telecaster?**

Not much. I've still got that one guitar I used with The Police, and it's still a great guitar. Actually, every time I pick it up, which is once or twice a year, I think, 'Christ! Why aren't I playing it?' I actually use a Steve Klein guitar with a Trans Trem, and that's a great guitar.

# MALCOLM YOUNG

DECEMBER 1992

*Malcolm Young was born in Glasgow and lived there until he was ten years old, at which time his family emigrated to Australia. Older brother George was already a musician and younger brother, Angus, was about six. 'I started playing guitar in Glasgow. It's one of those things, y'know, where I had a few older brothers kicking around who played acoustic guitar, and so there was always one around. I guess I started seriously picking it up when I got to Australia, but I knew how to get hold of the strings and a few chords and a few riffs at the time: the ones with three or four notes in – same as what we do today, really!'*

*The rest, as they say, is history: AC/DC formed in 1973, with Malcolm as the stalwart rhythm guitarist and Angus the wildman lead, and they became one of the most influential hard rock acts of the decade. One could even argue the band's effect on world politics... When Panama's ex-dictator, Manuel Noriega, took refuge in the country's Vatican Embassy, the American troops surrounding the building took one look at the situation and brought out their secret weapon: non-stop, high-volume AC/DC aimed directly at Noriega's supposed safe haven. The operation resulted in a bloodless victory for the forces of good. I asked Malcolm if he remembered which track they had used. 'I think it was "You Shook Me All Night Long",' he laughed. 'They just blasted it out really loud, just to drive him out.' I mentioned that there are many people who would have found that good enough reason to stay put. 'Nah, that's torture, that stuff,' he chuckled, warming to the theme. We then turned to his early days and his first guitars.*

**So the first guitar was an old acoustic?**

Yeah, I guess it was just an old Japanese acoustic. The older brothers used to go camping a lot and always ended up smashing the guitar, and so every week there was another acoustic arriving. So it was only worth probably two or three quid. The first serious guitar I got was a Hofner Clubman that I got given to me by George, my brother who was in The Easybeats. So it was a hand-me-down, y'know? So I got that, ripped the face off it and put a black cover on, and used that for a long time. Then I gave that to Angus, when I got my Gretsch.

**Is that the same one you use today?**

Yes, that's the same one I use on stage. It's a Jet Firebird.

**Presumably Angus didn't stick with the Hofner for too long...**

He had it for a couple of years – bedroom stuff, y'know? I think probably one of the first bands he was in he had the Hofner, when he was about 13 or 14.

**What led you towards playing rhythm guitar?**

Rhythm has always been my thing. When I used to listen to records, I used to listen to the drummer. Ringo's fills with The Beatles – they were always simple, but they stuck out in my mind. Lennon was conjuring up the feel within the track, y'know, and I sort of got into it that way, being a fan of John Lennon. So I ended up playing guitar a bit like a drummer, with that sort of influence.

**Who did you listen to, as far as the guitar was concerned?**

I used to listen to Jeff Beck. To me, he is one hell of a guitar player. When he attacked the guitar, it was rhythmic, the way a drummer would do accents. I used to listen to that guy a lot. I liked Pete Townshend too. He was a bit of an influence because of his big chords. Occasionally, he would come up with a little rhythmic part, here and there.

**Perhaps a bit of Jimmy Page, too?**

I liked a few of his things; they had a song called 'Good Times, Bad Times' and that had a good rhythmic riff to it. It really swung the whole track along. Again, they got more riffy, more heavy and I didn't get too much off on it. I liked the drumming big time! Bonham was shit hot with Zeppelin. I think there was a feud between Beck and Page, y'know, like, who was the original? I was more of a Jeff Beck fan.

**Rhythm guitar seems to be a dying art these days. It seems to carry a bit of a stigma, like you might be an inadequate lead player if you play rhythm. You've dealt with all that, presumably...**

Yeah. I'm content when it's firing. There is nothing worse than having nothing to feel when you're playing. It may be the building you're in, where it becomes playing by numbers – I really hate that. I hate playing under those circumstances. You tend to then have to generate the feel yourself out of frustration. I probably didn't realise that earlier on, because it was just raw aggression. These days, there is an art to it. When you are in the situation where it's just not happening you've got to take over, force everyone to take it up another gear. It's not a light-fingered guitar player's job, that's for sure. It's very muscular. I use thick strings, for instance: I've got a 56 on the bass E and a 12 on top. That allows me to really whack the guitar.

**The Gretsch that you use isn't really the traditional rock instrument, is it?**

I've actually tried to get spare Gretsch Firebirds, but they never sound the same. This one that I've got feels a lot more solid than the others. For some reason it's twice as loud as any of the others you pick up.

**Is that still the original bridge pickup?**

It's still the original. I've always had it rewound with the thickest-gauge wire that I can get in there. It's harder to get every time I want to get it rewound. People always say, 'Put the thin stuff on there – we can get more of it on there,' but that doesn't work. I'm looking for a pure microphone sound. I find that, with the heavy coil, you get as much of it on there as you can and that's the magic.

**It looks like your guitar has been dug about a bit over the years. The neck pickup seems to have disappeared along the way.**

That was never used. It always sounded shit, anyway. It was just a waffly, bassy, middley type of sound that never did anything, y'know? I pulled that out because the bridge one went at one time, and so I pulled it out and put the front in the back while the other one was being repaired. And the guitar sounded better with that hole in it – it sounded louder! Over the years, people have asked me how I stop it from feeding back, but for some reason, it just doesn't do it. Maybe the wood is waterlogged by now, or something!

**It may be that you've just learned to control it...**

Yeah, you get to know it.

**It doesn't look like you've kept the original bridge on the guitar...**

No, I think it's a Gibson. The original ones were a problem; they used to just sit on there. When you're playing pretty hard, you can just knock the bridge flying!

**You've covered the place where the tailpiece went with a sort of fish-head shaped piece of plastic...**

That was some kid in Sydney that put the bridge on for me. It's supposed to be some guy's dick. I never knew it until about two years later when he told me – it was just his little joke. He was having a good old laugh at my expense for a couple of years. I never knew. But I just kept it on, y'know.

**You've used that one guitar for most of your career. Have you had to have much work done on it?**

I remember a few years back, we got a deal from Rotosound – the first free string deal we got – and they changed to a sort of rough-wound string, or something. Anyway, about every two weeks or so, I would notice the frets down the bottom end, which is the only bit of the neck I use, just kept wearing out down there because of these strings. But I've probably had to re-fret about half a dozen times since I had the guitar. Now I prefer these wide frets, while a lot of kids seem to go for the narrow ones.

**Do you know what year your guitar is?**

I think it's a '62.

**Does it have a high action?**

It's about medium, I guess. With the heavy-gauge strings, at the beginning of a tour it gets quite hard on the hands about halfway through the set, so I ended up bringing the action down a bit. The neck is flat on top, it's not like it's semi-curved or anything. I find I can take the action right down on it – it's a brilliant neck. But I keep it about medium height, mainly for the tone.

**What do you use for a spare?**

Well, I've got another Gretsch that I've had basically changed into what my first one is. But again, it's not the same. There's a guy at Gibson called Roger Giffin who has made me a few Les Paul-shaped, hollow guitars, and he stuck a Gretsch pickup on them, and they go about three-quarters of the way there. But nothing comes near the other one – it's my Stradivarius!

**Live, you stay back with your amp...**

Yeah, that really comes from the early days when we just stuck close together. I originally used to play on the snare side of the drummer and I really liked it that side, but then as we rearranged the band on stage, I sort of missed out on that. But I still stay really close to the drummer. Even these days when we monitor up, we really only put the vocal through the monitor, because otherwise Brian wouldn't have a chance of hearing himself if we stuck the kit in there. And so the only place you are guaranteed to hear the drums is if you stick back there. Also, there's not much for me to do up front.

**You come forward for a bit of backing vocals.**

Even then it's a bit like crossing the M40, what with Brian and Angus out there!

**You do quite a lot of the writing in the band, don't you?**

Yeah. The ideal situation for us is to come up with a riff that you really get off on. If you're lucky enough to come up with one that really stands out, then that's a great way to start writing a song, or maybe if you've got an idea for a chorus or a line for a chorus. Angus can come up with a lot of good lines and riffs. If you come up with a good title you can think, 'It's got to be mean', y'know, wind yourself up.

**How do you arrange who plays what between you and Angus?**

We try and complement each other. Angus will pick up the strongest part for the record – the part that should be the lead part, or sounds like it should be played by the lead player – and I'll just feel my way around it.

**You use a lot of open-string chords...**

Yeah, the quality there is the thing. They're big chords and they can ring for ages. If you're playing in E flat, or something, it's like, 'Hang on a minute, this is wimpy!' Thank God we haven't got a rock 'n' roll piano player in the band. You can take any one of our songs and move them up and play them as barre chords, and they're just not the same songs any more. They've lost width or depth, somehow.

# STEVE HACKETT
MARCH 1993

*This interview was done a long time after Steve Hackett had left the folds of Genesis and potential megastardom. There had been quite a long period of silence, during which he took time to 'reorganise and regroup', the result of which was a solo album entitled* Guitar Noir...

**In the early Genesis days, you apparently used to suffer badly from nerves before a performance.**

In the very early days, yeah. It was because we used to try and mount a very big production with equipment that was not at all reliable. And so we all used to have this feeling in those days of 'will it or won't it fly?'

**How much is the 'ex-Genesis' tag a millstone for you?**

It's funny. It can be a millstone, but in some ways it can work for you. The record business is like that. If you want to be a survivor, you have to reorganise and regroup, especially if you don't want to work to the same formula each time. Maybe if your mission is to be an agent of change, then you have to commit professional suicide on a regular basis.

**Do you find that people listen to your albums and expect to hear Genesis?**

I think there are a lot of disenfranchised early Genesis listeners, for whom the current crop of songs from Genesis are a lot less adventurous.

**Obviously you've moved on, musically speaking, and it would be extremely unfair of people to expect you to have both feet placed firmly in *Foxtrot* territory.**

Right! There were some interesting parts to those albums, but when I listen to that stuff now it all sounds very serious and very earnest. The key word in those days was 'experimentation', and I think that is the thread that runs through my stuff today. In other words, I start a song and I don't know where it is going to end up. When I start writing, I just let the song lead me astray. I like the fact that you can start writing a ballad, but there is always this finger beckoning you and saying, 'No. You can make it more sinister than that...'

**It's been quite a while since the world saw you performing in a strictly rock context. Your last such project was GTR with Steve Howe, but that was in '86. Why the wait?**

Circumstances beyond personal control. [Laughs.] Sometimes you find yourself between bands, between deals. Anyway, the upshot of it is that we ended up building our own studio and starting up our own record company.

**How long did *Guitar Noir* take to record?**

Strictly speaking, ever since 1987! A year after GTR, I did an acoustic album called *Momentum* and toured it through '87 and '88. I more or less started on this round about then. There was at least one album's worth of material scrapped in the meantime. I had probably three or four albums' worth of material in various states of play, and having your own studio does enable you to take the most interesting parts of a jigsaw and stick them into a larger picture. So it sounds like it's taken an extraordinary length of time and sounds really indulgent, but in fact it was the reverse.

**You play a lot of nylon string on the album until around the middle, when you go into electric. This gives a kind of dual identity.**

There were at least two styles of arrangement that were growing over the years: electric versus acoustic. But the strongest material seemed to fall between those two camps, and so it was my manager's suggestion that we had the more thoughtful stuff first of all and build towards the electric band stuff. I think if it had been up to me, without that creative guidance, I would have come in with the heaviest track first of all – just like everybody else. But I'm very pleased that it starts out with the slightly unexpected. It's a more subtle introduction to the album. If I were to do it the other way round and choose my personal favourite from the electric stuff, I'd probably choose 'Vampyre With A Healthy Appetite' because it's so riffy.

**I see you are using a Stepp synthesiser guitar on the album despite its reputation for being problematic.**

Yes, it is about as reliable as Victorian photography. But it does sometimes produce unparalleled results. You need a lot of patience, but I really use it as a MIDI trigger for soft, atmospheric stuff. I don't think I've ever played anything fast on it because the triggering is not wonderful. What it does have, though, is a facility which, as far as I am aware, no other guitar synths have – touch activation. You can use both hands on the fretboard to produce the kinds of spread you would associate more with keyboards. That's the mode I tend to use it in, mainly for strings or sampled clarinets and trombones.

**You couldn't use it live, though.**

I don't use it live, no. I did try briefly after I recorded *Momentum*. The live show was mainly acoustic guitar with the occasional flute track. But then, right at the end, we did a thing which was Stepp and flute, and so there was a choir coming in. People couldn't equate the fact that a guitar was doing all these things. I know that Stepp are no longer around, but there are so many discontinued lines out there that I try to persevere with. The Gizmo, for instance. I had an interesting dream not long ago about the use of a Gizmo and so I've now got to implement it. Very strange, the way things come to you.

**What sort of classical guitar do you use?**

I've got three Yairis. I've been using them for about 20 years. I use one to record with which has a beautiful depth to it, while the other two I use for live work. They have the advantage of having a cutaway and are very evenly balanced. They are very bright, but each string is the same volume. If you are using them live with a desk out front, you have to use subtractive EQ to roll off some of the top end and mellow it slightly. They are purely acoustic and so I don't have to mess around with batteries.

**What about electric guitars?**

I've got a black Les Paul Custom with a Floyd Rose on it. But I find that it's not so much the guitar these days as who's actually playing it. With the recording techniques around now I don't think it is possible to tell any more whether anyone is using a single-coil pickup or a humbucker. I used to swear blind that I knew the difference, but now...

**What about amplification?**

I use a Groove Tube pre-amp with Marshall speakers to monitor on stage.

**You sing on *Guitar Noir*.**

I've done the occasional album where I was singing, but my singing never really got a good review. But recently, my manager suggested that I try pitching my voice lower. I tried it on 'Dark As The Grave' and it tended to colour the lyrics that I wrote as well. It was much more a case of almost spoken lyrics in places – like your actor who can't sing. I think that is a far more natural area for me. I always wanted a powerful rock voice with an edge to it, but I've had to develop character at the expense of technique.

# JOHN PETRUCCI

OCTOBER 1993

*During the '70s the music of bands like Yes, Genesis and Pink Floyd straddled many different styles. Rock, jazz, pop and even classical music were thrown into the melting pot and refashioned accordingly, often straining the credulity of audiences along the way. Eventually the genre became as unfashionable as flared jeans, but by the early 1990s, with a whole new range of music styles to draw on and, more lately, a resurgence of flares, the return of 'progressive rock' was long overdue. Champions of its return were Dream Theater, the New York-based prog-metal quintet that burst on to the scene with the albums* When Dream And Day Unite *and* Images And Words. *I spoke with guitarist and founder member John Petrucci in 1993, just as the band was beginning to enjoy considerable cult status in the UK.*

**So how did the band come together?**

We grew up together. We're all from Long Island, New York, except our singer, who's from Toronto. But three of us grew up, went to the same high school and graduated together. Then we met our drummer when we went to Berklee in Boston.

**We hear a lot about Berklee over here. What was your impression?**

It was great! We went right out of high school, and it was great for a couple of reasons: one was the environment – there were musicians from all around the world really intent on studying music and making it a part of their lives – and the school has a lot of resources. And so, if you're really determined and apply yourself, you can get a lot out of it. We were there for two semesters – only one year. We were playing so much we couldn't do both so we dropped out, and that's when it all started.

**Was Dream Theater a going concern at this point?**

Not exactly. At that time we were just putting things together. We were under a different name – Majesty – and we had our first singer. We weren't signed or anything, but eventually it all came together.

**Does the band share the same influences?**

I think our influences range from a couple of different extremes. One of them, which is probably obvious to most people, is the progressive influence of bands like Rush, Yes and Genesis. For some reason all of us are into that, but also we have a heavy influence: Metallica and Anthrax and all that type of stuff. We also have a pop influence: Peter Gabriel, U2, Journey, Billy Joel and stuff like that. So it's kind of a combination of those three elements that we all have a common leaning towards. Those influences vary even today as we grow. Everybody's listening to different types of music and gaining other influences, but those are the early ones.

**A lot of your songs have extended arrangements. Does that make for a tough slog in rehearsals?**

Yeah, it's fun. We just like being creative and challenging ourselves. Sometimes you can't say what you want to say in three minutes, but then sometimes you can, so we have things that are really short as well. On our first tour, we were playing small clubs, and it developed to the point where we were selling out clubs and moving on to theatres, and it's been really encouraging to see the development of a fan base. People seem to be passionate about our music.

There'll be packs of people coming to a lot of shows in the same area and they're into it – they know all the words. In Europe people aren't afraid to sing, and it's like we have a choir singing along with us. It's really encouraging!

**It's interesting to note that the majority of your fans were not born when 'prog rock' was popular the first time around.**

I think it's the medium we're presenting it in. I mean, the whole thing with the progressive music of the '70s that attracts all of us is that its musicians were trying to be creative and just do something a little bit different and experiment. There are a wide range of styles present in our music because there's no limit, no labels – you can do whatever you want! You can get into new age or thrash or...

**Who would you say was your principal influence as a guitar player?**

As a guitar player I'm really into Steve Morse and the Dixie Dregs. I was into a lot of different guitar players from Al DiMeola to Stevie Ray Vaughan, but Steve Morse is the one guy who I followed. I really respect his philosophies about music and guitar and I'm blown away by his guitar playing, technically and emotionally, every time I see him. He's the one guy who really introduced discipline into my playing.

**As the whole band was taught formally, does that help working with complex arrangements?**

Yeah, absolutely. A lot of the time we write the way any other band would write; just in a rehearsal, playing off one another But it does help if there's a complex arrangement, whether rhythmically or melodically, and you can write it out and give it to the other guy. Or if the keyboard player is going to double something I'm going to do, I can just write it out instead of sitting there and going through it note by note.

# FRANCIS ROSSI

FEBRUARY 1996

*At the time of this interview, Status Quo were celebrating their 30th anniversary. They had sold over 110 million records worldwide, spawned 49 hit singles and, adding it all up, had spent no less than seven and a half years in the charts. So it's probably safe to assume that most people know at least one Status Quo song. Resistance, as they say, is futile...*

*They celebrated in style by releasing an album of favourite covers (Don't Stop) and throwing an all-star party in London, which was in part a chance to record the video that went along with the album, and a live performance of their greatest hits especially for the fan club. All the celebrity co-stars from the album turned up to perform, including The Beach Boys.*

**The evening went very well.**

I think that's the idea isn't it, that it looks like there's no problem, but there were lots of panics that day. But it came off very well, I think, yeah.

**Getting The Beach Boys there was a real coup.**

Yeah, we couldn't believe it. Bruce Johnston is probably the most enthusiastic man in the world in terms of our business. He was very keen to do something, and when we started working the album and eventually found this track and sent it over, he said, 'We think we can get Brian Wilson on it...' and we were like, 'What?' As far as we knew, he'd checked out.

**So The Beach Boys recorded their part on the album in America?**

Yeah. They were actually touring and did some recording after gigs, which is something else to mention – you wouldn't get me in a studio after a gig! They eventually put Brian on in Los Angeles, and so a bit was done in Chicago, a bit somewhere in Toronto, a bit in Cleveland… [Laughs.] I tell you.

**Thirty years old and still rocking, it only seems a moment ago since we were celebrating Quo's 25th.**

That's the only thing that I get pissed about; at my age, it goes so fucking quick! When you're in your teens and early 20s, someone says 'five years', you think, 'Oh shit, it's miles away', you know. But it does seem like yesterday that we did the 25. I wasn't too keen on a big party, and I wasn't too keen on doing the album; the idea of it being covers and stuff. But then it kind of snowballed into what we actually did, so I don't know. So I've been around 30 years, oh fucking great! Who's interested? If we can say we've got two or three million fans in England, then that means there are 57 million people who don't give a shit. It's the same whoever you are. Even Michael Jackson – let's say Jackson's the biggest – he does 30 million albums in the States alone, which means 220 million people don't give a shit about him either! So you can be assured that whoever you are, most people don't like you, and I think that's a great way of keeping your feet on the fucking ground.

**That's an interesting philosophy.**

It's true, I can't see it any other way, because we're made to feel so important and 'Oh you're so special, and you're in the charts and you've done this and you've done that…' I think you can very easily get big-headed; we were, particularly when we were younger. I wish I'd thought about that some time back – most people don't like us and that's that sorted out.

**How were the songs for *Don't Stop* chosen?**

Lots of them we've ponced about with, rehearsed at sound checks or in the studio, and thought that it would be nice if we could do some of them some day. When you come down to do them, they are not as easy as you thought, or don't necessarily work. It's just making them work, getting that spark that makes you think, 'Yep, this is different enough to say it's ours.' But on most albums, if three of us like a song and two don't, then it goes with the vote. But with this one, if any one of us didn't like a track it just went by, and I think it's worked. The main thing about this album was nine times out of ten you knew the song, you know the melody, so you're working away arrangement-wise.

**The new album's content successfully blows away the 'three-chord wonders' tag that the band has been dogged with.**

Somebody noticed at last! That was a great joke for a while, but there are times when it hurts. It's demeaning. It isn't 'Three chords and you did it again, how do you manage?' And it is difficult to come up with good melodies over three chords or make it sound interesting. If it had been levelled at us that way it would have been fine, but it's always 'You're no bloody good, you only play three chords...', and I look at these people and think, 'Dickhead!' It gets on your tits sometimes. I quite often say, when everybody was keen on 'Nessun Dorma' that if you check it out, the main refrain is basically three chords. It's the same with the great classics: the main sections that we all know are only three or four chords.

**And it certainly sounds like Quo put a lot of work into each album or single that they do.**

More than people give us credit for, and it hurts. They just dismiss Status Quo as 'Oh dear...', you know. Or they say that all the singles were the same, and you think, 'Yeah, there was a similarity.' They were similar, but a true Quo fan will get his album and say, 'Of course they're not all the same!' Any album you care to name – of course they're not all the same. You couldn't say that 'Margarita' was anything like 'Down Down'. [Laughs] I'm doing what I shouldn't do, trying to justify myself and it's ridiculous!

**Did you use your famous green Tele on the album? It doesn't sound like it...**

Very good! I didn't use my Tele at all. About eight years ago, somebody came to the door and said, 'Here you are, Leo Fender said to give you this,' and they handed me a brand new G&L Asat. And I said, 'Oh, another Fender Tele', and I just put it by. But later on I started to play it and now it's the only guitar I like to play. I put it through a 30-watt Roland Cube, which I always use. So every single track was the G&L. Fender are going to make me a guitar and I want them to copy the G&L, so I'm not sure if their nose is a bit out of joint there. But it's a wonderful guitar. I never thought I'd be that much in love with a guitar; it's tremendous. It goes everywhere with me and I practise on it all the time. It's a fabulous guitar, I only wish Leo was alive to say, 'Yep, it did work.'

**While at Brixton Academy for the live show, I noticed that your pedal board was quite massive.**

It looks like a lot, but I've got a Roland GP8 which I use a couple of presets on, a Marshall Guv'nor and a Bluesbreaker, but I rarely hit those. I end up using the Roland every time, so I suppose I've somehow got to get those presets copied and get it right. I don't really need that big board on the floor. They're a pain really, I keep meaning to change it, but I'm terrible at change.

**However, a few things in Quo's gear setup have changed for the better.**

In the past Rick [Parfitt] and I would have 4 x 12s all over the bloody stage, and this would cause problems with the sound at the front, and we've been trying to improve that for the last four or five years, and slowly drop down the level of the back line. I think there's the same amount of power, but it's not the same spread. And of course with those in-ear monitors you don't shout LIKE

THIS! And you can actually sing a bit better, my voice lasts longer and my vocals are improving. I'm just a good all-round fabulous bloke!

**The current Quo back line consists of Marshall amps decked out in white – a touch of glamour, perhaps?**

Yeah, I wasn't sure about that, but Rick tends to go for that kind of stuff and so we said, 'Yeah, let's do it!' Marshall make the AC30s now. I didn't realise that so I've just acquired one of those. I think my ideal is to have one of those at the back to send to the front house and the Marshall, because I'm so used to it, behind me. I find it very difficult to use the G&L through the Marshall, there's just so much top in it, but Tonto [faithful Quo retainer] sets them up and gets a reasonable sound. As long as the front of house man is reasonably happy then we'll stay with that.

**What models are the snow-white Marshalls?**

I don't fucking know! Tell me some model names...

**Hmmm, OK, moving swiftly on, then – what other guitars are used during a Quo set?**

They're just a couple of old Teles, you know this thing about this green Tele shit... I've tried to use the G&L, but it's this mythical thing of 'Wow, the green Tele!' And that green Tele has given me more gyp over the years than anything! I've had the pickup changed in the last few years, the frets are steeper than I used to have, the action's slightly higher than I used to have, I've got a five-way switch, I've had the neck shaved...it ought to be like my G&L. I use a couple of old '58s that I've acquired over the years. It's just that I use a different one for 'Down Down' and 'Whatever You Want'. I just don't like the idea of people standing on stage dropping the Es down to D and going, 'Hey, look at me tune this guitar!' People don't need to see that, so I'll just grab another one. But I also don't like changes of guitar all over the shop. I try to keep those down to a minimum. I think, again, from an audience's point of view, it's, 'Oh, he's off to change his guitar, what's the matter with him?' It's like, 'Look at me, I can play this one as well!' I don't think they're interested.

**So the other stage guitars aren't in different tunings or anything?**

No, Rick tends to have various different tunings. Apart from 'Down Down', that's a G tuning with a capo on the fourth fret.

**What about 'Mystery Song'?**

That's a G tuning, brings you into the key of A. Rick loves his tunings, I don't know why.

**It seems to work for you.**

Yeah, can't knock it.

**Let's talk about some of those 49 hit singles – what about 'Caroline'?**

I remember writing 'Caroline' with Bob Young. It was written in '69. We went on holiday in the West Country and we wrote 'Caroline' and 'Baby Boy', which ended up on *Rockin' All Over The World*, and a few other songs. 'Caroline' was originally a slow shuffle, and then Rick suddenly went into that 'da da da da' and we said, 'Let's try it like that then.'

**What about the melody at the beginning?**

I always see that piece as French. I know it doesn't make any sense whatsoever. I don't always get that feeling, but if I do it takes me back to when we first did it, and I play it more like it should be. I don't know why, it just makes me think French... Screwed up old sod!

**The intro is played down in the first position, isn't it?**

Yeah, on the third and fourth string, the G and the D.

**You played the intro differently at the 30th anniversary gig.**

Last year when we went on tour, instead of opening with 'Caroline' we opened with 'Paper Plane'. I don't much like doing either of those songs and we were discussing it, and I said I still think that screaming thing with Rick's guitar opening and that little build-up into the song is a nice opening as it gives the sound guy more time. So instead of it being the normal intro, we suddenly got there that day – literally just as we were coming down the stairs for the live section, we were actually behind the drape – John said to me 'Are we doing the short front or the full front or what?' and I said, 'Oh just go by ear; whatever suits you...' And then as soon as Rick opened, I came in too early! We tend to be very keen like that. John and Andrew often found it a bit odd, you know; I like to throw extra bars in where they shouldn't be. We also have certain songs that we just call 'bars', because you can never quite figure where you are, it's just a bar to me. It's just one bar, a bit confused!

**Reaching further back into Quo history, you and Rick met at a Butlin's holiday camp in Minehead.**

What a piss! We nearly got thrown out of there. We had AC30s and we were too bloody loud, yet we went back in for the 25th anniversary, and when I think about the level we must have played in that room this time! [Laughs] To think we nearly got thrown out. We had this poxy little system – no volume. Shows you the sign of the times; if you're any louder, you're out. And we used to play the afternoon set with no bastards there and they still made you play it. However it was good training. I don't think we learnt as much as we could have done there, particularly myself in terms of practice.

**Practice?**

Yeah, I could have been a much better player years ago and it's taken the last five, six years maybe for me to realise it. I practise two hours a day, even Christmas day! I saw one of my sons, Nicholas, who's a lovely guitar player, and I thought, 'Shit, this is no good. I'm going to have to own up.' Because many times people years ago used to say to me, 'You should do a few scales, improve your playing', and I went, 'Yeah, I don't need that...' and I do! So now I have so much catching up to do it's not true, but my playing is improving.

**What's on the current practice routine?**

I'm studying the Joe Pass video at the moment. He's so hard to take in. I've got so far with it, but he's got so many alternative chords. In the key of C he's doing I VI II V, and he's going, 'Well, you can use a min7th like this...' and I go, 'Jesus Christ, now wait a minute, wait a minute!' He says, 'You can use an E7♭9', and I'm going, 'Really?' It tires you out listening to him, so I only listen for a while and I practise that for a bit and I go back. [Laughs] It's the slowest progress I've made in terms of learning. He was such a lovely player.

**Can we expect a Status Quo jazz album some time in the future, then?**

That would be funny, wouldn't it? No, it's not that I want to incorporate it at all. I need it for me. There's this thing when you get older – I want to put things right. I was a silly boy then, so I'll do it now. Whatever it takes, I have to learn, so I have this thirst for knowledge at the moment, much more than I did when I was younger, and I just want to be able to play these things. I said to Andrew [Bown, Quo's keyboard player] a couple of years ago that I wish I'd known this when I was younger. He said, 'Oh no...' And I said, 'What do you mean, "Oh no"?' And he said, 'Well, you wouldn't have written "Down Down" or "Caroline". You'd have started saying, "No, I'm going to have to throw something clever in here."' It's all right us saying we want to be musicians and all that shit, but if you're not careful...with a song like 'Caroline', I'd have started throwing ninths or thirteenths in, and what the hell for? So perhaps things have gone as they were supposed to. I was stupid at school. It was, 'No, I'm going to be a rock 'n' roll star, you lot can go screw yourselves.' And I was right: I did make it, I suppose. But they were right: I missed the knowledge. I have a thirst for knowledge at 47 years old, what a dickhead! What a time to wake up!

# TY TABOR

DECEMBER 1993

*Every so often a band comes along and defies convention to such an extent that audiences, tired of that 'same old, same old' from other rocking combos, just keep flocking back for more. Such a band is King's X, who steadfastly refuse to be categorised or employ a formulaic approach to producing their music. In any given King's X album, listeners can find in equal parts metal riffs, prog-rock movements and Beatles-esque harmonies. Often, the result of such resolute defiance can be filed under Just Plain Weird and kept under the safe lock and key of almost total obscurity, but not so with Ty Tabor's band. King's X maintained a loyal – even zealous – fan base, as I discovered when Ty and I talked shop in 1993, prior to the release of the band's* Dogman *album.*

**Your first record was released in '88. How long had King's X been together before then?**

Eight years. We got together in 1980; we all met in a town called Springfield, Missouri. We were all there for different reasons, and we actually formed the band in 1980 and got a record deal in 1987. We'd been together seven years when we got signed and then had the record out in '88.

**Where did the name of the band come from?**

Well, originally we got the title from our manager. He knew of a band that his brother was in called King's X in the 1960s, but they had long since disbanded. He had always liked that name and so he mentioned it to us – but it really comes from a Texas game that's like tag, so it's sort of a Texas phrase.

**Many people in Britain must refer to you as King's Cross?**

On the first couple of albums we were still encountering that, but we haven't encountered it in a long time. But yes, for a long time people thought we were called 'King's Cross'.

**What style did you set out to play when the band was formed?**

Blues-orientated rock. Way back in the '70s I was really into it – I mean, old Aerosmith was real bluesy, you know what I mean? I really loved all that stuff in the early '70s, so we started out with more of that influence. Things had changed by the time we made the first album in '87, though.

**Who else was an influence?**

Well, The Beatles were the first really major influence; I was heavily into them. But I was also into bands like the original Alice Cooper band, and there's some early Bowie and early Kiss that I was into. I really liked Bad Company when they came out – and Boston, too.

**What age were you when you started playing?**

I don't really know exactly. I don't remember what age. All I know is I have a tape at home of me playing guitar and singing a song when I was eight years old, so it was very young, I guess.

**Were you in bands at school?**

Yeah, I just kinda grew up playing, you know? With all the kids in the neighbourhood, there was always somebody who had a drum set or something, and we would jam and sometimes bands were formed out of that.

**Was your first album, *Out Of The Silent Planet,* influenced by the CS Lewis science fiction trilogy?**

The title's from that book, yeah. That particular space trilogy by CS Lewis I really like; I think it's some great writing. We never actually had any kind of overall album concept like that. A lot of people have called the first two albums concept albums, but they really weren't as far as we were concerned. Maybe the songs sort of have a thread of unity in them that makes them seem like that, but it wasn't intentional.

**King's X are certainly no slaves to musical trends or fashion.**

Well, we've always been out of fashion – even when we try to be in fashion we're out of fashion. We just finally had to come to the realisation that we were never going to fit in anywhere; that was the way we had to view it. As long as we tried to fit in we never could, so we finally had to accept we are who we are, so let's do what we want to do and who cares about fashion or fads and what's going on?

**Were the next couple of albums after *Gretchen Goes to Nebraska* – *Faith, Hope, Love* and *King's X* – as successful for you?**

They were more successful for us, as far as record sales and hits on the radio in America and all that stuff. The third album sold probably four or five times more than the first two albums, and it made our mark in America. We had a top-three hit and a big video on MTV from the third album, and the same thing happened with the next record. It's just that they were lesser albums in our eyes than the first two – we were reaching a dead end.

**So, in a way, the different approach you employed with *Dogman* was to revitalise things for the band?**

Well, we've always been considered a 'live band' and we've always had complaints about albums never even coming close to representing that live energy. We've always known that and it's always bothered us. So this time around we wanted to make more of an effort to get at least some of that live energy into the studio and [Pearl Jam producer] Brendan O'Brien seemed to be the best way to do that, because it's something he seems to have a knack for. We wanted to work with him to see if we could do it, you know? To see if we could come up with something more 'live' in the studio.

**I gather that a lot of *Dogman* was recorded using a first-take approach?**

Yeah, literally. I mean, there's a lot of first takes in there – a lot of first-take solos where we just rolled the tape and whatever happened, happened – and we were going to keep it, you know?

# CHARLIE BURCHILL

OCTOBER 1994

*In the late '80s and early '90s, Simple Minds were filling stadiums with the party faithful, turning out in aid of Nelson Mandela and generally, it has to be said, going ballistic. Then Virgin EMI released* Glittering Prize 81/92 *and we thought it may be all over. But it wasn't...as guitarist Charlie Burchill explained when we spoke in 1994. It was simply a time for getting back to basics.*

**Simple Minds has had some personnel changes lately.**

Basically, we're a duo. [Laughs.] When we play live we forge a band together and it's not really that different. In the '80s we were a collective of five people, but it had many different forms. People would leave and others would join, but basically we started off as a duo and it's kinda ended up back there. In many ways, especially at the moment, it's an advantage because we are using the economy of the situation to the benefit of the songwriting. We wanted to clear out some of the big, bombastic sound that we became known for, and we've been able to do that naturally because it is just guitars and voice now. At the end of the '80s our keyboard player left, and we lunged into the album *Real Life* when we really should have taken a gap then and looked at what we were and what we were going to try and achieve. But we didn't and just went straight into it and emulated the keyboards as if he'd never left. But after that album and tour, we realised that we had to take stock of the situation and lose some of the old reference points and, of course, that's much easier said than done. It really did take time, but we didn't stop working. We continued to write songs and wrote about two or three albums' worth of material. But we wanted a really clear-cut direction on this album, and so we were very selective about what we were doing. In between times we had a retrospective album, which at least kept a certain amount of public focus, but essentially we've been really taking stock of the situation and trying to lose a lot of the baggage we were carrying from the '80s.

**These days your guitar is very much up front, grabbing centre stage and no longer merely a stooge for great washes of keyboards.**

We originally wrote songs on the guitar – that's what started us off and that's how we got our record deal. Keyboards take up so much space and they soften things and have a tendency to give things this big grandiose thing, and for a long time we've been trying to get space in the music.

**How do you and Jim [Kerr] go about songwriting?**

I'll sit down and play, either on a piano or guitar, and Jim is always writing in his notebook: observations that he's picked up and so on. He'll listen and take something and say, 'That's great, let's focus on it.' From there, we manage to get some idea in demo form on a cassette, and he takes it away and almost meditates on the music, just plays it continually, time and time again. Things start to merge for him from the music – it could be a mood or the suggestion of a line or a theme – and so then we go back and try and make the thing work. But it's a very intangible, illogical thing. Sometimes something appears out of mid-air and it's very exciting.

**What about the Mandela concerts?**

There were two of them: one when he was still in jail and one just after he was released, and that was incredible. We met our greatest heroes there: Lou Reed was there and Neil Young. And Mandela, of course. When he gave his speech we were standing behind the curtain and it was a real thrill. Not long after that, we were playing in Barcelona and he turned up. He was in the city opening a sports centre, came on and gave a speech before we played. The Mandela show was amazing, it was such an uplifting event. He did a great thing: he took all the artists backstage with the media, and he said that when he couldn't hear any voices, he could always hear the voice of the artist. That kind of summed things up because at that point people were talking about the politics of the thing, and somehow he defined the feeling that I think most of the artists had when they got involved and the reasons why they chose to become involved. It was quite an event.

**For the first concert, Simple Minds took on house band duties for many other artists who were appearing.**

We did about seven or eight songs and we had tons of people out there. We had Little Steven, Neneh Cherry and Youssou N'Dour and we had to rehearse with them, too. We'd been playing 'Sun City' for some time and Little Steven came in and said, 'Hang on, hang on, the riff's not right...' And he showed us the riff, and the way he did it was just so great. He was so funny, such a character. He's got so much energy, and it was great working with all those people because you learn so much. We also played behind Peter Gabriel when he sang 'Biko'. Peter gave us our first break, y'know. We toured with him, and usually you have to pay to go on a tour with a big act, but he brought us on tour and there was no money involved or anything. It was just so brilliant, they looked after us so well.

# KIRK HAMMETT

OCTOBER 1992

*Metallica's self-titled 1991 album brought the band unprecedented mainstream success, a success maintained by a mammoth world tour. Backstage at their 1992 Wembley Arena gig, I overheard two crew members locked in conversation about the length of this particular world tour...*

*'My wife had a baby six months ago,' one piped up. 'When I left home that baby wasn't even thought about and by the time I get home it will be a year old!' Such is life on the road, but Metallica have a unique way of dealing with one particular aspect of globe-trotting rock mayhem: jet lag. In order to keep things on an even keel as far as the various time zones of planet earth are concerned, the band lives on US time, irrespective of where they happen to be. The catering staff are used to oddball feeding times and the band have become accustomed to going on stage at what feels, to them, like lunchtime. Thus everything runs as smoothly as possible within the enclosed microclimate that is Metallica. Despite everything, though, marathon tours can take their toll on a player, and so my first questions related to how exactly one manages to stay in shape...*

**How long has this tour been going on?**

Fourteen months, but we've still another six months to do.

**That must be pretty hard on you as a player. So how do you keep in shape?**

I play a lot in my hotel room. I don't go out and carry on like I used to. Basically, I just sit down with a little Pignose amp and a tape recorder and play all night.

**What guitar do you use for that?**

A Strat from the Custom Shop at Fender.

**I had you figured as a dedicated humbucker user...**

In the beginning I was a single coil man. But then I started putting humbuckers in all my guitars and now I'm back to the single coil thing, but just for playing in my hotel room. On stage I still have humbuckers in everything...

**What sort of things do you play when you practise?**

I have chromatic exercises I run through, I play scales, I run through my modes in every key. It depends what I feel like playing, because I've got into the blues lately and I'm learning all these licks I should have learned 10, 15 years ago!

**But the early metal bands drew very heavily upon the blues influence...**

Yeah, I hear it totally now that I'm familiar with all these blues licks, and so I'm starting to apply that sort of thinking to the more modern type of playing. I feel now that I can express myself better than I ever could in the last 15 years. I've even gotten into the Mississippi Delta style, fingerpicking blues. The Robert Johnson stuff is incredible! I've been listening to that a lot.

**Does this mean that Metallica is set to become more blues-biased in the near future?**

I don't know. It's more like a hobby with us, so I don't know if it would ever be that strong. The influence is there, but I don't think it will creep its way into the songwriting because with that we have a certain focus. But you never know, it's really too early to say, but all of us have our little musical platforms.

**Metallica have a no-compromise attitude towards volume on stage, and you're renowned for being one of the loudest bands on the planet. Seeing as an electric guitar becomes an almost entirely different animal at high volume, how do you compensate for that when you practise?**

As long as it sounds good when I go out on stage then it works for me. And if I'm practising and it sounds good it'll work for me too. Making that transition isn't so bad, unless I want to do something that relies heavily on feedback or ambience. But I don't practise at full volume – I don't know anyone who does. It's very rare when I'm practising at home that I'll need feedback or a lot of ambience. My practice setup at home is basically just a small Marshall combo and a wah pedal for certain sounds. If I want a different sound altogether I have a collection of Fender amps. I have a Twin Reverb, a Vibroverb, a Super Champ – which is louder than those two put together. And I have a variety of outboard gear which I use if I want to get that 'big hall' sound in my little room. But if I want to play real loud I just go down to my basement. I have a stack down in my basement and just crank that up.

**Do you play an acoustic on tour?**

No. James does; he has one of those Chet Atkins Gibsons. All my acoustics are vintage, but I don't take those out because they're a bit too fragile. I have an old Dobro – it's one of those wooden ones with a metal resonator. Then I have one of the Robert Johnson Gibsons, which is great to play with slide because you get that tone. Then I have another Gibson, a '50s model with a big old cutout – that's beautiful. Those are all steel-strung guitars, but I have a regular nylon-strung one as well. I'd like to get a Martin D45. I saw one in a catalogue for $100,000, which is a bit more than I would care to pay.

**You could buy your own fighter plane for that...**

Yeah, or a guitar factory...

**How do you keep the material fresh on such a long tour?**

On the last tour I basically played the same thing every night and I suddenly came to the realisation that I wasn't progressing as much as I should. I was going out and playing five nights a week, and I realised I should be a hell of a lot better than I was. So on this tour, because I'm playing so much off stage, I have the opportunity to work on certain things, certain licks here and there, and then the next night I can go out and actually play them live. There are certain songs now that I leave open for improvisation; I play something different every night instead of playing the solo from the record. Obviously I don't do that with every song because a lot of people like to hear certain things as they are on the record. But learning things in the hotel room and trying them out on stage the next night leaves it fresh, but gives me room to interject new ideas and see if I can pull them off or not. I also play an open solo, and I play that differently every night. The last tour I had the whole thing note-for-note worked out and it got a bit boring after a while. This way it stays exciting, and sometimes I pull it off and sometimes I die a death. But, hey, that's the chance you take.

**Is there a specific point in the set that you look forward to every night?**

I enjoy playing it all. When we take breaks – when I'm at home or on vacation – my chops go down drastically because I'm enjoying my free time and doing things I don't usually have time to do. So when I'm on tour my guitar playing hurts a little bit, and it usually takes three or four days to get my chops back. But you never know how the gig's going to go. Sometimes if I've had a particularly bad day and I go out there thinking I'm going to have a particularly bad gig, I'll have a really great one. If I've had a great day and I've been playing a lot and I feel real confident, it sometimes doesn't come together on stage at all. It's a weird thing. Having said that, my playing never sinks below a certain standard, although sometimes it's hard to tell if you're actually improving, because you're so close to it. But I'm beginning to tell – all these off-the-wall licks finding their way into my regular playing. So that gives me an idea of where I'm headed. By the end of a show my fingers are pretty loose and I feel pretty good, so I use the opportunity to go to my hotel room and play some more. The two situations complement each other, although there was no intention originally for it to turn out that way...

**You're famous for your monster rhythm sound. My understanding of the ultimate metal rhythm sound is to remove a good amount of mid-range while boosting the low and high ends...**

Yeah, to a large degree I still scoop a lot out for the rhythm sound, but for lead I add a bit of mid. For the lead I also have an Ibanez Tube Screamer.

**You drop-tune for some songs...**

Yeah, on 'Master Of Puppets' we dropped it down to D and live we look it down to C sharp. The problem with that was that every time me and James played, we played with varying degrees of attack on our guitars, so we were constantly out of tune with each other because the strings were flapping around so much.

**Didn't you compensate by using a heavier-gauge string?**

We didn't know that back then! [Laughs]

**But even with 10s they're going to flap around, tuned that low...**

It was especially bad for me because I played a guitar that had a floating bridge, which didn't really help things. But now I play it on the Jackson and the bridge is stationary, so it helps it to stay in tune a lot better.

# NUNO BETTENCOURT

DECEMBER 1992

*This interview was carried out just before Christmas. At the time, Nuno's band, Extreme, were at their peak. 'More Than Words' had been an unexpected hit for the band, and the album it was taken from, Pornograffitti, had quickly become regarded as being something of a riff-laden heaven for would-be rock guitarists everywhere. After having battled through the Christmas shoppers and a bomb scare in central London, I arrived at the band's hotel to find Nuno had a bad cold and wanted to save his voice for the evening's performance in Bournemouth. So the whole interview was a bit of an uphill battle: answers were short and the whole atmosphere in the hotel room was gloomy, to say the least. Despite all this, however, I still think this particular interview gives an accurate snapshot of Nuno's attitudes towards playing at the time.*

**You cite Eddie Van Halen as your first major influence. Was there a specific track or solo that really inspired you?**

Nothing specific, really. All of it, although I started a little later than when they came out. I suppose it was pretty much their *Fair Warning* record. When I heard that sound, it really got to me.

**What was the first electric guitar you ever had?**

The first one I had was just something that was lying around my house. I think the first one I actually bought was an old Kramer.

**Presumably you were in different bands at high school?**

Yeah, although in the early bands I was actually playing bass. I think I just started playing too many notes on the bass, though.

**What material did you cover in those days?**

Everything from Aerosmith, Rush, Pat Travers...

**You tune your guitar to E flat; were you doing that in the early days?**

Yeah, I've always done it. It's just a heavier sound. When I started playing, it just felt better to play on.

**Do you use a heavier string gauge to compensate for the loss of tension?**

No, I use .009s.

**Detuned? That must make things pretty loose...**

Yeah, but it isn't as loose as you would think.

**Do you have a fairly low action?**

Actually, when a lot of people play my guitar they don't like it too much, because the action isn't as low as they would like; it's pretty high. I like to bend a lot of strings, and if you try bend with strings too low, then it's kinda hard. I like to have something you can grab hold of.

**One of the most outstanding aspects of your technique is your approach to**

**rhythm. It seems that rather than use a static, chordal approach – four or eight to the bar – you employ a constantly moving figure, a bit like counterpoint.**

Well, when it comes to rhythm playing, it's not down to how you hold the pick or anything like that, it's where your head is at. That's where it comes from. It's really just how an individual wants to play rhythm. Technically it's not a big change from playing regular stuff, regular chords. It's just a matter of mentally applying something. It's funny, because it's always been there. If you listen to any old Van Halen records, there's a lot going on that I think people miss out on. He was such a flashy guitar player for his time that everybody kinda overlooked his rhythm playing. Combine somebody like him and Jimmy Page and Angus Young, and you've got yourself some rhythm playing, you know. And that's pretty much what it is with me – you should be able to play power chords like Angus when you feel they should be there. I think a lot of younger players end up worshipping one person too much. If you take in a lot of different people, you'll feel it a lot more.

**It's like your picking hand is moving constantly in 16th note rhythm when you play these rhythm parts.**

It's important, because instead of just having the hand do it – you know, I try and do that as much as I can, moving in 16th notes or whatever – but even if your hand is not moving then your body has to be moving. The clock has always got to be moving and that's what makes it so that at any moment, at any time, you can actually hear something, whether it be an upstroke or a downstroke – whatever. Your hand is always moving. It's always somehow rhythmically involved. You gotta be sorta like a drummer inside yourself.

**You also put in ultra-fast triplets in your rhythm style...**

Yeah, it comes from having a sort of 'drumming wrist' – always thinking like a drummer.

**That would fit with the 16ths thing, because that would be your hi-hat hand.**

Right.

**The triplets come quite naturally to you, presumably...**

As I say, it was just probably an evolution from playing drums for such a long time. I've never really played heavily. It was just that wherever there was a drum set, I played it. Nothing major, you know, just enough to help me out.

**How do you think your style has changed since the early days of Extreme?**

I just think it's got more balanced. I don't think it has changed that radically, really. As time goes on you just tend to put more stock into areas of your playing that you think are more important. That's what changes, really – just your approach to what you think is important.

**Where do you think your guitar playing is going now?**

I dropped out of the guitar olympics a long time ago. I'm not really worried about physically getting somewhere I haven't been before. I take it song by song and play for that, you know.

**So what advice have you got for people who are still struggling to learn guitar?**

Even though you're into guitar and you want to be able to do all these fancy things and get to a point of capability, I think it's really important not to ignore songwriting and basic rhythm playing and the simplicities of it – the beauty of a simple chord change. If you can get that together while you're learning and while you're developing, you'll end up a lot more brilliant in the end.

# STEVE ROTHERY

MARCH 1994

*I seem to remember that I rang Steve Rothery on his mobile for this particular interview. He was in Sainsbury's car park at the time. Hell, even rock stars run out of cat food... Marillion's album* This Strange Engine *had just hit the streets, another in the series of critically unfashionable prog rock albums the nad released during the mid-'90s... Don't get me wrong – I am, in general, a fan of all things prog, and you can be sure that somewhere in my closet there's a pair of flared jeans and a trenchcoat.*

*Steve is another player whose guitar sound is an integral part of his band Marillion's sound. Well known for complex arrangements which are faithfully recreated live, I asked him first about the gear he needs to accommodate the band's material.*

**Marillion strive to recreate their often complex music as faithfully as possible live on stage. What sort of gear do you need to cover the guitar side of the business?**

My amps are the same as they've been for a while. I've got a couple of Marshall Master Volume amps with two 4 x 12s and two Roland JC-120s. In the rack, the main controller is a TC2290, which controls various effects like a BOSS DS-1 distortion, a Dimension C, a BOSS rack-mounted chorus, some Rockman modules going in to a Quadraverb, again controlled by the 2290. Then everything goes into a Sound Sculpture, which is a 16-way programmable matrix, allowing me to send either the dry signal or the 2290 signal to either, both or all four of the amps, or even blend everything together. Occasionally I'll use my TCM 5000 in there; I used that for the *Afraid Of Sunlight* tour, but not so much this time – it's too much of a studio item to drag around the world. That's pretty much it! For me, a programmable delay, a Boss DS-1 for the solos into the JC-120 and some sort of chorus and delay for the clean picking sound and the Marshalls for the grunge – that's the essence of what I do most of the time.

**What about guitars?**

My main guitar is still a Squier Strat with EMG SA pickups and a Kahler tremolo. The other guitar is a Steinberger six and twelve (double neck), which was custom made for me. It's got three single coils for each neck. Then I've got a couple of acoustics: a Takemine Santa Fe and a twelve-string.

**So the guitar retinue is quite lean, then?**

Well, nearly everything I do in the studio is on the Strat anyway – occasionally I'll use a Les Paul or whatever else is to hand, but I tend always to go back to the Strat, really. For me it has a little bit more character than anything else. It's a little bit harder to play, especially where it comes to bending or very fast stuff, because the action I have isn't that low. I prefer it a bit higher to get some tone, really.

**Do you use a heavy string gauge, too?**

Not that heavy, no; I use 9-46s. They're Hybrid Slinkys, so they're pretty light, really.

# ANDY POWELL

MARCH 1997

*At the beginning of the '70s, Wishbone Ash practically invented the idea of using twin lead guitars, often playing very tight harmony parts. Years later the name lives on... The line-up has changed significantly and often as the years have tumbled by, but the band's sound has remained faithful to the original brief. The core of this sound is undoubtedly Andy Powell's Gibson Flying V, which has itself become something of a Wishbone hallmark.*

*So, with the band still going strong, with sold-out shows all over the world, I felt it was appropriate to start with Andy's early years. And I got the story behind the band's unique musical invention.*

**You started playing guitar at a young age.**

I started playing guitar about the age of 11. It was the normal thing where various people in the neighbourhood got guitars and the word got about that somebody had got a brand new Gretsch or something, and you had to go round there to see it.

**Who was your earliest influence?**

The first person who really caught my ear was Hank Marvin and The Shadows. I saw him just recently and he's lost none of the finesse – he just has such a great touch. He was very melodic, and I think that early influence just stuck with me, the tone and everything. We started to form little groups and play at places like Saturday-morning pictures during the intermission and at youth clubs.

**Since the early '70s, you have proved almost inseparable from your Gibson Flying V.**

I'd seen pictures of Albert King with one and I knew that Dave Davies in the Kinks had one and it was just such a wacky-looking instrument. I didn't really go out seeking one, we kind of found each other. There was a little shop in Denmark Street called Orange Music, and I was just looking around and they just happened to have two mint mid-'60s Flying Vs that had sat in the packing cases for five or six years, because they were considered a bit too way out. So I picked one out and just fell in love with it. The sound of it even before I plugged it into an amp was just a beautiful vibrant tone. As you know, if the thing sounds good acoustically and feels good, you know it's going to be good when you plug it in.

**How did Wishbone Ash come to be formed back then?**

The band was actually formed by [bass player] Martin Turner and [drummer] Steve Upton, who came from the West Country. They came up to London as a three-piece with Martin's brother Glen playing guitar, but Glen decided London wasn't the place for him and went back to Torquay. So they just started putting ads in the papers and did the usual audition route. At that time they met Miles Copeland [now Sting's manager] who was looking to get into the music business and he'd seen them play at Hampstead Country Club and was astounded that they didn't have any backing or a record deal. He recommended that they find another guitarist, and so they put an ad in and were thinking of maybe a guitar player and a keyboard player. As it turned out, they narrowed it down to Ted Turner and myself, but couldn't really decide between the two of us. So they said, 'Why don't you both come down and we'll play together and we'll see what happens.' And it was sort of, 'Why not use two lead players?'

# DAVE 'CLEM' CLEMPSON

AUGUST 1992

*Once upon a time, Vauxhall used the Clapton track 'Layla' to advertise its cars on UK TV. Everyone assumed that they used the original, but it was in fact rather a clever copy, as I found out when I spoke with ex-Humble Pie and Colosseum guitarist-turned-session player Clem Clempson. 'It was just a session I was booked for,' he told me. 'I didn't even know what it was until I got to the studio.'*

**Trying to recreate something as well known as 'Layla' must be like trying to forge a Picasso. Was it a fairly daunting task?**

It wasn't difficult at all. I mean, it's just a simple guitar riff really, not a Mahler symphony or anything. I didn't consciously try to get close to the original sound, but I think my style has always been fairly close to Eric's anyway, plus I generally use a Strat in the studio. The producer had written out all the parts; there are actually seven guitar parts on there, doubled in different octaves.

**Were there any other jingle sessions where you had to recreate an original?**

The soundalike things don't happen very often. But one incident that amused me was that I was booked for a coffee commercial, and the producer phoned me up the night before the session and said, 'I don't know whether you've heard it, but it's an old Humble Pie track called 'Black Coffee'...which was fantastic, because I had to go into the studio and copy myself! It was great because [former bandmate] Steve Marriott was on it as well and I hadn't seen him for a couple of years. But he was the same as ever – just went in and did it in one take. That was the last time I saw him.

# the
# BLUES PLAYERS

# ERIC CLAPTON

APRIL 1994

Back in 1994, getting an interview with Eric Clapton was harder than gaining an audience with the Pope. It took around eight months to finalise a time and a place with EC's management, and that was with a fair amount of cat-and-mouse, not to mention the letters and faxes that travelled between offices in the meantime. In the end, the interview took place on the 11th of April in the coffee bar at Olympic Studios in Barnes where Eric was recording his From The Cradle *album.*

After the interview was published in June of 1994, timed to coincide with Guitarist *magazine's tenth anniversary, it was syndicated around the world, turning up in the most unlikely of places including Japan, Spain, the USA, Holland and France. It's even been published a couple of times since, but never in its complete, unabridged form – until now.*

Eric Clapton has enjoyed a long and illustrious career, chasing in and out of the limelight with peaks and troughs scrupulously documented by the world's media, eager at once to create, infiltrate and often demolish the ivory towers of his celebrity. Hailed variously as God, drug addict, alcoholic and, more recently, the Prince of Sartoria and all-round nookie monster, that day he looked fit, tanned and happy, the cadaver of his troubled past long since laid to rest.

Eric and I spoke just after his yearly set of shows at the Royal Albert Hall. Aficionados of the annual 'Clapton Proms' knew that in previous years he had chosen to feature special, dedicated blues, rock and even orchestral nights. But for this season, which also celebrated his 100th appearance at the venue, he decided upon a slightly different course, telling me that the shows represented *'everything that goes on in my head musically'. This meant a noticeable blue hue to the first 55 minutes or so of the proceedings, which saw Eric chopping and changing between vintage Martin acoustics, Dobros, a Gibson L5, a Byrdland, a Les Paul (really!) and a white Clapton signature Strat.*

*What was in Eric's head musically at that moment – as it had been for some time – was his beloved blues project.*

**From The Cradle is obviously a labour of love...**

I'm recording this album as much as I can with everybody on the floor at the same time – horns and everything. We're trying not to overdub anything at all, and so mistakes and everything go in.

**A bit like the old Chicago days?**

Yes, I suppose so, although I think even they overdubbed sometimes. But for the purpose of getting it the way I want it to feel, I want everything live and it means playing everything, and I'm getting a bit sore because I went off and had a little holiday after the Albert Hall and [my fingers] get soft in the sea. It's hard to keep this up; the only people I know who can do that are BB King, Robert Cray and those boys. They work all the time and so they've always got perfect facility. I tend to get a bit lazy and then it takes me a while to get back into it.

**It's something of an anniversary for you, too, because I checked up and found that The Yardbirds' first single came out in June 1964.**

Did it really? Good God...

**In a way this studio is pretty much your old stamping-ground, isn't it?**

This is where a lot of the early stuff was done, yeah. This is my idea of a recording studio. If you asked me about a recording studio, this is where I would mentally refer to, because I came here more than anywhere else, and it's between where I was born and where I used to go. Down there is Kingston and

Richmond, then London's to the north. It's in the middle of all of my stamping-grounds and I think I must have recorded here with just about every outfit I ever played with. The Yardbirds I don't think came here, but just about everybody after that came here, except John Mayall, and did a lot of work here. This is a proper recording studio – always has been in my term of reference. This is the real thing, y'know.

**Can you remember what it was that turned you on to music in the beginning?**

Well, the first thing that rang in my head, rang any bells, was black music, all black records that were R&B or blues orientated. I remember hearing Sonny Terry and Brownie McGhee, Big Bill Broonzy, Chuck Berry and Bo Diddley, and not really knowing anything about the geography or the culture of this music. But for some reason it did something to me – it resonated. Then I found out later that they were black and that they were from the Deep South and they were American black men, that started my education. In fact the only education I ever really had was finding out about blues. I took a kind of elementary fundamental education in art, but it didn't rivet my attention in the same way as blues did. I mean, I wanted to know everything. I spent all of my mid- to late teens and early 20s studying the music: studying the geography of it, the chronology of it, the roots, the different regional influences and how everybody interrelated and how long people lived, and how quickly they learnt things and how many songs they had of their own and what songs were shared around... I mean I was just into it, you know? I was learning to play it as well and trying to figure out how to apply it to my life. I don't think I took it that seriously, because when we're young we don't. It was only when other people showed an interest that I realised I could make a living out of it.

**What was it like for you when you started playing in the clubs?**

Well, anybody that had any idea of how to play any instrument could just about hold their own because there was no competition – there was no one around. There were only a handful of bands, and anyone that could play Sam

And Dave was OK. When I started out, Stax and Motown were in the clubs and anyone who could play those songs, any drummer who [could] play that feel, or anyone who could approach that, was a master. I came from the blues and so to my way of thinking I had even more of a grasp of that kind of thing. To my reckoning R&B came from the blues, so I felt I was in some kind of inner sanctum, mentally or spiritually or whatever. And there was no one around. If you could play anything in a halfway convincing fashion you were the boss, and there were so few of us. If you were pretty good you could work all the time and you'd get fairly well paid, and you were successful. It was easy to be successful, very easy if you had what was necessary, which was the right musical taste, I think.

**What about the guitar, though? When did you first hear the guitar and think: that's what I want to play?**

I think on the early Elvis records and Buddy Holly – when it was clear to me that it was an electric guitar, then I think I wanted to get near it. It was fine with the white rock 'n' rollers until I heard Freddie King, then I was over the moon. I knew that was where I belonged, finally. That was serious, proper guitar playing and I haven't changed my mind ever since. It's exactly the same for me now. I still listen to it in my car, when I'm at home. I listen to Muddy Waters, Freddy King, and I get the same boost that I did then.

**The first guitar of yours was a Hoyer, wasn't it?**

Yeah, it was a Hoyer acoustic from Bell's in Surbiton.

**Did it have nylon strings or metal?**

Funnily enough, it looked like a gut-stringed guitar, but was steel stringed. An odd combination.

**But it wasn't too long before you got your first electric?**

I got a Kay double cutaway. I got one because Alexis Korner had one.

**That can't have lasted too long either, because by the time you were in The Yardbirds you were using Telecasters and Gretsches.**

It didn't stand up too well. I think the neck bowed and it didn't seem to me that you could do much about it. It had a truss rod but it wasn't that clever, and the action ended up being incredibly high. I remember at some point I didn't want it to look like it looked any more and so I covered it in black Fablon! Can you imagine what it sounded like after that? Let alone what it looked like, this matt black plastic finish. And then it moved on. I sold it to Roger Pierce and at some point there I ended up with the ES335TDC and then I got into Fenders. I had a Telecaster and a Jazzmaster and then a Strat – oh no, I didn't get a Strat for a long time.

**It's well known that in the early part of the '60s nobody could get 'the sound' that you were hearing on records out of British-made amps. How did you overcome that?**

Just by turning them flat out! I thought the obvious solution was to get an amp and play it as loud as it would go until it was just about to burst. And that's how it sounded. When I was doing that album with John Mayall, it was obvious that if you mic'ed the amp too close it would sound awful, so you had to put the mic a long way away and get the room sound of that amp breaking up.

**That was when you discovered Marshalls, wasn't it?**

Yes.

**What were you using prior to The Bluesbreakers?**

I was using Vox AC30s and things like that, but they didn't do it for me. They were too toppy. They didn't have any mid-range at all.

**Did you use anything to drive them or did you just whack them right up?**

Whack them right up and still they didn't distort, as far as I can remember. They may have distorted but I can't remember that they did so in an attractive way. It didn't really get thick, it just got edgy.

**Do you harbour any romance for that period at all? I think it was Mark Knopfler who said that in some ways he misses the old days where you could turn up at a club with a guitar and an amp and just do your gig.**

Well, yeah that's true, although I don't picture myself doing that these days. I'm going to see someone play tomorrow night and it's funny for me now to think of walking into a club and seeing another band play. I do it every now and then and it all comes back to me, and I feel that this is where I belong. I mean, I grew up playing in clubs – that is my spiritual stamping-ground – and every time I walk into a club I feel like I'm going to be asked to play, but I don't get asked to play. I don't know what it is, whether people are intimidated to ask me to play or get reverse snobbishness about it. So I go in and I probably don't get asked to play. Back then there were so few people around that if you did go into a club you knew everybody there. If you went to see someone play you already knew those people. There was no intimidation – there was no inhibited stuff at all. It was just simply that you hung out with these people and you would play with them all the time. So in that respect I miss that camaraderie. Even then, there was competition, but it was friendly; now I think it's much more aggressive. I went through that 'dinosaur' thing ten years ago and so God knows what it's like for me to show up somewhere. I don't know what they think of me now if I walk into a club. What do I represent to young players? I have no idea. I don't know where they've gone in their heads now, what they think, what their influences are. It's probably nothing to do with what my contribution was. I have no idea.

**I don't know, because I teach guitar and I see 12-year-old kids coming in with Hendrix albums, which is great...**

Because they're making the connection back to that root, yeah.

**Everybody assumes that you were with The Yardbirds a long time or that you were with The Bluesbreakers a long time, but in actual fact it was only a matter of months in both cases.**

No, I went very quickly through all those things. [Laughs] I mean, Cream was like a year and a half or something, and even with John Mayall I was only half there. I was so unreliable, so irresponsible. I would sometimes just not show up at gigs, and that's how you'd get Peter Green asked to play – because I was not there, and that was happening a lot. I went to see John last year to actually make amends. I'd been looking back and realised how badly I'd behaved, I mean...

**There was the infamous Glands incident where you formed a group and then took off for Greece.**

Yeah, just took off – took off and left him high and dry!

**Let's talk about the whole 'Clapton Is God' thing. Were you uncomfortable with it?**

I thought it was quite justified, to be honest with you! [Laughs.] I suppose I felt I deserved it for the amount of seriousness that I'd put into it. I was so deadly serious about what I was doing. I thought everyone else was either in it just to be on *Top Of The Pops* or *Ready Steady Go*, or to score girls or for some dodgy reason. I was in it to save the fucking world! I wanted to tell the world about blues or just get it right. Even then I thought that I was on some kind of mission, so in a way I thought, 'Yes I am God, and quite right.' My head was huge! I was unbearably arrogant and I was not a fun person to be around most of the time because I was just so superior and very judgemental. I didn't have any time for anything that didn't fit into my pattern or my scheme of things.

**Before that time you'd actually played with Muddy Waters. How did that come about?**

I think Mike Vernon [Bluesbreakers producer] put the whole thing together. I think Mike got them into the country, or maybe they were on their way through to do a tour or something, and he got Muddy in the studio and got me in there with them. All I can remember is just being incredibly scared, clumsy and overwhelmed, you know? Completely overwhelmed.

**In those days nobody really knew Muddy outside of the immediate blues fraternity, though, did they?**

Nobody really knew that much about him, no. And the blues thing was going through some funny changes. If you played electric guitar, you'd sold out. Josh White had done a lot of touring of Europe and Big Bill Broonzy too, but Josh came later and picked up the slack. He would go on and do 'Down By The Riverside' and 'Scarlet Ribbons' and things. It was very middle of the road blues and folk, and it was all acoustic. Then Brownie McGhee and Sonny Terry would tour and they made it palatable. They kind of acquainted everyone with the blues via the acoustic guitar, and so I think when Muddy came over the first time he brought an electric guitar and it wasn't very well received. So he wasn't everybody's cup of tea. It was only the purists who knew about Chicago blues.

**It must have been overwhelming for you because you were only about 20 at the time.**

Yeah, if that. I couldn't take it all in, I couldn't take it on. I felt really stupid because I was a little boy trying to play a man's music, and these were the men. They were actually just past their prime so they'd done it; they'd done what I'm still trying to do. I felt really clumsy. I thought I didn't really belong, but I just felt very grateful for the opportunity.

**How does Cream fit into your perspective now? It must have been a very intense 18 months.**

It was very intense and it actually seems like a longer time. It seems like we were together for three or four years but, in fact, it was very short. I think my overall feeling about it now is that it was kind of a glorious mistake. I had a completely different idea of what it would be before I started it and it ended up being a wonderful thing, but nothing like it was meant to be.

**It was meant to be your band, wasn't it?**

It was meant to be a blues trio, yeah. I just didn't have the assertiveness to take control. So I let Jack do the singing – well, it's not a question of 'I let' anybody, it just worked out that way. Jack was already singing, he was the singer, and those two were the powerful, dominant personalities in the band. Ginger did the business and they sort of ran the show and I just played. I just went with the flow in the end and I enjoyed it greatly, but it wasn't anything like I expected it to be at all.

**In the Cream period you virtually ran the whole gamut of Gibsons: your Firebird, 335, Les Pauls, SGs – the very famous psychedelic SG.**

Yeah, yeah...

**Were there any particular favourites? I hear you've still got your 335.**

Still got that 335 and I love it. I still get it out every now and then. The 335 was a big favourite, and that particular Firebird, I had some great times on that; the single pickup was a fantastic sound. I think that SG went through the Cream thing just about the longest. It was really a very, very powerful and comfortable instrument because of its lightness and the width and the flatness of the neck. It had a lot going for it: it had the humbuckers, it had everything I wanted at that point.

**That's the one you've got in the film of the last concert at the Albert Hall, with the famous bit in the middle, when you describe 'woman tone'...**

[Cringing] Embarrassing, so embarrassing...

**No, it's great. I actually skived off English at school to go and see that film in Kilburn.**

Oh, that's great.

**You've played as a guest on many different albums, but the most unusual must be your contribution to Frank Zappa's *We're Only In It For The Money*.**

Yeah, we were pals. It started when I went to New York with The Cream and The Who to do the Murray The K Show. We used to go down the Village to find out what was going on. There was The Fugs and The Mothers, and you'd be able to go into the Café A Go Go and see BB King play and just everything. New York was unbelievable. The Mothers were at this place called The Garrick Theater and there would be nobody in the audience – nobody. They were experimenting every night. They'd have odd people – bag ladies and marines – on the stage, and Frank would come off and sit in the audience and talk to someone while the band played. It was madness. He took me home one night to his house and he made me play. He plugged me into a ReVox and made me play straight on to tape with a rhythm machine or something, and told me to play everything I knew – all the licks I knew. And he sort of put it on file. I thought it was really sweet and I didn't mind doing it. I was just very flattered that he was interested, because it was clear this was a music intellectual I was meeting and so I was very flattered. He was very manipulative and knew how to appeal to my ego and my vanity, and I put everything on this tape. I think he just had files and files of tapes of people and I was in there somewhere. And then I went back – I don't know if it was the next trip to New York – and I called him up and he invited me to the studio. He'd already had someone inside a piano – he'd climbed inside the piano – and he said, 'I want you to pretend to be Eric Burdon on acid.' And that's what I did. I was just talking there, 'I can see God' and all this stuff, and it was just funny to be involved with these people. I felt like I was being incredibly hip and fashionable but, God... I mean, I've had some funny times with Frank. There was another time I went to LA and I knew he had a party, so I went round to his house and someone opened the door and put a guitar in my hands and it was already plugged in like they'd been tipped off I was coming, and I walked straight into this trap, you know? Another time I went up and jammed with him. I went to see him play and he invited me to play. When I went out to do my solo, he did that famous thing of doing hand signals to the band and they went through about ten different time signatures and fucked me up completely! I could not make head nor tail of it!

**You had to love him though...**

I love him dearly – a wonderful man.

**Looking back now, are you able to put all this sort of stuff into context objectively? Are you able to look back at the player you were then and actually think, 'Yeah, that was OK' or 'That was a bit dodgy'?**

Yes, fairly. I think all of it was OK until drugs and drink got involved. My motives were just clearer, you know? I don't think my facility has really got much better or worse. I mean, I've just finished doing a blues in there, a Freddie King song, and it doesn't sound that much stiffer or that much faster either, than when I was doing the John Mayall or the Cream period – maybe a bit more fluent, a bit more confident, maybe. But what's clear to me is at that period and this period I was much more in touch with the actual making of the music, and there was this long bit in between where I was more inclined to get out of it. It was some point towards the end of the '60s and all the way through the '70s I was out, you know? I was really kind of on holiday and being a musician was my way of making the money to be on holiday.

**That whole thing started with Jimi's death in a way. The dates are almost coincidental, aren't they?**

Yeah. It was funny how that all picked up. The '60s were great when we were all doing drugs recreationally. We were all under the impression that we could take it or leave it and it was more like weekend binging: you do whatever you were doing and then you'd get stoned one night, or you'd take acid, and then you wouldn't do it again for a while. Then it got to the point where those of us who were addictive by nature just carried on doing it and we'd do it all the time. And it kinda got fucked up. I think we lost the thread then. In a funny way… I suppose this may be a bit presumptuous, but it kind of opened the door for punk and all these things to come in, because there was no continuity from the musical pattern that evolved in the '60s. It kind of got scrambled and lost with all the drugs and opened the door for all the anarchy, bitterness and anger. The musicians of the '70s didn't really have a very clear legacy. The legacy got very fucked and very self-indulgent. I think that the whole thing about The Sex Pistols was that they were really pissed off at our indulgence – the indulgence of the '60s and that self-righteous stance.

**Jimi actually jammed with Cream, didn't he?**

Mm. First time I ever met him, we were playing at the Central London Polytechnic. Harvey Goldsmith was the promoter – he was the Entertainments Secretary of the Students' Union – and Jimi came along with Chas Chandler. I don't know how long he'd been over here, maybe a couple of days, but he got up and played. He was doing Howlin' Wolf songs and I couldn't believe this guy, I couldn't believe it. Part of me wanted to run away and say, 'Oh no, this is what I want to be – I can't handle this.' And part of me just fell in love. It was a really difficult thing for me to deal with, but I just had to surrender and say, 'This is fantastic.'

**You became good friends, didn't you?**

Oh yeah, instantly, instantly.

**The music was the huge point of reference between you.**

Yes, yes…

**I don't think people realise how much of a blues player Hendrix was. In a lot of ways it's obvious now, but in those days it didn't seem to come into it.**

No, I know. I think a lot of people thought, 'Oh yeah, the Band Of Gypsys thing was the best.' Or they look at different eras of his music making in terms of his peak or his most prolific or his most creative. But the core of all his playing was blues and that's what really used to upset him the most, was that he got this fixation about selling out. He got very down on himself and very cynical about his acceptance. He thought he was going commercial all the time and yet he couldn't stop himself, in a way.

**It seems that perhaps the bubble burst a bit for you when Jimi died. Previously, you'd been using Marshall 100-watt amps and Gibson guitars, and you'd been going up and up in the power stakes in the same way that Jimi was. And yet, when Jimi died, you switched over to smaller amps and started using a Fender Strat. Was your switching to Strats around the time of Jimi's death a conscious tribute to him on your part?**

Yes, I think it was. Once he wasn't there any more I felt like there was room to pick it up. And also I saw Steve Winwood playing one and something about that did it for me. I'd always worshipped Steve, and whenever he made a move I would be right on it. I wanted to know, because to me he was one of the few people in England who had his finger on some kind of universal musical pulse. I always watched his next move and thought, 'There's something to be learned from this.' I went to see him play at the Marquee and he was playing a white-necked Strat, and there was something about it… Because he was white and he was playing a Strat, made it all right for me.

**It's a story that has been told often in the past, but can you tell us how you came by your most famous Strat, 'Blackie'?**

Well, it ties in with that period, actually. It was the Derek And The Dominos period or maybe before, during Blind Faith. I was in Nashville and I went into this shop called Sho-Bud where they had stacks of Fender Strats going for virtually nothing because they were so unfashionable and unwanted. I bought a big pile of them all for a song – they were really cheap like $300 or $400 each – and I took them home and gave them out. I gave Steve one, I gave Pete Townshend one, I gave George Harrison one and I kept a few. And I made Blackie out of a group of them: I took the pickups out of one, the scratchplate off another and the neck off another and I made my own guitar, like a hybrid guitar that had all the best bits from all these Strats.

**You almost played it to death, too, didn't you?**

Yeah, I wore it out. It's pretty well inaccessible now…

**Isn't the E string almost hanging off the neck now, where it's been worn down?**

Yeah, there's not much of the neck left! [Laughs] It's worn away on either side and on the back with wear and tear.

**So what made that Strat unique for you?**

The fact that I made it. It was one of the last guitars that I kind of road managed myself, really. Therefore it felt like it was invested with some kind of soul, you know…

**We've reached the Derek And The Dominos period, and this marked the beginning of your liaison with Duane Allman, who would have been another influence around this time, wouldn't he?**

Yeah...

**When did you start playing slide guitar?**

I've always played slide – not electric, always – but I played slide when I was playing acoustic in the pubs. I tried to play like Furry Lewis and other of the more primitive rural blues musicians, and I also tried to be a little bit like Muddy. Then it sort of went on one side, but it's always come and gone. I've never really stuck very hard at it. I've done a couple of Elmore James songs on this album where I've come back to it again. I do love it, but somehow or another it doesn't have the madness. When I got into Buddy Guy, there was something about the madness of his playing, it was like someone jabbing you with his forefinger that I fell in love with – the staccato madness of it that you can't do on slide. Slide is much more rhythmic, in a way, and much more of an accompaniment than anything else.

**Was Duane Allman an influence on your slide playing?**

Yes, very much so.

**The story of you meeting has it that you just went to see him in concert...**

Well, we'd started the Derek And The Dominos album and we hadn't really got very far. I'd written some songs and we had played gigs – some touring in England – and we'd got a kind of persona. But in the studio it was very one-dimensional and it didn't feel like we were getting anywhere. There was a bit of frustration in the air, and Tom Dowd has always been a very clever mixer of people. He's always been a great one for being a catalyst and putting different combinations of musicians together to get an effect. I don't know whether he saw an end result or not, but I think he just wanted me to see Duane. In fact, I'd been talking about Duane because I'd heard him play on 'Hey Jude' with Wilson Pickett and I kept asking people who this was. So he took me and all the rest of the Dominos to see The Allman Brothers play in

Coconut Grove, after about two weeks of us being in Miami, and introduced us to them. I said, 'Let's hang out – come back to the studio.' I wanted Duane to hear what we'd done and we just jammed and hung out, got drunk and did a few drugs. I think they were going to be around the Miami area and he just came in the studio, and I kept him there and we made the record. I kept thinking up ways to keep him in the room: 'We could do this. Do you know this one?' Of course, he knew everything that I would say and we'd just do it. A lot of those things like 'Key To The Highway' or 'Nobody Knows You When You're Down And Out' are first or second takes, and then I'd quickly think of something else to keep him there. I knew that sooner or later he was going to go back to the Allmans, but I wanted to steal him! And I tried, and he actually came on a few gigs, too. But then he had to say, almost like a woman, 'Well, you know, I am actually married to this band and I can't stay with you.' I was really quite heartbroken. I got used to having another guitar player and, because it was Duane, it was fantastic. But I felt like I had to have another guitar player in the band and I had Neil Schon come in for a little while, having met him through Carlos Santana, and then by that time we were getting really fucked up and the band was on its way out.

**Because the Dominos didn't last very long either, did it?**

No, that's right.

**Eighteen months or so?**

Yeah, yeah...

**That was the beginning of your dark period, wasn't it?**

I don't know whether it can be fairly placed at the door of drugs or relationships or life issues as much as I just had to get away. I had been doing so much. I'd been out there for a long time, playing and playing with no break. I do that a lot. I do work quite hard – I always have done – and at that point for some reason a combination of things put me into a kind of fairly necessary retirement. And I needed it, in a way, because I remember at the end of that period that I was starting to fall back in love with music. I remember listening to music very hard and wanting to play very much, but I had to get almost off the scene to get that enthusiasm back because I'd lost it. Derek And The Dominos were recording in here when we broke up, and I went into that dark place. I was coming in and I didn't give a shit about the music any more. We'd come in and just argue all day and have a go at one another, and then one of us would blow up and split. The music didn't matter. I didn't like the sound of my guitar, I didn't like the way I played and it took me a while to go away and come back to it. When I came back I came back with a different point of view, a fresh enthusiasm and a kind of ability or an open-mindedness to learn about new music, because that's when I heard reggae and that's when I took that as a place to join in, to learn or to muck about with. Then there was JJ Cale and Don Williams, and all these things were on top of me – I was just like a kid again in a sweet shop.

**You toured a hell of a lot in the '70s.**

Toured and recorded and got out of it. I had a great time, but it was all fairly directionless. In a great way. I mean, I don't regret any of it, to be honest. I think there was no other way for me to go, in a way. I'm just very grateful that I survived it and didn't die, because I was often in some very seriously dangerous situations with booze and drugs. I used to do crazy things that people would bail me out of, or where I was risking life and limb in cars, or in different life-threatening situations, and I'm just grateful that I survived. But the music got very lost. I didn't know where I was going and I didn't really care. I was more into just having a good time and I think it showed. I think I got fairly irresponsible and there were some people that liked it, and other people that got very pissed off. And my guitar playing took the back seat. I'd got fed up with that thing about 'The Legend' and the rock hero and all of that. I wanted to be something else and I wasn't really sure what it was. I was just latching on to people and trying to be like them to see if something else would emerge, and all that did emerge in the long run is what I am now. I don't really know what that is as a definition, except it's more in tune with what I was at the beginning – which is a blues musician.

**People have said of those days that if they came to see you, nobody could actually predict what the concert was going to be like. Maybe Legs Larry Smith would turn up and maybe you'd be wearing a plastic raincoat...**

It would depend very much on who I'd bumped into that day, who had managed to corner my attention, because then I'd just go off with them. I was just like a grass in the wind – I went anywhere. I was literally anybody's, depending on what they were holding – you know, what drug or what drink they were on – and I'd go with them. Then there'd be the gig in the evening and I'd be wherever that was, wherever I'd been taken.

**That period ended dramatically around '84/'85. Suddenly there were projects like *Edge Of Darkness* and the Roger Waters album *The Pros And Cons Of Hitch Hiking*, which saw you playing with much more fire and power. But it was probably Live Aid that was responsible for re-establishing you in many people's minds. Did the reaction you received surprise you?**

Yeah! I'm not sure even I was able to take it all in, you know? What I remember about it was that it was the simplest way of being clear to me how important I was, because I've always been a very, very self-effacing or low self-worth sort of person. I beat the shit out of myself a lot. But when they told me where I was going to be on the billing I didn't get it. I thought, 'What? Really?' and that really did a lot for my acceptance of myself: other people's opinion. And that reception...actually, yeah, it was mind-blowing.

**It was a tremendous ovation...**

Yeah. And I think you don't know about that until you're put on with a lot of other acts and see how you fit in with the musical spectrum; how they think of you, compared to everybody else. And so, from that point on, I started to give myself a bit more of a pat on the back and be kind to myself.

**Which all leads up to where you are now, which is making a blues album.**

I'm making a blues album because it's come full circle, hasn't it? I mean, it is 30 years and I'm doing what I want to do. I'm fulfilling myself for other people, too, because I've always been badgered about this. You know, people are always saying, 'When are you going to do this blues album you're always going on about?' And I'm doing it. And it then will free me up to either carry on doing that or do whatever it is I'm going to do. I've been doing everything else until I did the blues album, and now I'll open up the door for whatever is next, and it will be interesting to see what that is.

**At the Albert Hall this year not only were you using a Les Paul again...**

Because they were Freddie King songs. This album is paying respect as much as possible to the records the way I heard them and felt about them, and so when I'm singing and playing, I'm trying to be me being Freddie King. Of course, that doesn't happen because it still comes out as me, but I'm doing it as much as I can. In the way we record it, for instance: all on the floor at the same time, the instruments I play and the way I sing it – everything, to try and be as true to my recollection of the experience. Not that I want to copy the record that closely, just the experience – the emotional way it felt to me.

**How did you go about choosing the songs for the album or the live set at the Albert Hall?**

Well, they're just the songs that I've always loved out of my record collection. The various blues masterpieces, for whatever reason, in my taste, that have had some kind of profound effect on me. Like that Jimmy Rodgers song 'Blues All Day Long', there's something about that. The beauty of it, the balance of the instruments, the way it was recorded and the strength of it has always taken my breath away, and always will. I don't do it quite the same way, but what I'm trying to recreate is the emotional experience I got when I heard it. And the same with all of the songs. There's something about all of them that I played at the Albert Hall that did something to me emotionally and took me to some beautiful place and made me feel better, or gave me cold chills when I heard it. So I try to make that happen again by playing it.

**Do you think there are any modern blues songs being written that do the same sort of thing?**

Oh, yeah. In fact, I would like to do a couple of Robert Cray's songs. There are so many off all his albums and I think I ought to do one. There are other people, too, but he's the first one that appeals to me, because he is the last of the great heroes, and he is a player, too, and a writer. So I'll probably do a couple of his things.

**You played some Hendrix at this year's Albert Hall gigs, too…**

Yeah.

**You've recorded Jimi's 'Stone Free' and 'Little Wing' in the past. Why haven't you recorded more, seeing as you were so close?**

I got very jealous of Jimi. I was very possessive about Jimi when he was alive, and when he died I was very angry and I got even more possessive. I got so possessive that I didn't want anything to do with it. If people talked to me about Hendrix I would just turn away, I wasn't interested in their perception of Hendrix because I felt like they were talking about an ex-girlfriend or a brother who had died. In some way I just thought, 'I'm not talking to you about it. I knew him, and he was very dear to me and it's very painful to hear you talk about him as if you knew him – you fucking didn't! I don't want anything to do with it.' It's taken me all of this time to heal. I don't know how long the grieving process is, but in my experience it's a fucking long time, and it's taken me this long to be able to pick up a guitar and play a Hendrix song. It's a long time, and maybe that's the way it is for human beings. It is for me, anyway.

**Why did you choose 'Stone Free'?**

Well, the thing with 'Stone Free' was that Jimi told me when he first played it to me that it was the one he wanted as the A-side instead of 'Hey Joe'. And so I thought 'Oh, OK', because to me it was better than 'Hey Joe'. When I heard 'Stone Free' it blew my fucking mind. And I thought, they're going to put 'Hey Joe' out because it's commercial. He wanted 'Stone Free', it was the first recorded thing that I'd heard of his, and so that was the connection to our friendship.

**There have been lots of books written about you. What do you think of them?**

I think they all take it far too seriously and that's a trap. It's a bit like the 'Clapton Is God' thing – they all follow on from that. *Survivor* has got a hint of that. It's all a bit reverent, isn't it? I don't really see myself as being that heroic. I was just lucky to be in the right place at the right time and gifted and very fortunate to have survived. So I am a survivor, but it all ought to be taken a little less seriously, I feel.

**Are you amazed by the furore about you and your status as a player that is still out there?**

Is there?

**Yeah!**

Really?

**We [*Guitarist*] ran a poll in the magazine to ask readers who they would most like to see featured, and you won it.**

Oh really? That's really nice.

**One guy even wrote on the bottom of his entry, 'Have you got something against him, or what?'**

[Laughs] Well that is great... Oh I dunno. I think if it's due to anything it's just the fact that I'm fairly honest about what I do. I'm not labouring under any great pretensions to be brilliant. I just try to do the best to be there and carry on working, and do it as simply and unaffectedly as possible, because there are a lot of temptations to latch on to this as it goes by or latch on to that as it goes by. But to be true to myself, I think it's easy for people then, isn't it? Because they know who I am, I'm not bullshitting them. I'm being true to what I do and true to me, and I think people like that and they can identify with that and they see a strength in it. All I really want to do is to play with dignity and self-respect and to pass that on, and to give that to people when they hear it.

**Did the multiple Grammys for *Unplugged* take you by surprise?**

Yeah, I must admit I found it all a little bit overblown. I mean, I thought the album was quite rough, to say the least. I think most of the recognition and applause was wrapped up in another gesture – which is beautiful and I don't want to put that down at all. I appreciate all of it. But I felt it was all a little bit blown out of proportion. And frightening too, because it was like a peak that could have done me in. If I'd taken it too seriously, it could have done me in.

**Singing 'Tears In Heaven' and 'The Circus Left Town' must be so difficult for you.**

There's a fine line, a very thin dotted line you have to walk on, out of respect for the emotion of the song and the event that brought it about and succumbing to the power of the emotion. It's been close on occasions, where I could choke and not be able to do it, but then what would happen? We'd have to stop and then it would get mawkish and it would get embarrassing. At the same time, to back off and pretend that it's about nothing and just play it as if it was a song that had no meaning would be pointless. So there's somewhere in the middle that does require a fair amount of discipline, concentration and focus to stay in the right place and not step off the tightrope either way.

**Are you going to record 'The Circus Left Town'?**

Yeah. I wanted to talk to the record company about making this blues album and recording another one alongside it and putting out a double album, but at the moment it seems that they're not in agreement with this. It's not just 'The Circus Left Town': there's another one that I wrote about my son called 'My Father's Eyes', which was also part of the *Unplugged* programme, but didn't get in there. There are a handful of songs that are in that mould, and some other stuff too, which is more rock 'n' roll, so that will be on perhaps the next studio rock 'n' roll album, if that's what's going to happen. But at the moment all I can see is this blues thing and being true to that.

**Are you aware that there are choral versions of 'Tears In Heaven', and that it's often performed in churches?**

No... Wow, good God. That's amazing.

**Have you got any advice for today's guitar players?**

Yeah – listen to the past, you know. I've run into a lot of players in the last 10 or 15 years who didn't really know where it was coming from. They thought it came from Jimmy Page, or they thought it came from Jeff Beck, or they thought it came from Buddy Guy, or that it came from BB King. Well, it comes from further back. And if you go back and listen to Lonnie Johnson and Robert Johnson and Blind Blake and Blind Boy Fuller and Blind Willie Johnson and Blind Willie McTell, there's thousands of them that all have something that led to where it is now. And actually, the beauty of it is that you can take one of those things and make it yours. With learning too much from the later players, you don't have that much opportunity to make something original. Whereas if you go back into the past, and even go beyond the guitar playing... For me, I listened to King Oliver, and I listened to Louis Armstrong, and I listened to Jelly Roll Morton, and I listened to Thelonious Monk, and I listened to Charles Mingus, and I listened to John Coltrane and I listened to Archie Shepp... I listened to everything I could that came from that place that they call the blues, but in formality isn't necessarily the blues.

**A lot of those guys are jazz players.**

They are, but they all would acknowledge that if you can't play the blues, you can't play jazz anyway. So, listen, listen, listen, and go back as far as you dare; that's what I still do today. I still listen to Leroy Carr and Scrapper Blackwell for their beauty and simplicity, and to get a feeling, because that's what it's about. It's not about technique, it's not about what kind of instrument you play or how many strings it's got, or how fast you can play or how loud it is or how quiet it is. It's about how it feels and how it makes you feel when you play.

**Finally, you once said you had two ambitions in life: one was to play one note in a blues solo that could bring an audience to the verge of tears, and the other was to sleep with 10,000 women. Have you found that note?**

No – and I haven't slept with 10,000 women either! Still got both of them to do, isn't it amazing? If I live that long.

# GARY MOORE

MARCH 1995

*After playing fiery hard rock during the '80s, at the beginning of the 1990s Gary Moore officially turned back to the music he grew up listening to. The blues was a formative influence on his playing, but often such a dramatic mid-career change of tack has unfortunate results, and for many only the doldrums await. But happily not so in Gary's case. His first blues outing,* Still Got The Blues, *created an entirely new momentum that spurred him on to release two further blue-hued projects:* After Hours *and* Blues Alive. *But possibly the project closest to his heart was* Blues For Greeny, *an album of Peter Green's music. In 1995 I was invited down to the studios to hear some rough mixes of the album while it was still very much in its formative stages.*

**Tell me about *Blues For Greeny*.**

Basically it's just that: an album of Peter Green's music, although it concentrates more on the blues aspect as opposed to his more poppy things. I've ignored the obvious things like 'Albatross' and 'Man Of The World'. In fact, the only single of his I've done is 'Need Your Love So Bad', which I've been playing for a long time and so it means a lot to me. It's a great song and I love Peter's version of it, but I've taken the guitar solo on a lot further at the end. The original is much shorter than people realise, actually. As soon as the guitar comes in at the end it's gone.

**Peter was more celebrated for 'Albatross', although 'Need Your Love' was the bigger hit...**

That was because 'Albatross' was an original song, and it was the first instrumental to come along for a long time and be very commercially successful – that was his answer to The Shadows, I suppose.

**There is a bit of controversy regarding which guitar Peter used for the original recording. Some say it was a Strat...**

A Strat? It was a Les Paul. Why would they think it was a Strat? It's very deep that sound; you wouldn't get that depth from a Strat. If you listen to the warmth on the low end, it's a very soft sound. It doesn't have the cut that a Strat would have.

**Some say they can detect the presence of a tremolo arm...**

No, there's no tremolo, that's finger vibrato. I've seen him play it and I've seen him do it exactly like that live, and it's always been on a Les Paul.

[While at the studio Gary previewed several tracks from the album: 'Long Grey Mare', 'Merry-Go-Round', 'If You Be My Baby' and 'I Loved Another Woman'. 'Apart from those,' he told me, 'there are things like "The Same Way" from *A Hard Road*, which was either the first or one of the first vocals Peter ever did. I've tried to go from John Mayall onwards, through Fleetwood Mac, up to when he left.']

**So there is a strong chronological aspect to the album?**

Yeah, but it's not put together in that way. The songs are compiled as they fit together, as opposed to chronologically. There are a couple of more obscure songs that I've chosen from the Fleetwood Mac period, things like 'Love That

Burns' and 'If You Be My Baby', which is more the rough-and-ready side of Peter's music.

**The end results speak for themselves, but what was it that initiated the project in the first place?**

I don't really know, to be honest. I've wanted to do it for a long time and I just felt that now was a good time. It was like going back to the old roots again, because I felt that in a blues sense I'd drifted away very much from the essence of what I started to do when I did *Still Got The Blues*. When I did that album I started off doing stuff more like this. It was more contained, much more low key, with just a bass player and drummer. But by the time the album came out and we went on the road, the whole thing had got bigger and bigger, and it became like a rock thing again. The whole thing got blown out of proportion and I ended up playing very loud with a big distorted guitar sound, and I lost the essence of it. It was very successful and everything, but that's not the point. The point is that musically this is more where it started off, so I've gone right back to that very bare feeling. 'Merry-Go-Round' is just done with bass and drums; it's very dry and very pure. It's got that essence of what Peter was about, which was that very stripped-down, minimal way of playing, and that was something I hadn't done a lot of on record before, but something that I really enjoy listening to.

**Did you consciously try to emulate Peter's guitar sound on the album?**

Well, I used his guitar! When you pick up that guitar, it's kind of hard to play any other way, and so of course I wanted to play along those lines. But I also wanted to come through myself, which I think I've done. It's just obtaining a balance between those two things. Obviously I don't play the same way as Peter, but I could do a passable imitation of Peter Green. If you gave me a guitar I could sit here and probably get closer than anybody else. But there's no point in coming across like an expensive bar band. You want to let whatever it is you do come through in the music. So I didn't just want to clone it and do everything exactly the same as he did. I've tried to be faithful to the original songs, but put a bit of myself in there as well. Definitely the vocals are quite different, and I think that's something that will set it apart. There are places where it is very close to the original in terms of the sound and everything, like I think 'Love That Burns' is close – we've used the same horn line and everything. There's something about it; the sound became very similar to the old version. There was a sort of nasal sound to the whole track and the way the guitar sounded like it was bleeding down the vocal mic, which brought out all the mid-range. So there's a lot of that on that particular track, and that's probably the closest I get to the way he plays on the record.

**How did you come by Peter's Les Paul in the first place?**

Peter said to me one night, 'Do you want to borrow my guitar for a while?' And I said, 'Fuck – yeah!' I mean, what are you going to say, 'No, don't bother me Peter, I'm busy?' So he gave me the address and I went down and picked the guitar up at his parents' place. He lived with his parents at that time in South London, and I picked the guitar up and I had it for a few days, and I couldn't believe I had it in my hands. I was so scared that anything might happen to it because I lived in this bedsit in Belsize Park, and I had to take the guitar everywhere because there was no lock on my door. So wherever I went this guitar had to go too. He called me up and said, 'What do you think of the guitar?' And I said, 'Well, it's fantastic!' He said, 'Do you want to buy it?' I said I couldn't afford it, but he said it wasn't the money he was interested in, he just wanted it to have a good home. So he told me to take my main guitar and sell it and whatever I got for it I could give to him, so it would be like swapping guitars. That was how he offered it to me. I had an SG at the time, and so I took it into town and I sold it for £160 or something like that, and he came up to my flat for the money and gave me 40 or 50 quid back. He said, 'I'll tell you what, I'll just take what I paid for it which was 120 quid.' But then he said he wouldn't even do that, and so I think I ended up giving him £100 or £110. I said to him if he ever wanted it back I'd give it to him, but he said, 'No, I'll never ask for it back…'

**The guitar had a close brush with death a few years ago.**

I was in a bad car crash and the guitar was in the boot of a car. It was a very strange experience… I had a dream one night that somebody stole the guitar, and sometimes when you have these dreams they come true. I was leaving for the studio to do some demos and this guy picked me up in a car, and just as I was leaving I said, 'I want to bring the Les Paul with me today because I had this terrible dream.' And he said, 'Oh you're getting really paranoid!' So we put it in the boot of his car and were driving to the studio when we stopped at the lights at Chiswick flyover, and this great big fucking truck just came up behind us just as we were about to pull away from the lights and BOOF! Straight into the back of us. I just opened the boot and although the guitar was in a flight case, its neck was completely broken. So the dream wasn't entirely wrong – someone did take it from me. But we got it repaired amazingly well, we put a steel bolt in the neck. It was in a terrible state, though. The car was written off, so you can imagine.

**Apart from that one incident where major surgery was required, what about everyday maintenance?**

It was refretted quite a while ago, but the thing is that until now I haven't been using it on a regular basis. I mean, I've been using it for one or two songs – 'Midnight Blue', stuff like that – but it hasn't been my main guitar for the last few years, so there hasn't been much wear on the frets. But if I start using it all the time now, I know it's going to need a refret, which I really hate the idea of because you just think it's going to be different. You know what guitarists are like: they're all so neurotic about things like that!

**On *Blues For Greeny*, was there any attempt to recreate the feel of a '60s recording in the studio by having all instruments playing together live?**

We all played live, but I played in the control room a lot of the time because I don't like wearing headphones. But we still played all together and we could see each other, so it was just like me being in a booth, all screened off, except I had the luxury of being able to hear everything coming through the speakers. This is the livest studio record I've ever made, actually, even some of the vocals are live. Equipment-wise I used a little Fender Vibroverb reissue, a Matchless amplifier and a '60s Fender Bassman. A lot of the time we were going through a 4 x 12 Marshall cabinet. The key elements in recreating Peter's sound are basically that guitar and the touch, really. You can't recreate his sound to the point where it's the same, you can only approximate it – but luckily I've got the guitar. Peter always had a clean sound, and I think it's down to the playing after that. It's down to the touch and sensitivity of the player, and the phrasing and the space that you leave. It's all those things.

**Some of your playing on the album is very intimate, suggesting the guitar's volume control was rolled right back in the studio.**

Well, when I'm playing I fiddle with the sound a lot, changing the tone, so at times the guitar would get full, at other times I'd back it off. It's just depending on how I feel at the time really. 'Merry-Go-Round' is very close to Peter's old sound I would say. It was on the first Fleetwood Mac album, the second or third track on there, and it comes in and it's very dry. It's like, 'Wow', I don't think I'd heard anything that pure before. It was so basic, just with the bass and drums behind it. So the guitar was very in your face – very present with no echo or anything like that.

**How did you come to meet Peter?**

I'd seen him play with John Mayall just after Eric had left the band, when I was 14. He had a Selmer amplifier, which was rented because no one could afford to bring their own gear, and he had to play 'All Your Love'. I thought it was going to sound like shit, but the moment he plugged in he went into that lick at the start and I remember the whole room was vibrating. It was an amazing experience just to hear a guitarist walk on stage and plug into this amplifier, which I thought was a pile of shit, and get this incredible sound. I'd never heard anything like it, and I thought, 'God, if I could ever get a guitar to sound like that or even better, to have that guitar...' He was absolutely fantastic, everything about him was so graceful. Anyway, later on when Skid Row opened for Fleetwood Mac at the National Stadium in Dublin around 1969 or 1970, I was only 16 or 17 at the time, and Peter had said to this DJ guy who was hosting the show that he'd like to meet me. I was really thrilled because Peter was one of my big heroes, and so I just went up and said hello and he said, 'Oh, I really like your playing, do you want to come back to the hotel afterwards and we'll have a chat?' I had to go and play another gig after that but he waited for me back at the hotel, and I went up to the room and there was Mick Fleetwood and Peter sharing a room, and he had the guitars on the bed. We both sat there and talked all night and played together, no amps or anything – there weren't any practice amps in those days – so we just played and talked all night. It was great. Then I travelled with him to the next gig and he persuaded his manager to bring Skid Row over to England, and then we stayed in touch after that for quite a while. I used to go up to his house and stuff, and hang out there and play with him sometimes. I hadn't seen him for quite a few years. I saw him a couple of times when I was recording *Back On The Streets* in the late '70s. He was downstairs in the bar at the studio and I said, 'Come up, I want to play you this track.' We'd done this slow version of 'Don't Believe A Word', which was very much in the Fleetwood Mac style. The Les Paul was leaning against the chair in the studio and he came in, walked across and brushed it with his hand – that's why it's given me another 20 years of magic ever since. It was losing the old vibes having been in my hands for a while, so he put some of the old magic back into it for me. And then he came up the stairs and sat in the control room and we played him 'Don't Believe A Word' and he said, 'That's like something Fleetwood Mac would have done...' and we went, 'Er, really?'

**One of your lasting memories of Peter was a nightmare gig at London's Roundhouse.**

I'd met him the night before, and he asked me to play with him. So I was struggling to get to the Roundhouse on the tube, all the way across town from the East End. I ran up to the door, Les Paul under my arm, and said 'My name's on the guest list, I'm playing with Peter Green.' The guy on the door told me that Peter was already on stage, so I had to run round to the back of the stage, get my guitar out, plug into this horrible amplifier with a dodgy lead which was just buzzing the whole time, and get up and play. He just sort of looked at me like, 'You're late!' But I think that was his last major gig. It was such a bring-down for me, because I'd always wanted to play with him properly, and I'd played with him in a room before and it was great, and then I had to plug into this horrible amp. And he had his Fender there, a little Twin, and he had this beautiful sound. I sounded like a joke, but that's one of the lessons you have to learn...

**Are there going to be any live dates to support the album?**

I'm not going to tour with it, but we might do a couple of things here and there, or maybe some festivals in the summer. But I'm not going to do a full-blown concert tour with it, no.

**Is that decision based upon the intimacy of the music and the fear that it may not weather well at larger venues?**

I don't know. I think on the surface it is, but I think this stuff can work anywhere because the music is so powerful and soulful. I mean, if you go to a rock gig and someone plays a ballad it can still really come across, even though there's a hundred thousand people there.

**One tends to associate Peter's music – and perhaps blues in general – with the small clubs.**

Yeah, very much so. But I'm not crazy about playing in clubs anyway. I always think it would be great to play clubs again, and then when I do I don't like it because I just feel sometimes it's a bit too intimate. I mean, we did a club, the Marquee, with BBM, and the band nearly broke up! The volume was terrible and it was awful, a nightmare. It was the first gig we'd done together and we were under a lot of pressure. But the monitor desk was down on the floor with the crowd – we couldn't even have it up on stage. All the luxuries you get used to... You come from rehearsing in the Academy in Brixton and you play the Marquee. It's kind of round the wrong way, isn't it?

**Since your blues renaissance a few years ago, you have worked with many legendary figures including BB King and Albert Collins. Are there any players you'd still like to work with?**

Not many of them left... I really enjoyed working with BB King, because I think a lot of his style was handed down to me through Peter. Obviously he was into BB and everything, and so when I play with him I feel he's a lot easier to play with stylistically than, say, Albert King or Albert Collins because you can relate a lot more to what he's doing. For a start we both play in standard tuning, whereas the other guys had their own ways – totally alien ways of playing – and the more you try and play like either of the Alberts, really, you've got no chance. I mean, nobody could play like Albert King. I've never heard anyone get really close. Stevie Ray could to a certain extent, but if you look at it, there's no way you could play like those guys because it's such an unorthodox way of playing. Albert King's tuning alone is just the weirdest thing, and the fact that he's playing upside down, pulling when you're pushing, it's like – you can't win! And Albert Collins – no one could play like that except him and he knew it. He told me that it went back to when he had no bass player and it was just him and a drummer, so he'd have to fill the sound out, try and play the bass at the same time. So it all came out of necessity for him. I don't know where the F minor tuning came from, that's still a bit of a mystery to me.

**Not to forget the other remarkable facet of Albert Collins' playing – his capo.**

Ah yeah. It was just, 'Hey, what key are we in?' [Laughs] He didn't give a shit what key it was in, which made me think, 'Why would he tune to F minor to begin with? Why not E minor and go from there?' He used to listen to different music as well and he used to play some country stuff; it wasn't just blues when he started out. But he was amazing just to be around. I remember when we did the *Still Got The Blues* tour, he played with us for four months or something, so I was up there every night with him and a lot of the time I wouldn't bother to play. He'd come on and I'd, like, stand back and play one chord every couple of bars and watch him, and I learnt nothing. It wasn't until about a year or two afterwards that the influence started to come through. That's the weird thing, you know. Hard as I tried to be like him on the tour – nothing. It wasn't until I got away from the whole thing that I was able to pick up a few things that he did, and even then it was very fragmented. Just the attack on the notes and stuff like that, and a bit of phrasing, but that's as close as I ever got.

**Do you ever see yourself involved in a blues project like Clapton's From The Cradle, where authenticity is the watchword?**

I don't know. It's something he does so well because he's more of a historian than I am. He's always been more into that, whereas I'll always just enjoy listening to it and playing it. I don't claim to be an expert on the blues or anything, whereas Eric... You could talk to him about any aspect of the blues and I'm sure he would know the whole history of it, which is probably why he did the album like that, more of a history lesson.

**For all the comparisons, you've never played with Clapton.**

No, he's never asked me. I love Eric's playing. If it wasn't for Eric, this world I live in wouldn't exist. When I heard the Bluesbreakers album, like a lot of guitarists of my generation, that was the thing that turned the world upside down for me. When I heard that guitar, that was as powerful for me as Robert Johnson was for Eric. To hear a guitar become the main voice in the music and to be that forceful and so direct, it was amazing. There was nothing like that before and nothing like it since either, really.

# PETER GREEN

## DECEMBER 1995

*It just happens like that occasionally. Sitting in the office amidst the pre-Christmas tinsel and cheer, the phone rings and it's the Howard Hughes of blues guitar... In December 1995, news had been filtering through to the magazine for some time about the apparent return to form of Peter Green, British blues legend. I'd been quietly romancing Peter's management for several weeks, but never thought I would get to talk to the man himself. In the end, our quick chat was a bit like one of those two-minute trolley dashes that people win in supermarkets: you end up with an awful lot, but after a couple of hours you begin to think of all the items you could have gone for...*

*What do you ask an infamously reclusive blues legend in the first interview he's done since his dramatic exit from the music world 25 years previously, when time is of the essence? Well, you start with all the apocryphal stuff, clear up a few mysteries if you can. For instance, there was this controversy over which guitar Peter used on the original recording of 'Albatross'...*

**Gary Moore insists it was a Les Paul, whereas a consensus of we guitar hacks pleads the case for a Strat. So who's right?**

It was a Fender Strat. [He sounds as though the session took place only a few days ago rather than nearly 30 years ago.] A brand new Fender Strat, straight out of the box. We hired two for the recording and that was one of them – a sort of tobacco sunburst colour. There's a Les Paul on there as well, though.

But the chords and the main melody are on a Strat with the high melody parts on the Les Paul. Danny Kirwan plays the harmony parts.

**Well, that's settled then. Any other surprises?**

There are two bass guitars on there, too. John [McVie] came in and said he had an idea for using two basses, and it was an experiment and it worked, so we left it on. You listen and see if you can hear them.

**Another subject that people have speculated about for years is the way your famous Les Paul (now in permanent residence with Gary Moore) was rewired to give an out-of-phase sound when both front and back pickups are selected. Theories abound, but what really happened?**

I didn't have it rewired. It's just backwards, that's all. I didn't use the neck pickup very much, and so for some reason I took it off. I can't remember why. I played it for a while with only one pickup, but when I put it back on, I just put it on backwards with the screws pointing towards the tailpiece instead of near the neck.

**But surely the magnets were reversed at some point?**

No, it's just on backwards, that's all.

**But this really turns things around – where does the out-of-phase sound come from?**

People keep telling me about this out-of-phase thing, but I don't know anything about it. It was just round the wrong way. If you take the cover off, there are two pickups underneath which look like Strat pickups close together, but I didn't touch those. It must have been like that already, unless Gary's done anything to it...

Your command of the blues is, of course, legendary. Every note seemed fuelled with genuine passion, fire and an outstanding maturity that was yours and yours alone. Where did it all come from?

My main influence was Eric Clapton, then Buddy Guy, Elmore James, Jimmy Reed, John Lee Hooker – although not for his guitar playing, more his songs. John Lee Hooker's style is impossible to copy – you can't get near it – but his songs and the way he taps his foot when he sings... It's very hard to emulate.

If Clapton was your principal influence, it must have been difficult to step into his shoes in The Bluesbreakers, surely?

Yes and no. [A long pause] I didn't think of it like that. It was blues music, that's all. Blues music and guitars. In a way it was difficult...but I didn't really think about it like that.

What about those rumours that you've returned to the studio and are recording once again?

Yes, and I'm really happy with the result. I'm just experimenting, but what's coming out is better than anything I've done before.

There was also a story that you have bought yourself a Telecaster...

I haven't bought anything, but I've been loaned some guitars by Fender and Gibson. I've got a Telecaster and some Strats, and I've got a Gibson Firebird and a black Gibson Howard Roberts Fusion, which is really nice. It's a sort of semi-jazz guitar, you know? They offered me some Les Pauls, but I've had enough of them. They say they're the greatest guitars in the world, and I don't know. They probably are and I used to use them, but I've had enough of them.

In the '60s, you were renowned for using Selmer, Orange and Fender Dual Showman amps. What have you got with you in the studio now?

I'm not using any amps. I'm going straight into the desk. I don't own any amps. I have one amp, I found it in my house in Richmond. I don't know how it got there, I don't remember, but I gave it to my brother Mickey. It was a Peavey, it was really strong and loud.

# JOHN LEE HOOKER

SEPTEMBER 1998

*

*John Lee Hooker doesn't talk. He growls. Speaking to him, as I did in 1998, you can see where the unique vocal delivery comes from – it's an intrinsic part of the man himself. 'Well, thank you,' he rumbled when I congratulated him on the release of his latest album,* The Best Of Friends, *which celebrated his work from the previous ten years. The last decade had seen the legendary bluesman team up with luminaries from the rock and blues world, the resulting albums representing a massive upturn in John Lee's popularity and fortunes.*

**You first picked up a guitar during your early teens. Your stepfather, William Moore, was your first tutor, correct?**

I started playing when I was a kid, about 12 or 13. I was living with my stepfather and my mother, and it was my stepfather who taught me how to play. He gave me a guitar called a Stella. The stuff I'm playing now, that's his style. Then, when I was 14 or 15, I left home. I just took off, y'know? I didn't want to stay in the south and work on the farm. I figured there had to be a better way in the world and I headed north. Then, when I recorded 'Boogie Chillun", I got a hit on it.

**Did you play gigs in the south?**

No, I wasn't making records then. I didn't start making records until I got to Detroit.

You made the move north during World War II and started to work on the automobile assembly lines. What sort of venues were you playing in those days?

Oh, theatres and small nightclubs… I was playing the blues, I guess, same as I'm playing now. I've just updated that same thing.

Who were your influences on the guitar around that time?

Eddie Kirkland – you heard of him? Him and me, we played together for many years an' he learned from me and I learned from him.

Records like 'Dimples', 'I Love You Honey' and 'I'm Ready' came out over the '50s and '60s, but your career really hit an all-time high after the release of the album *The Healer* in 1989. How the album came about in the first place had a lot to do with the celebrity admirers you had collected around you at the time. The list of willing collaborators on that album was a long one – a testament to the popularity you'd amassed already. But the one man who was instrumental in the sound, style and direction of *The Healer* was Carlos Santana.

I was living in California, in the same city I'm living in now, and he used to come on my gigs all the time. Sometimes we'd be on the same gigs, his band and my band, we'd be on the same show. The first time I heard him, he was on one of my shows and I listened to him and got talking to him. We decided we wanted to do something together, so we did it and it turned out good.

'Good' is probably an understatement. The album's title track won you a Grammy and a follow-up album became almost inevitable. Another man who took a very active role in bringing you to the world stage was Van Morrison.

I met Van Morrison in Europe. He loved my style and he really can sing, so we did some things together. He's a good man.

Other song partners who were originally long-term fans include Bonnie Raitt…

She used to come to my shows all the time. She used to love the song 'In The Mood'. I met her and we got talking, and she was really, really big at the time. When we came to record together, I asked her which song she wanted to do and she wanted to do 'In The Mood'. That was the one thing she wanted and she's a really good girl, and I think she did justice to the song.

**Ry Cooder has shown up on a couple of your albums as both guitar player and producer.**

We just bumped into each other at gigs. My agent put us together to record and he produced me. He's a good man, a good guitarist – good all round.

**You met Robert Cray after hearing his *Bad Influence* album. You invited him to open for you on tour and the two of you are now firm friends.**

He's a very nice young man. I met him when he was living in Portland and he was playing small clubs. We recorded together. I like him a lot.

**So you've worked with a whole host of superstars during the last ten years… Do you have a favourite?**

It's pretty hard to say. I worked with them all and I love them all, and all of them are really nice people and good to work with.

*Best Of Friends* is a compilation of some of the best of your collaborations during the last ten years, including a couple of new tracks. The most notable of these, perhaps, is a rereading of your original hit, 'Boogie Chillun", with Eric Clapton lending his considerable weight to the proceedings. Was this the first time you two had met?

No, we'd jammed in England. He's a great guitar player and a great person. I'm looking forward to seeing him again. I'm always glad to see him.

'Boogie Chillun" probably sums up everything good about the blues; on the original, there's just you with your guitar, stomping foot and sub-bass vocals. The famous 'Last night I was laying down...' lyric has even turned up in live performances by Led Zeppelin. The song's influence has obviously burrowed deep and embedded itself in modern rock. It's been 50 years since the original recording of 'Boogie Chillun"...

Yeah. Whatever...

What sort of guitars are you using at the moment?

I use Gibsons or Epiphones.

What sort of amplifier do you favour now?

Fender Bassman and Rhythm King – I play both.

One of the major characteristics of your style on guitar is your rhythm. It seems that your thumb keeps a four-to-the-bar bassline going while your fingers sound the top strings with an upstroke. As a guitar style, it's quite unique, but where did it come from?

My stepfather. He just taught me his style, a sort of rhythm and lead style. It's a strange style...

During your early years, you preferred to play solo rather than with a band...

I played solo. I like playing by myself, I can get more into it.

That, of course, has changed now...

Oh, it's changed a lot.

**What do you listen to these days?**

[A long, reflective silence] I used to play Albert King and Albert Collins...but now? Most of them are gone...

# ROBERT CRAY

*Throughout Robert Cray's work there is a strong soul influence, which gives his blues-based albums a unique flavour. This rich strain of originality hasn't gone unnoticed, either – Cray is certainly no stranger to the Grammy nominee list. Also, when someone like Eric Clapton refers to a player as 'one of the greats', the world just has to sit up and listen. When I talked to Robert in 2000, I was eager to hear his story from the start.*

**What is it that first directed you towards the guitar?**

Everybody in my neighbourhood got a guitar when the Beatles came out, and I was one of them. [Laughs]

**So The Beatles were an influence, you might say?**

Well, I guess…in a way. Because of the popularity of the guitar and seeing them play on TV and all that stuff, then I guess so.

**Who else?**

My friends. Everybody in my street had a guitar and all we did was listen to the radio and tried to steal everything we could from there. Also my parents had a great record collection when I was coming up, and it wasn't until I started hanging out with some of my friends when I went to high school at about 15 or 16 years old that I went back to my parents' record collection. At that age, I had some friends who were listening to Buddy Guy and BB King, and so we starting hanging out together and listening to their records and it all went from there.

**So did you put bands together when you were still at school?**

No, actually before that I had been in a band when I was quite young. We played soul and psychedelic!

**What, all at once?**

Yeah, my father was in the army and so we moved around quite a bit, and when I started playing guitar we lived in the Seattle, Washington, area. We were there for a couple of years, and then we moved to Virginia where the soul music was pretty popular. We played songs like 'Knock On Wood' and then we played 'Purple Haze' – it went kind of like that.

**How did that go down with audiences?**

We didn't have that many audiences, we only played two gigs! When you're 14 or 15 years old it's more of a dream than any major reality, that kind of thing. But then there was a succession of high-school bands, where we played all kinds of things up until late high-school days. After then it was blues and rhythm and blues.

**When you were learning to play, who were the key players you focused in on?**

I was big on BB, Buddy Guy, Magic Sam… I would listen a lot to Jimi Hendrix, Eric Clapton and Freddy King, Otis Rush and guys like that. I'm just a big blues guitar player fan and Jimi Hendrix is always in there.

**After the early days, who became your principal influence as a guitarist?**

Well I did get an opportunity to hang out with Albert Collins quite a bit. He also played our high-school graduation party, and I was really enamoured with his playing and personality and all. So I think probably more than anyone, Albert Collins had an influence on what I do. But there are a lot of people: BB King was a big influence, Jimi Hendrix, Eric Clapton...

**Did you ever attempt to work out Albert Collins' unorthodox tuning?**

Ah, no. I think his tuning was something like a C minor or D minor and he'd just use a capo for whatever key the song was in.

**Collins played with a very 'snappy' style, pulling the strings away from the neck with his fingers. Your own style occasionally reflects this, although you play with a pick.**

Yeah, Albert played with his thumb and forefinger, which actually led me to use a heavier pick, and sometimes I'd play with my fingers as well. He just had a really strong attack and that's what I've always liked about him. He reminded me of someone like [organist] Jimmy McGriff. I questioned him on this once, because Albert played organ a little bit as well and Jimmy McGriff was one of his favourite organ players. Albert would comp like an organ player and he would ride up to the high notes on the high end of the guitar just like an organ player would.

**So you're not playing with a pick 100 per cent of the time – sometimes it's fingerstyle?**

Well, a combination of both. Some of the blues techniques that you pick up on are fingerpicking ideas. I'd grab an idea from Buddy Guy, but also by watching Albert Collins play, things like that. I'd watch Albert play and use his thumb like a plectrum, and I'd see him pulling the strings up so much that it was a wonder he was able to keep strings on the guitar!

**You have since played with BB King and Eric Clapton. It must have been a great thrill to play with the people who had such an influence on you as a player.**

Yeah. I think it's pretty much like anybody else who's a musician, y'know? You listen to somebody's records and you're playing your guitar at the same time, pretending you're on stage with them... And to have that happen later on is pretty wild.

**Clapton covered your song 'Bad Influence' on his album *August,* and later on you co-wrote 'Old Love', which appeared on no less than three of Clapton's albums – *Journeyman, Unplugged* and 24 *Nights,* the latter of which features you on the blues nights section of the album.**

I first met Eric at the Montreux Jazz Festival in '85 or '86. We had been asked to do some dates with him, and so we were meeting up there for the first time and then going on to do some dates. We went backstage at the rehearsals during the afternoon. He had recorded the song 'Bad Influence' for his *August* album, but it hadn't come out yet.

**You never use an awful lot of gain on the amp, do you?**

No, not really. I'm using 35-watt amplifiers and running them about half – maybe just slightly over – but that's about it. I think what probably happened for me was that I always played through smaller one-piece amplifiers for the longest time, and I never got a huge amplifier with lots of power in it. As a matter a fact, I do have some Twin Reverbs, but I didn't like them. I liked 40-watt Super Reverbs with 4 x 10s, and so I just never really cranked it up.

**Do you actually have an organised practice routine?**

I don't. I really don't. I try, y'know, but I just end up grabbing the guitar and playing. I don't go through a routine of running scales or anything like that. I still like to put on an album, get the vibe and play along. Or I just go over something that I need to re-learn from our own material.

**As a writer, how do you approach new material?**

I start putting a song together when an idea comes. I don't sit down and say, 'I'm going to write a song.' I can't do it that way – I'd just sit in the room and look at the walls. I have friends that do. They get together and say, 'Let's write a song', and I have done that with other people, but I don't do that with myself. If I have dead time around the house and I'm in the mood, there will be music in my head and I sit down and start playing.

**Where do your best ideas come from? Does the process start with two chords that go together, or is it a snatch of lyric or something like that?**

No, maybe there'll be a melody in my head and I'll be out in the garden and have to rush back in the house and pick up a guitar. But it's not like putting a couple of different chords together. I start singing the melody and if I get something that doesn't come naturally, I'll figure it out.

**Do you come up with things in the studio or go in with complete songs?**

We try to go in with complete songs. There are some ideas that pop up in the studio, but we don't like to waste time in the studio, sitting around, and so we like to get everything pretty much set beforehand.

**When did you first start using Strats?**

I got my first Strat in '79. Before that I had played a Gibson 345 and an SG Standard. I got the Strat because I'd seen a concert with Philip Guy – who's Buddy's brother – and he was playing a Stratocaster through a Super Reverb, and it just sounded so clean. He had just the slightest amount of reverb on it, which just gave it a shimmer, and it was like he was cutting glass or something.

It was the coolest sound I ever heard, and after that I went out and instantly started looking for a Strat.

**What were your specific requirements for your signature Strat?**

It didn't need much; the only thing I wanted to have was the neck feel right. I wanted the radius of these two different Strats that I had – a combination of the two because I enjoyed playing both of them. The first Strat I had was a 64 and I found a 58 a little later on, and so I had to take both guitars and try to find a medium with the width and all that. That was my only prerequisite, other than it didn't have a whammy bar, just a stop tailpiece.

**You're known as a player who uses quite heavy-gauge strings, but when we've spoken before you've always said that you don't consider them as such.**

I was going to say that again, as a matter of fact!

**Well, we might as well cover that ground again...**

[Laughs] OK, I use an 11 on top, then I go to a 13, 18, 28, 36, 46.

**With fairly heavy-gauge plectrums?**

Yes.

**What advice would you pass on to people who are setting out to learn blues now?**

I listen to my favourite records that I used to look to when I first got excited about it all now and again. The hardest thing to get out of those records is why they play the way they do – the emotion behind it, the passion, and so on. I think you have to listen to a record and grab hold of that spirit and then it takes you to how, why and what made them play the notes that they do, whether it's a flurry or whether it's one pretty singing note, just to put a dab of colour on a piece of paper. If you listen to a song that way and try to play it that way, it's magical; that's where you get that spirit from.

**Are guitars important to you?**

I can pretty much take them or leave them. I decided at one point that I was going to grab hold of a couple and I did grab hold of that 58 and I have a couple of 64s, but after that I pretty much gave up on it because I thought paying a ridiculous amount for a guitar was useless! If I get a guitar from the custom shop, hey – it sounds great and it plays great, so I'm not worried about it.

# BUDDY GUY

MARCH 1996

*Run your eye down the roll call of blues legends and it won't be long before you find Buddy Guy. In the mid-'90s, where there seemed to be some fiery new blues hotshot launching a career every five minutes, Buddy was one of the very few 'originals' we had left. Without him and his contemporaries to fire up players worldwide with an enthusiasm for the blues, music itself could have taken a very different turn. Take the blues out of contemporary rock music – or pop, jazz and funk for that matter – and what you have left is a wholly spineless affair. A tasteless stew. Makes you shudder to think about it... But fortunately blues thrived in the hands of T-Bone Walker, Muddy Waters, Willie Dixon and, of course, Guy, who passed blues' burning brand on to Clapton, Peter Green, Jimmy Page & Co – and we were all spared having to listen to British folk music for the rest of our lives as a result.*

*Anyone who has witnessed a Buddy Guy concert will tell you how Buddy can manipulate expertly an audience with a unique brand of showmanship that is genuinely all his own. He'll come to the front of the stage, reduce the volume of the band to almost a whisper and sing to you (often without using a mic) using every sinew of his wiry frame to project his blues message. The blues congregation go home duly blessed when Buddy's been preaching. When I spoke with the legendary bluesman in 1996, his recent live album and video releases inspired me to ask how his charismatic stage presence evolved...*

**How did your stage presence evolve?**

Well, I learned a lot of my stuff from the late Guitar Slim, and some of the great guitar players and horn players and keyboard players. I saw that actions speak louder than words, and I never thought I was a real good guitar player or a real good singer, so the late Guitar Slim used to show me some stuff – you know, he would go and hit his guitar and if he stepped off the stage these people were, like, eating it up. They were, like, going crazy, and I thought if I ever learn to play this well I want to be like that, so I copied a lot of stuff off Slim an' the great T-Bone Walker years ago. This is the way to entertain people! I think you owe that to people. You know I played in sub-zero weather and I played in places that were so hot I was gonna cancel it, and you look out at these people and there's water running down their faces, or people with overcoats on, and they think that much of you to come out and hear you play, I think you owe them 110 per cent of yourself.

**It must be difficult to keep up that rapport with an audience in the bigger venues, though?**

Yes, especially when it gets so big; the big stadium sort of thing where the stage is so high and you're so far away from them. It worries me when I can't get down there too. Man, you can have a good look at women down there, you get close to them and have a good look, it makes me feel young again!

**And singing acoustically, too...**

Yeah, well you know, that's it. Back in the earlier days we didn't have all the big huge speakers and the big amplifiers and things, and you could do that. I learned a lot of that from Muddy. Muddy used to go down with his band, play so soft you'd have to put one finger in one ear and turn the other one towards the bandstand to hear what he was doing. BB King can do that, too, and I would say, 'It's so great – the dynamics – man, I got to learn this.' And I just worked on that real hard, and nowadays when you do that, my audience will say, 'Now you see that; that's him doing this.' You know, that's not a fake coming out of the amplifier or the rest of the guys doing the playing or the singing. It's just so for real when you do things like that.

**Obviously a lot of people are eager students of the blues. What can you pass on to them?**

You never can learn enough with any instrument. I don't practise as much as I used to, but when I was really into my late teens and early 20s I kept a guitar by the bed with the radio turned down real low, nobody would hear it except me. And every time a guitar would come on and you'd hear something, you'd grab the damned guitar right then and get as near to what you heard as you can. If you could sleep with that guitar in your hand, it wouldn't be too much guitar. Yeah, you need to fool with that thing as often as you can and as long as you can and if you love it like I do, you would be one of the best. Spend as much time with it as you can, more than you can, even though you know you've got to put it down sometime. Every chance you get, you put that damned thing in your hand and you fool with it.

**Many feel that players almost have it too easy now with videos, tutors and magazines to help them on their way. With so much purely visual reference material about, it's almost as if the ears aren't given much of a chance to develop.**

Right. I had to just listen to the record and if I missed it, I missed it, and unless I had the whole record I just kept slipping the needle back until I got something similar to it. That's what made it so hard for me, but these young kids now can buy a video and watch it over and over again. I had nobody to tune my guitar and I couldn't watch the television to see what the guy was doing. I had to try to figure out what he was doing. I just had to imagine what he was doing, and that's very much different to what you got today. But I don't care how much you watch TV, you're not going to be an Eric Clapton, you're not going to be a Jeff Beck. I don't care how much you watch him, there's something that comes out that's coming from you anyway. Muddy Waters' shoes are still under the bed and nobody's gonna fit those shoes. And Stevie Ray Vaughan and all those great people like that, they only come along once in a lifetime. What do you do? You just practise that thing as best as you can and listen to all music, you get ideas from everything and you wake up one morning and think you have something you've created.

**What was the most important lesson you learned as a young player?**

Willie Dixon taught me how to respect. How to respect an audience that put up with you before you got good. After you got good they sit there and that's the treasure, to have people come out and watch you play and enjoy and laugh and smile. You can make them happy because through life we all have something to make us unhappy, whether it's your wife, your job, your health or whatever, and you can come out. And if I can play a few notes that can make you forget that for a while, that's a tremendous feeling to have, man. That you can do something like that. When I see someone smiling and clapping their hands I think, 'Whatever problem you had yesterday or the day before, you don't have it now while I'm playing this two hours.'

**What turned you on to the Stratocaster in the first place?**

The late Guitar Slim, with 'Things I Used To Do'. That's the first one I saw, and he beat that damn thing up so much, man, it was dragging off him and falling off him. And he was blowing my head off, the way he was clowning and playing and walking slow with that guitar. And he could drop it and pick it up and play it, and a lot of acoustic guitars around before that thing came out you couldn't drop because it would bust wide open. So when I saw that Strat I thought, 'That's the guitar for me.' It could take so much wear and tear, plus its sound. I mean, Leo Fender made the kind of sound from that thing that was unforgettable, with him and his Fender Bassman, that's just one sound that would carry me away from here.

**Do you use all the pickup variations?**

Yeah, if I have to. Very seldom I go back and use that real high one. I did a lot of that back in the Chess days, and I tried to get this effect that had the Leo Fender Bassman sound a lot, and I just loved that.

**If you had the chance, are there any blues players, living or dead, that you wished you had a chance to play with?**

Robert Johnson had passed before I came along and I think every guitar player in the world would have liked to play with him. I tease Eric about this: I played with Lonnie Johnson, Fred McDowell, Son House and I played with Muddy, and the first time I met T-Bone I was there in London. And I met Elvis – February '65! I would have liked to play on the same stage as Elvis, I mean, who wouldn't want to be up there with that guy? I had a chance to jam with Hendrix, in a live format, not in the studio. There are times when somebody like BB or Eric, when they play they look round at me and say, 'Come on, play!' and I say, 'Look man, you play, I'll listen. I'm trying to learn something...'

**So your tastes are by no means confined to the blues?**

No, no, man. I went to bed with my radio tuned on the spiritualist station and I woke up this morning and clicked it to jazz. I don't just listen to blues, I don't want to get hung up on that. I get a lot of ideas from jazz people, and we all, as blues players, we got a lot of spirit, a lot.

**Who do you think are the most important blues players around at the moment?**

I think BB King still is, man. I mean that guy invented this thing, and if you go watch him play, man, you hear something and you say, 'Shit, I just gotta go back to school!' And sometime I'll pull up a tape like John Lee Hooker, and those slide guitar players have got something that we non-sliders don't have. Otis Rush can do a tremendous job with that and try to play like the slide, and that's when you go and say, 'Oh shit, look here what I've found trying to play like a slide player!'

**Then of course there's Eric...**

Yeah, I played with Eric quite a few times. Eric and Keith [Richards] and all those guys. Man, those guys are the best friends a musician should have. Oh, yeah, they done so much for us: Eric, the Stones and Beck. These guys have always been there. The late Stevie Ray Vaughan was the same way, and I'm the proudest man in the world to have friends like that.

# ROBBEN FORD

*Once upon a time, the guitar playing of Robben Ford was one of the music industry's best-kept secrets. Scanning the credits of albums by artists such as Barbra Streisand, George Harrison, Joni Mitchell, Miles Davis, Kiss and Burt Bacharach would often reveal his name, but it wasn't until Robben's 1988 solo album* Talk To Your Daughter *that his playing found the acclaim it had so long deserved. Since then, he's continued to release solo albums that combine both jazz and R&B sensibilities with a double helping of good, tasteful guitar playing.*

*Of all the guitarists playing the blues today, few have as unique a melodic approach as Robben. With his musical learning rooted in jazz-kissed blues, he manages to bring a fresh slant to what many regard as a thoroughly staid genre. Our first interview took place in Manchester in 1992, after Robben had played a particularly spectacular gig at the polytechnic. I remember being so hopelessly shell-shocked by what I'd seen and heard that night, that I got hopelessly lost on my way back down south in the car. I've interviewed Robben several times since and what you read here is a kind of medley from two or three of them.*

**The success of *Talk To Your Daughter* was received with some surprise.**

I knew that I had an audience out there somewhere. I was surprised by the Grammy nomination; that shocked me. In fact, when my manager told me, I thought surely it was a mistake, I didn't believe it. It was only disappointing frankly that my record company was so short-sighted – they didn't know how to get it out to more people.

**Backtracking a little, in 1986 you played guitar for Miles Davis, whom you have often cited as your greatest influence. What is your most enduring memory of Miles?**

His music, obviously. He is my number one musical icon. He has been the most inspiring of any artist that I've ever been exposed to one way or another. His endurance and his longevity are particularly inspiring. He kept on making that great music and playing great up until he passed away. He could walk out and just be so good, and that is probably the thing that most impressed me about him. I liked the way that we'd be on the bandstand playing, and he'd just be walking around and playing and just look at you and kind of tip his head. You'd play and then he'd start playing when he wanted you to stop! The very first night I played with him, he's up there blowing, and he walks over to me and says, 'Play somethin', Robben.' That was the coolest thing and I love that memory of him. It's really great to be able to play with your icon, your main cat. It felt like I was being christened, y'know. It felt like he was saying, 'You're OK, you're a good musician', and that kind of engendered some confidence in me.

**You've retained much of your jazz sensibility in your attitude to playing blues. But are you a jazz player who plays blues, or a blues player who is well versed in jazz?**

Basically I see myself as a musician. [Laughs] My first and strongest influences were all blues players, and I played blues so much when I was in my mid- to late teens and early 20s. I went from blues to jazz and the jazz that I was attracted to was all basically simpler forms of all the great players. I liked the modal periods of Miles and Coltrane, where you had fewer chords and more emotional expression, so that's just an extension of the blues. Of course I've played a lot of music over the years and learned things from those experiences, and I've played with a lot of different artists and I always kind of see things as the same. Playing with someone like Joni Mitchell or Miles Davis, there's this thread that runs through the whole thing, which is really just love of music, and it doesn't matter what the style or form is, the heart of the thing is always the same. It's like looking through a prism.

**Back in the days when you were a sideman, who are the other people you worked for that have left a mark on you personally?**

Well, the experience of working with, in particular, Joni Mitchell and Jimmy Witherspoon, those two are the other outstanding ones for me, and it's because they are the masters, all of them. That brings out the best in me: somebody who is brilliant on their own and knows how to let you bring the most you have to them, and those people were like that.

**How much freedom did Joni Mitchell, for instance, let you bring to her material?**

We all worked together. We were all in her rehearsal studio and we learned these things together and helped each other. When I first joined her band, I was the youngster who was basically learning the whole thing, and all these other people were so developed already. They were great musicians and they knew how to do this. It was very new to me so I was being helped a lot.

**Was Miles the same?**

Well, the music that I got was somewhat developed. The music that I was first playing for him I had to learn off some poor tapes and some very poor charts, so I had to come up with my own stuff, and I never had a rehearsal with him or anybody until I had my first gig with them, so it was a leap into space! He seemed to like what I was doing; I only heard good things from him. There were a couple of times when he asked me to do something – do something like this here, do something like that there — so he must have liked what I was doing.

Apart from obvious serious chops on your instrument, there are a few things about your style that are sufficiently different to be worthy of mention. For instance, you hold your pick back to front with the wider, butt end being employed to pluck the strings...

Well actually, whenever I sat and practised the guitar for some reason, I just naturally turned the pick that way, and then I would play gigs and I would have the point out. At some stage I just thought, 'Well, if I'm practising the other way round I might as well do it that way on the gig.' For some reason I was literally doing two different things, and so I made a conscious choice to go ahead and use the butt end of the pick. I think it's the smoothness. Maybe if you have a broader piece of the pick hitting the string it makes a difference. Somehow I found that a better feeling, less...pointy, I guess.

Your string gauges are .010–.046 and your signature guitar bears a Gibson-type scale length, which is a good balance. Melodically speaking, your main deviation from the norm as far as the blues is concerned is your preference for including the major sixth in the standard pentatonic scale as opposed to the more common flat seventh.

It was a sonic choice. The pentatonic scale, everyone thinks of in terms of the flattened seventh or the black keys on a piano, and I went this way because it was a sound I liked. I use both, of course, but I like that sound because I heard that kind of thing from Mike Bloomfield and BB King. They both use that little device there. You know, those two guys were just so important to me.

BB King is renowned for his blend of both major and minor scale for blues lead lines, which has inspired your own almost Dorian scale powered soloing. You're not afraid to dip into the diminished scale for the occasional trip 'outside' the blues framework. Harmonically, your chords lean heavily towards jazz, too.

I learned my chords from Mickey Baker [referring to the renowned jazz guitar method written during the '50s]. That's where I got my chords, and there's that thing that I learned with the Miles Davis band, which is quite a bit different, using 4ths and creating a 12-tone situation. But what I play is definitely traditional chords. There's nothing really different, although I guess the way I use them is my own.

**Whereas textbook blues harmony seeks nothing more adventurous than the odd 7♯9, you favour a more expansive, extended seventh vocabulary.**

Yeah, I like those altered chords, I like using them: flat fifth chords, raised ninth chords, thirteenths, and so on. They can add a lot of character to a blues.

**Do you have to rearrange some of the parts of the recorded pieces for live performance, being a three-piece without the keyboard, rhythm guitar or harmonica that you find on the albums?**

We have had to change things a bit but not too much, and yeah, we do work the songs out as a trio. I have to change my guitar part sometimes and we have to redo the songs, but not too much, not that that would make a difference to the listener, I don't think.

**On *Talk To Your Daughter*, the tune 'I Ain't Got Nothin' But The Blues' is where the tidal pull between blues and jazz is most prevalent within your style.**

Oh yeah, absolutely, but I've kind of moved away from it with my music because it's so stylistic. I like playing music that's a little more open so that you can stretch it out further. A piece like 'I Ain't Got Nothin' But The Blues' is kind of in a box. The music that I'm gravitating towards – and always have – is a little more open than that. Obviously we're playing blues, but where we can go from there is wild, we can take this thing really far out and we do. You play something like 'I Ain't Got Nothin' But The Blues' and you've kind of got to play it just like that, you know, play these chords and you need to stay within certain boundaries – the style is very specific.

# WALTER TROUT

*One of things that you notice about Walter Trout is that he never seems to stop touring. Like fellow bluesman BB King, he's rarely off the road, and so interviews are usually snatched while he is somewhere in transit between the towns and cities of the world, his trademark nicotine-yellow Strat enjoying a few hours' respite before the blues onslaught begins anew.*

*Perhaps Walter is still not considered part of the blues mainstream, but you have to admit that any guitarist who has a playing CV that includes stints with Canned Heat, John Mayall and John Lee Hooker must have an interesting story to tell...*

**What first drew you to the guitar?**

I guess the thing that drew my ear to the guitar in the first place was the folk boom in America in the early '60s. Then along came The Beatles and they presented people of my generation in America with a new look at our own music. That really got me turned on to the electric guitar, and then my older brother brought a Paul Butterfield album home and said, 'Listen to this guy...' I heard it and I was just shattered; I walked around for a couple of days unable to talk.

**How soon did you start playing in bands?**

By '68/'69 I was out playing in club bands, working a lot. I grew up in New

Jersey, along the Jersey shore where there was a large scene of nightclubs, and if you played enough dance music for people, you could work.

**The covers band scene saw you playing material by a lot of different bands in very many styles.**

For a period of time we had a horn section and so we might do a song by Chicago Transit Authority, followed by something by Blood Sweat And Tears, then something by Otis Redding, BB King, The Rolling Stones, followed by 'Got To Get You Into My Life' by The Beatles with the full horn line. So it was quite a cross-section of musical styles and I loved playing all of it.

**It's a big step from playing in cover bands to playing with John Mayall's Bluesbreakers...**

It was kind of a fluke, really. A friend of mine told me that he had been on the Redondo Beach pier the previous Sunday afternoon, and there was a little nightclub up there with some old guys playing blues. He said he bet if I took my guitar down there the following week, I could sit in and play. I went up there with him and got up and jammed with them, and they told me to stay up on stage, so I played all day. At the end they told me that they'd like me to join the band. I started playing with them and one of them would come up and say that he was playing with Big Mama Thornton and she needed a guitar player. I'd go, and suddenly I'd be in her band! Once, I was doing a show and she was double-billed with John Lee Hooker. When Big Mama Thornton finished, John Lee told me to stay on stage and then suddenly I was in his band. Through playing with John Lee Hooker I met Canned Heat, because they have quite a close connection. They called me up right after Bob Hite died and told me they were going to reform and do a tour of Australia and would I like to do the tour? It ended up with me playing with them for five years, and while I was playing with them I got a call saying that John Mayall had put together the original Bluesbreakers with Mick Taylor and John McVie, and he was doing some shows in America and Canned Heat were going to go out and open for them. So I met John Mayall and we did some shows and I ended up being with John for five years!

**You're famous for using your yellow Fender Strat…**

I've been using the same guitar since 1974. It's a hard-tail 73; one of the ones that collectors tell you that you're supposed to hate, but I love it. But it's all collector bullshit because it is my belief that there are good guitars and bad guitars. I've picked up a 58 Strat and it's played really badly, then I've picked up another one and it's played great. I'll pick up another 73 Strat and it plays like shit, but I pick mine up and it plays like butter. I bought my Strat brand new, off the shelf, from a little store in California. It's turned yellow now, but it used to be white. It was blazing white when I bought it, so bright it would hurt your eyes. About 1980 I was in Alaska with Canned Heat in February and it was 40° below zero. We were touring in this little six-seater aeroplane, and all I had for a case was just the regular Fender Tweed and it was in the hold. I carried it out of the plane, into the club and into the dressing room and opened the case and started hearing this incredible cracking sound. I looked down and, from the bottom of the guitar where you hook on the strap, slowly right up the body of the guitar about 10 million little finish cracks were beginning to happen because we'd gone from the cold to the warm. I stood there yelling with my head in my hands, just watching the finish on my guitar crack up completely. So, from there, I was playing in all these smoky bars and the nicotine went into the finish, and so that's the reason why the guitar is yellow now. I can scrape the guitar and the yellow comes off and there's bright white underneath. It's got a lot of soul. It's been refretted about ten times. I get big fat frets on there and they last maybe three years. Other than that it's all original, apart from a brass nut. The reason for that is that I'm prone to doing things like going down to my bass E string and playing an F on the first fret and bending it up to a G or even an A. When I did that originally, I would bust the original nut. There'd be little pieces flying off.

# JOHNNY WINTER

AUGUST 1992

*Stevie Ray Vaughan, Albert Collins, Billy Gibbons, Johnny Winter… The chances are, when you think about Texas blues guitarists, you'd be hard pushed to find a common denominator between them in terms of style. Each flies the blues flag in his own unique way, but all the while there's a perceptible epicentre, which nevertheless fights shy of any real definition – not that I wasn't going to try and get one out of Winter when I interviewed him in 1992. I had just enjoyed the privilege of watching his live act from the side of the stage at London's Town & Country venue, and had a head full of questions…*

How would you define Texas blues?

There are so many different styles of Texas music. You would know immediately if you heard a Delta song. And you know right away when you hear a Chicago blues song and you know if it's a New Orleans song. But there are so many different styles in Texas, and I think that's what I liked about growing up there: you could just hear so much stuff. You had to be able to play a lot of different things in the clubs or you'd get killed! You had to play Cajun music – the French Cajun two-steps – and in parts of Texas there was a lot of Mexican music. And of course there was the Louisiana and New Orleans stuff, as well as jazz and country. You can't get away from country.

**The experience of running the gamut of various Texan styles seems to have benefited you...**

All that stuff just kinda blends into blues, but it is real hard to compare someone like Blind Lemon Jefferson to Albert Collins. Then there's people like Lightnin' Hopkins and T-Bone Walker. There's a lot of difference in the Texas musicians. It's real hard to listen to someone and say, 'Oh yeah, this guy's definitely playin' Texas music.' But there are just so many different styles of music involved. You don't know what you're going to get with a Texas musician, but it's usually going to be a pretty well-rounded thing. I think that's probably the one thing: Texas music has just got more variety to it than the Delta stuff or Chicago or New Orleans. But it sure was a great place to grow up – you heard all kinds of stuff on the radio...

**You began playing clarinet at age five. Before long you had switched to ukulele, and graduated from there to guitar at the age of 11. Your first group was a vocal duo with your brother Edgar, very much in the Everly Brothers tradition. By the time you reached your teens, you had been exposed to rock 'n' roll...**

That was the most exciting time. I was about 15. I made my first record and I started playing in nightclubs, and I had my first drink. It was a real exciting year: all the stuff was brand new and you could be driving to the gig and hear your record on the radio. I was just a little kid, living at home and going to school – 15, but boy it was real exciting. You're out there playing for people, you've got girls chasin' you and stuff... Now that was real nice! The first CBS record, *Johnny Winter*, is one of my favourites. *Progressive Blues Experiment* was another. I made a record with Sonny Terry, called *Whoopin'*, that I also like a lot. There are a few others, but those records are the ones I enjoyed the most.

**Do you still enjoy playing live?**

Oh yeah! To me that is the most enjoyable thing: playing and having an audience involved in it. Making records is a lot of fun, too, because you know that you have it there for ever, and after you're dead, hopefully, people are still listening to it. That's nice, but you still don't know what people think of it until you put it out, so it's just not quite the same as playing for people. So I guess that is my first love.

**Do you still enjoy the travelling?**

Probably not as much as I did when I was a kid; the travelling part is hard. I guess what I would really like is if I could get my own club and have everyone come to where I was. It's still interesting, but not like those first few times outside the States when I'd go sightseeing – y'know, checking everything out. Now I've been most places, it's just like going to work and doing your gig. Sometimes you don't know if you're in Philadelphia or in London or California or wherever; crowds don't really change that much.

**Do you think your style has changed much through the years?**

Yeah, I think so. Not a lot, but I keep changing. Hopefully I also keep progressing, or really there's no reason to keep going. In fact, I'll change with the last record that I heard. If I hear someone I really like on a record, or even at a gig before I play, then the chances are I'll be playing some of his licks. I've gotta be real careful about listening to tapes before I go out there, so I don't put on something too far out.

**Another aspect of your playing is your slide work. Who were your early influences in this quarter?**

Robert Johnson, Muddy Waters and Son House were the first people that I really heard. When the Robert Johnson *King Of The Delta Blues* album came out, that was one of the main things that made me want to play slide. Early Muddy Waters stuff; his stuff was the first slide that I heard and I didn't know what it was. I didn't know if someone was playing steel guitar; it sounded like they were fretting the guitar and slidin'. I'd never heard anything like that before. Eventually, just from listening to albums, you could tell what tunings they were using, because a lot of them weren't using a regular tuning. Most of them would tune to a particular chord. There are so many good people now, but back then they were definitely the big three – although, of course, Elmore James was in there too.

**Your own slide guitar style is pretty unique. Do you use glass or metal slides?**

I use a metal slide. It's a piece of pipe that I got at a plumbing supply place; I bought a 12-foot piece of pipe and had it cut into pieces a little over an inch long. Even today I still can't find one in a music store that fits my finger. I use it on my little finger. When I first started playing, there wasn't anything like that in the stores. I tried a lot of things, like test tubes and lipstick holders and medicine bottles... I used the crystal in my wristwatch – all kinds of things. Then a guy in Denver called up and told me that I should go to a plumbing supply place and try a piece of pipe, because that way you can find one that fits your finger, and I've been using the same slide ever since 1967, I believe.

**Have you ever tried the traditional approach of snapping off a bottle's neck?**

Yeah, I've tried a few bottles. They were always a little bit big, and I just liked the metal a little bit better. I just think you can get more sustain that way. But I love the way Ry Cooder sounds, y'know; he uses bottles and just has a great sound.

**During the late '70s, you collaborated with and produced albums for the legendary Muddy Waters, and in so doing were almost single-handedly responsible for the great bluesman's comeback. What are your most outstanding memories of Muddy?**

Just all real good memories. Muddy was one of the nicest people I've ever met, and yet you wouldn't guess that he would be such a sweet guy. His records were so earthy and you can't imagine such a nice guy singing all this nasty music! But a lot of times Muddy used to say, 'You should have seen me when I was young, I was a real hellraiser!' I'm sure he was, but the last few years when I knew him he'd gotten a lot of respect from people and he wasn't having to struggle any more, and I think he knew the people loved him and he liked that. He was real glad that he was getting some acceptance. I didn't see any of that crazy side that he always told me was there. I was told stories about him and I know that he was pretty much a hellraiser, but when I knew him, he was just a really nice guy. He was also a very firm bandleader; he didn't take any shit. If he didn't like something, he'd let the musicians know exactly what he wanted or expected from them. But he was real good at being nice and diplomatic at the same time. He didn't have to scream at people to get his way. He just told them and he knew that they knew they had better do it that way or there was gonna be trouble!

**You played with John Lee Hooker, too. Would you say there was a marked difference between him and Muddy?**

Yeah. Although they were both Mississippi bluesmen, with John Lee you'd never know when he was gonna change chords. He'd sing until he got tired and he'd start playing guitar, and then he'd do that until he got tired and then he'd sing again. It wouldn't be what you might think of as being in time, and so you really had to listen and be real careful, because John Lee was gonna play his stuff and you better fit into it, because he wasn't gonna fit in with you! But I was real familiar with his records and so I knew it was gonna be that way. In fact, it was really kinda fun to have to take a guess at when he was gonna change. But their music was really deep blues, Mississippi Delta stuff, and so the feeling was the same, although they went about it differently... They both had real distinctive styles.

**Your albums are a mix of blues standards seasoned with a few of your own tunes. I wonder if you prefer arranging songs to writing them...**

Yeah, I do. But also I just don't like the songs I write as much, usually. I just have a hard time writing songs; it's just not what I do real well. If I felt like I could write enough songs for a record that were good, I would, but it's not where my real talent is. I wish I was a better songwriter.

**Throughout your career you have veered away from the blues into other areas. Are there any areas that you still want to explore outside the blues framework?**

Well, of course, I've played some rock 'n' roll – stuff like that. The only other thing that I've thought I might do one day is do a country album. I've grown up hating and loving country music, too. Sometimes you just didn't want it to be there 'cos it was the only thing you'd hear on the radio in Texas, before rock 'n' roll. But I think I could make a good country record. Someday, if ever I found the right producer and a label were interested, I'd like to give that a shot.

**Is there anybody around now that you would like to play with, having had so many and varied collaborators in the past?**

Man, I'm sure there are... But most of the people I've either played with already or they're dead now. I'm always on the lookout for the guys who are around. I guess the '50s was my favourite period for the blues and so the guys that were making records – most of the Chicago people who were playing in the '50s and who are still around – are the ones that I am always interested in playing with.

# LESLIE WEST

NOVEMBER, 1993

*Mountain were hailed as the natural successors to Cream when they burst on to the scene in the late '6os. The formula was the same: brutal blues-based rock with sweetly screaming, gutsy guitar. But the Eric Clapton role was now in the hands of a very large man with a very small guitar. In the UK, though, the band didn't manage to scale quite the same heights as they did Stateside, although many had a sort of unconscious relationship with the band via the fact that London Weekend Television decided to use Mountain's 'Nantucket Sleighride' as its signature tune. This, of course, means that Leslie was in for a fat royalty cheque every time he visited these shores. 'I never have to bring money with me when I come over here,' he told me with glee. 'In fact, when we played Knebworth a few years ago and we did "Nantucket Sleighride", the audience reacted like, "Oh that's the group that does that song," because the TV never announces who it is.' We started out at base camp...*

**Tell me how Mountain came to be.**

Actually I was only in two groups: The Vagrants and Mountain. A lot of my friends were in hundreds of groups before they had their first record, so I was pretty lucky. The Vagrants broke up because we didn't have the songs. Felix Pappalardi had produced two singles for us and we were going to do an album together, but he only had two weeks before he went over to do *Goodbye Cream* in Britain, and we had no material. I had thought we'd get Felix in the studio and I'd write songs with him, but he didn't have enough time. We were sitting in the studio with Felix and he said: 'Look guys, you don't have any songs. I've got two weeks and it's not enough time to write songs and record an album…' so The Vagrants split. But Felix said to give him a call if I ever got another group together. Then he went over to England and did *Goodbye Cream*, and he came back and I called him and we went into the studio – and he threw me out! He didn't like my drummer, I didn't have a bass player, I was using an organ player who was playing bass pedals on a Hammond C3. Somebody said to Felix, 'Well, why don't you play the damn bass?' – and that's how we started Mountain. The first album was *Leslie West Mountain* and then *Climbing, Nantucket Sleighride, Flowers of Evil, Avalanche* and all the rest of them, but then Felix didn't want to go on the road any more. I had met Jack Bruce through him, and I flew over to England to make two phone calls. I was going to call either Joe Cocker or Jack Bruce, and I figured if I called Jack I would only have to make one call – if I called Joe I still had to get a bass player! So I called Jack and he was going to Germany to do some gigs with Jon Hiseman from Colosseum, and I asked him if he wanted to start a group, and he said 'Yeah, of course.' So with Corky [Laing – drummer] that was it: West, Bruce and Laing.

**There must have been some good times.**

Playing with Jack was my dream of a lifetime. After we worked with Felix initially, with The Vagrants, I got Cream's *Fresh Cream* and *Disraeli Gears* and I looked at the credits and said, 'Hey, wait a minute, this is the same guy who produced us!' I couldn't believe that he was producing my favourite group! So when I got to play with him and then Jack, it was like fulfilling a dream; I mean, it was just hard to comprehend. I learned more from playing with Jack than anybody. Somebody said one of the reasons I've been able to stay around so long was because I've had some great bass players, which is sort of true. I've had Stanley Clarke play on my IRS album, *Alligator*, and I've played with Jack and Felix, and now Randy Coven, so I've been very lucky that way.

**I guess that if Cream was your favourite group then it follows that Eric Clapton was one of your favourite guitarists?**

Oh yeah! But for some reason, his style now is anti-Cream, you know? The tone he used to use, the guitar he used to use...it's almost like he's not using them on purpose. Albert King was my other hero. It seemed like he had one lick and he turned it around sideways, upside down, and played all these variations, but it was all the same lick! I was amazed this guy could stretch one string, because he played upside down, and when he would stretch the E string, it was on the bottom rather than the top, and I was wondering how the hell is this guy stretching that string so far.

**Did you ever get to meet him?**

Yeah, my first show with Mountain was at the Fillmore West with Johnny Winter and Albert King. Albert's amps didn't work and I had to lend him mine and so I met him, but it was my first gig and I was so nervous. We were supposed to do a 45-minute show, and we were so nervous we got through the set in 20 minutes. But Albert King was more my style than BB King: BB was more of a showman, a nightclub singer/player, and Albert King's style was more, I would say, rock, so I tried to emulate him whenever I could. So Albert, Clapton and Hendrix were my three favourites.

**So it was principally a blues influence?**

Oh yeah, you don't have to be black and broke to have the blues. You can be Jewish and have nice cars. If you wake up and have a fight with your wife, you've got the blues. If you step on the cat and the cat scratches you, you've got the blues. But anyway, that's more or less where my playing comes from. A lot of guys say, 'My playing is based in the Mississippi Delta...' and you know damn well that they haven't listened to any Robert Johnson records or John Lee Hooker or anything like that. But my roots are in The Who, Stones, Cream, you know? I never listened to that old music until I listened to these guys and found out where it came from. If it wasn't for the British showing us where this stuff came from...I mean, all you did was take the music that started in the US and make us aware of it. Everybody thinks it was the Americans that discovered the blues, but it took the English to rediscover it for us – for which I'm very grateful, by the way.

**What was the guitar you used with Mountain?**

A Les Paul Junior. I turned Mick Ralphs on to them, and we used to go through Texas in the '70s when we were touring and we hit every pawn shop there was. Actually, Felix gave me the first Junior that I used in Mountain. It was basically a hunk of wood with a pickup on it, the cheapest guitar that Gibson ever made. But it was all I needed – it had one pickup, a tone control and a volume control, and years later when Van Halen came out, basically all he used was one pickup. The only thing is they eliminated the tone control. Well, I happen to like using the tone control with the treble rolled off, because Clapton used to have this tone called 'woman tone', the same tone he used in the solo on 'Sunshine Of Your Love'. It's actually my favourite tone: very warm, not metallic and no matter how loud you play with that tone, it just never hurts. The Les Paul Junior was my primary guitar, although my first guitar was a Stratocaster. I bought it with the money I got for my bar mitzvah. I remember going to Manny's Music and buying a '58 Strat, and a few years later when The Vagrants started, they all had new instruments and my Strat was already about six years old and all beat up. And so, like an idiot, I traded it in. I'd love to have that guitar now, man...

When I started Mountain with Felix, I used an SG Junior and the thing would never stay in tune. So he had this old beat-up Junior, and he said, 'Try this thing,' and I never gave it back. In the end I gave it to Pete Townshend. I played on 'Can't Get Fooled Again', 'Baby Don't You Do It' and 'Behind Blue Eyes' when they did *Who's Next*. They came over to the States and they were at the Record Plant in New York, and Kit Lambert called me up and said, 'Pete wants to record an album, but he doesn't want to overdub. He wants you to play lead.' So we went down and we did it. But when they got back, I think they thought that it didn't really work because I was playing lead. But I've got a tape of it. And when I finished the sessions, I gave Pete my Junior and an old tweed Fender Champ and he wrote me a really beautiful letter. I'd love to be able to release one of those cuts one day. I had the greatest time seeing how they recorded, because that was a unique group, I've got to tell you.

**One of your more surprising appearances over the past few years was playing a transvestite rock musician in Spielberg's film *The Money Pit*.**

Yeah! We were on the Deep Purple tour in '85 in Europe, and I signed a contract to do this film. Actually it was between me and Meat Loaf. Martha Quinn, who used to be a video DJ on MTV, had recommended me for the role, and so I had to leave the Deep Purple tour and come back to the States to do the movie. It was unbelievable. When Steven Spielberg does a movie... I mean, we had to sign a contract saying if you lost the script, you were fired. When all those effects started and the house started crumbling down... I mean, that house was built on the studio. They duplicated a house that was a real house out on Long Island, and to see how they duplicated this house... It was just a front, but you could never have told that one was a prop and one was a real place. It was just amazing. When that guy does a movie, he doesn't really miss, does he?

# SONNY LANDRETH

FEBRUARY 2001

*Long before this conversation took place, I'd heard about this slide player from America's Deep South who was not only one of the hottest players around, he had also developed this seemingly impossible technique where he'd actually fret notes behind the slide – something that gave him access to all sorts of chord voicings previously unattainable to a slide player. Later on, I heard some of Sonny's albums and was dutifully aghast. What's more, Mark Knopfler kept quoting him as being one of his all-time favourite players. In fact, when I interviewed Mark, he showed me a brand-new resonator guitar he had had made for Sonny, which had been specially inscribed. Thus, an interview was seriously overdue. It was Sonny's 1992 album* Outward Bound *that started turning heads on an international level. It wasn't until 2001, when he released the* Levee Town *album, that I had the chance to talk to him. The album was a heady mix of swamp-fuelled Zydecko and Deep Southern country, but it was Sonny's slide that caused the biggest ripples on the guitar waters...*

**How did you develop your slide technique?**

When I first heard slide I didn't even know what it was. So I did a little research and tried figuring it out and trying it on my own. I got totally frustrated with it and couldn't begin to figure it out, but I stuck with it and started getting better at it. Once I heard Robert Johnson, that inspired me to combine his style with Chet Atkins' fingerstyle; I put the two together and that was a big step for me.

**Did you start experimenting with tunings back then or did you stick with standard tuning?**

At first, I didn't know about open tunings, and then I got a Mel Bay steel guitar book – I actually had a little Fender lap slide with six strings and a single pickup – and that's how I learned about G and E tuning. That was when I started to experiment, especially with E because of the common notes with standard tuning.

**Where did the technique of fretting behind the slide come from?**

I guess it was just a burst of inspiration. I don't know when exactly it was, but I guess it was around 1970 or '71, but I'd got a little frustrated just playing blues. If we went to a minor blues and I had the guitar tuned to an E chord, it could make things very difficult. So one night I was playing at the 12th fret, using all six strings, and I could see where my problem area was, which was the third string – the G#. I could see the G natural behind it and so I thought, well, what happens when I press this? So I pressed the G natural behind the slide and strummed a big E minor chord. That opened the window for me because once I had done that, I realised that there were all these other notes back here too, and that's when the whole thing opened up.

**Does this mean that you have to play with quite a high action?**

Actually you really don't – it's less than one might think. When I started out using the steel guitar approach to the bottleneck, I had a really high action. I put a high nut on an old Gibson Melody Maker, but then I would go into music stores and start playing acoustic guitars, having tuned them to an open E, and I'd get on fine. So that's when I began to sand down the nut a little at a time until I got used to a lower action. The other thing that was a factor in learning to improve was using heavy-gauge strings. I went up to a .013 to .056 set – which was like a medium acoustic set – and with the tension that it adds and with the thicker string, you get a bigger sound and more sustain. So you don't need as high an action as you might think.

**You use the slide on your little finger, don't you?**

That's correct.

**Do you favour glass or metal?**

I started out with metal. I had a friend whose family had a motorcycle shop and he gave me a handlebar, and so I had a lifetime supply! I just got out a hacksaw and started making slides. Then my dad got a glass cutter and we cut the necks off some wine bottles, and the first time I played with glass I really loved the sound and the feel. So that was it for me; I kept up with the glass from then on. I still like metal and I use different types on tracks, but I'm pretty much a glass guy.

**What about further slide influences?**

I went on to Lowell George and Duane Allman, Elmore James, Sleepy John Estes and Mississippi John Hurt – some more of my Delta blues guys. I just went on and on.

**Any contemporary players you especially like?**

I'm a huge Robben Ford fan. I got to work with Robben a few years ago and he's big on my list, too. But really, the guitar bands that came up during the '60s, '70s, '80s; I've always been open to players and individual styles. I'm pretty much about tone and phrasing, and so it's guys with their own sound and identity who really hit it for me. Like Mark Knopfler: you hear him and you immediately know it's him. He's an amazing player, musician and songwriter, and we've got to be good friends.

**What about your solo career? When did that really begin?**

Well you know, the first album I ever recorded got released in the mid '90s. I recorded it back in 1973 and I never thought that it would see the light of day. I recorded it in Houston and it was all acoustic, and at least half of it was instrumental and solo style guitar, the other half was with a rhythm section. That was the first album I ever wrote and recorded. And then, there were a lot of tracks I recorded in another studio, and essentially two albums came from that. There was one called *Blues Attack* and the one after that was called *Way Down In Louisiana*, which came out on Sony. That was in 1985, and the next album I did officially was in 1992, which would have been *Outward Bound*.

**What's your main guitar?**

I have a collection of guitars and amps, but for this album [*Levee Town*] I went the vintage route with a 65 and a 66 Fender Strat. I used the 65 more: it's a wonderful, very special sounding Strat. I also used a 1960 Les Paul sunburst and one of my road Strats, which has DiMarzio Fast Track pickups in it – that's a tried and true sound for me. I used some acoustics: 30s Nationals, a Collings OM Style acoustic, a Taylor 12-string and a couple of Bourgeois acoustics: one's an OM-style guitar and the other is more like a J-45. I used my old Martin D28 that I've had for around 25 years, too.

**What about amps?**

For the most part I used the trusty Demeter, which I've been using for many years. It's a three-channel, 75-watt amp and I've probably done about 80 per cent of my recordings with it. I also used a Dumble Overdrive Special – Alexander has tweaked it for me and it's a really great amp.

# the
# JAZZ PLAYERS

# MARTIN TAYLOR

NOVEMBER 1999

*I've known Martin Taylor since the early 1990s, having worked with him on his techniques column for* Guitarist *and, subsequently,* Guitar Techniques *magazines. We've also written two books together, a tutor and his autobiography, and so I guess you could say that his particular story is one with which I'm already very familiar. One thing is for sure: he continues to lead the world in the art of fingerstyle jazz guitar and has proven to be a worthy successor in the same lineage that gave us the legendry George Van Eps and Joe Pass. No stranger to the heady heights of guitar polls the world over, Martin was awarded the MBE in 2002 for his services to jazz. Looking back, however, it turns out that he was taking his first formative steps with the guitar at an age where most of us were still struggling with nursery rhymes...*

**Exactly how young were you when you first picked up the instrument?**

I believe it was four. That's what I've been told, anyway. I can't really remember the very first time I played guitar because there were always guitars about the house. But I can remember my dad coming home with a ukulele – one of these Hawaiian things, red with a little palm tree on it – and I started messing around with that and driving everybody mad. My mum asked my dad to show me some chords, to make it sound more musical, and so he showed me a few and that really gave me the bug. A friend of mine who lived across the road got a guitar, and when I saw that I thought that was really what I wanted, and so my dad bought me a guitar. It was made in Russia and was like a classical guitar, only it had steel strings on with an absolutely horrific action. But I got this guitar and I just couldn't put it down. I just became obsessed with it and I just played all weekend and I couldn't wait to get back from school to start playing again.

My dad and his friends used to be around the house, and they'd put Hot Club or Eddie Lang records on – a lot of the early pioneers of jazz, really – and I just loved the music. I really liked what I heard and started to try and pick out the melodies and, particularly when I was listening to Django Reinhardt, when it got to what I would call the 'fancy bits', I asked my dad, 'What's that?' and he told me that he was improvising, and to think of it as making up another melody on the spot.

**So really your musical journey was a non-stop ticket to jazz rather than, in many other players' cases, arriving there via blues or becoming disenchanted with rock 'n' roll.**

Well, first of all my dad was a jazz musician. Also, because I was so young, I didn't have any of the peer pressure to be into a certain type of music or a certain band. Not that jazz was the only music I would listen to. I remember going to see Jimi Hendrix at the Albert Hall with my brother, for instance... I thought he was fantastic!

**Did your early experience on the guitar incorporate learning scales and so forth?**

I can remember my dad sitting me down and showing me some scales on the guitar and I got them under my fingers. What that did more than anything was to start to unravel the mystery of the fingerboard in terms of where the notes were in relation to each other. But in terms of getting dexterity together, I just used to play and I've always been like that – I would sooner use the time I have practising something I'm going to use rather than doing gymnastics or exercises.

**An awful lot of jazz is taught from the point of view of scale theory. Do you consider this approach invalid?**

I think it's a discipline to familiarise the pupil with the fingerboard and to give them the basic dexterity needed to play the music. But I think it's a mistake to teach everything in terms of scales and modes. One of the major criticisms people make about jazz is that it just sounds like someone going up and down scales, and I can always tell if someone has learnt that way when I hear them play. One of the things that can happen is that you take up an instrument to make music, and you become tied up with the technicalities of the instrument itself and the music is put into the background.

**Given that Django was possibly your earliest influence, who else was it who provided inspiration during your formative years?**

It seemed to be all the early guitar players because those were the records that my dad had. I came across an album by a Hammond organ player called Shirley Scott, and I put it on and I heard this very tasteful, sparse guitar playing, and it was Kenny Burrell. That turned my head completely and I started to look more at the American guitar players like Barney Kessel, Charlie Christian and Herb Ellis. I've always been attracted to jazz players who have a blues element. I think a lot of people forget that jazz is basically a more complicated form of the blues – blues with a few more chords.

**Did being in situations where you were playing with older musicians ever take the form of an apprenticeship of sorts?**

Well, yeah, because the way I got into playing professionally was a way that almost doesn't exist any more. If you wanted to take up an instrument and start playing, then you got together with other people who played, and got into a band and you played at weddings, and then you got into a professional band and did summer seasons and went on the cruise ships. You played dance halls, did radio broadcasts and things like that – an old-fashioned apprenticeship. Now, if someone wants to become a jazz musician, they go to college.

**How did you meet with jazz violinist Stephane Grappelli?**

I was in a duo with the bass player Peter Ind and I also had a duo with Ike Isaacs, as well as working with the Tony Lee Trio. Ike had worked with Stephane and so had the bass player that was working with Tony Lee. I first met Stephane in 1976, although I didn't start working with him until '79. He just called me up and asked me to do a few dates with him in France and I went over and did about a week, and he asked me to do a tour of the States about two or three months after that. I worked with him for just over ten years, but it was always on a very informal basis. It wasn't like a full-time job, but it certainly was a good one.

**Was it another intense period of learning?**

Stephane was one of the first musicians I'd played with who had the combined talent of being a great musician, but being able to communicate with the audience at the same time. That fascinated me and so I sort of informally studied him, sitting next to him all those years. But that was the biggest thing I learnt from him, just communicating with an audience.

**It must have been a fantastic thrill to play with someone who shared the stage with Django.**

Yes. It was funny, because I used to make a point of thinking when I sat next to Stephane every night that I must remember all this as a special time. For a musician to be this close to someone who has been such an influence in music doesn't come along every day, and many musicians go through life without ever having that experience. Stephane and Django were the first European jazz musicians who formed a group that had its own sound – a European sound.

They weren't trying to emulate American musicians, they gave it their own sound and they were our musical forefathers.

**A while ago, you brought out an album that was a tribute to jazz pianist Art Tatum – were piano players an influence on your chord melody approach?**

No, not really. It started in my childhood – my mother used to play lots of records by Tony Bennett, Frank Sinatra and Nat King Cole, and all those arrangements were by people like Nelson Riddle. I loved that orchestral sound and the way a singer could sing one note and underneath they'd change the harmony and it would change the whole feeling of that note. I would hear folk players, classical players and blues players playing very complete parts, but I didn't hear any jazz players doing it at that time. I just wanted to be able to sit down and play something on my own. The only jazz musicians I heard who could do that were piano players, particularly Art Tatum, who was such an incredible virtuoso, but there was also Bud Powell and Fats Waller and people like that. I started to try and do that sort of thing on the guitar and then I heard Joe Pass play, which I just thought was wonderful. Then I heard George Van Eps. I guess that my way of playing is more like Van Eps rather than Joe Pass, because, although there is a lot of improvisation going on, it's all very arranged with different lines going on, whereas Joe's playing was very spontaneous. For me, where playing solo guitar is concerned, I don't think of myself getting better on the guitar, being able to play more or anything like that. I just think in terms of musical freedom – actually being able to play the ideas that I have. That doesn't mean trying to play things that are complicated or fast – in fact I don't play as much as people think. When my solos are transcribed, there isn't as much going on as you think, it's just that I try to give the impression that there's more happening. It's actually breaking everything down to the bare bones, because a guitar player has to suggest things are happening in his playing that fall beyond the scope of the instrument. I think all guitar players will know what I mean when I say that you have all these ideas, but somewhere between your head and your fingers, there's a communication breakdown. That's a thing that has to be overcome somewhere along the way.

**So how does the process of writing a chord melody version of a tune begin?**

Usually, it starts with the melody, but in jazz it isn't enough to have a good melody – you've got to have an interesting enough harmonic structure to mess around with. If you've got a ballad with a really fantastically strong melody, then I would keep that and reharmonise it in the same way that an arranger would with an orchestra. But you've got to have an interesting structure to begin with.

**Is there then a set process from that point on, which eventually produces the finished article?**

Well, I could show you a method, but I don't always use it! I have a way of showing people how to put the three things together – bass, melody and harmony – but I don't actually think that way. After a long time of doing it, I've built up a vocabulary of how I can do things. So it becomes like the way you speak; you know the words and you know the letters that make up the words and you know the grammar. But when you speak you don't necessarily think about the individual words, letters, grammar, and so on. If you did, you couldn't talk. So when it actually comes down to talking about the process of playing, that's when I get really stumped, because when I'm playing I don't actually think about what I'm doing. When I'm playing and it's all happening and it's all coming together, I get to the point where I'm not even conscious of playing... In fact, I'm not even conscious that I'm holding a guitar. It's very difficult to describe it, but it's just music. Obviously that doesn't help anyone who wants to know the process, but I know all the things I need to know to put the whole thing together, but now I've got them, I don't need them any more.

# JOHN SCOFIELD

MARCH 1994

*This interview took place at the time when fiery fusionists John Scofield and Pat Metheny recorded an album together, called somewhat mysteriously I Can See Your House From Here. Scofield actually confided during the interview that the title came from the punchline to a particularly tasteless joke – the sort that musicians will roll around the floor with laughter at hearing, but one that is probably best kept away from that sensitive area called public taste. Sick business, jazz...*

*Arguably one of the most difficult tasks in professional guitar playing is that of defining yourself with an immediately identifiable sound. It's an awkward trick to pull off, but if anyone working in the genre can be accused of having squared the circle in this respect, it's John Scofield. I asked him first how his signature sound evolved.*

**You've got an immediately identifiable sound on guitar. How did that evolve?**

The guitar is so difficult to get your own sound on, and if I've come up with that, I think it's been by luck. It's just sort of been shaped over a long period of time. I first put my sound together during the '70s, I guess. It was harder then to get a sound on a guitar because they didn't have all the gizmos and stuff that they have now. Right now you can go get a multi-effects system and immediately sound like the new Van Halen record just by using the presets. Distortion, chorus, compression – it's all right there. Back then that wasn't happening, but I liked the sound of distorted blues guitar and I tried to bring that to jazz. But it was really hard to do because all those effects were not available and pre-packaged; you had to fish around and find stuff yourself. I just wanted to overdrive an amp to try and get a blues sound in a jazz idiom, whereas most of the jazz guitar players wanted to get more of a Wes Montgomery or Jim Hall sound.

**The previous generation of jazz players would go for front pickup with the treble rolled off.**

Yeah, exactly, through whatever amp was around – almost an acoustic sound. I love those players, but I thought I could get more of a horn-like quality, and then I discovered the stereo chorus pedal in the early '80s. I mean, Metheny had been using digital delays and chorusing with big expensive rack-mounted jobs, but when the chorus pedals first came out I loved them. Mike Stern was addicted to them. He was playing through two amps and a chorus pedal, and I said, 'Hey, that's it for me!' But it's got to be one of those cheap Boss or Ibanez chorus pedals. It can't be any fancy chorusing units; they don't sound right, they sound too spectacular.

**So you're an analogue kind of guy?**

I guess I am, although I don't make it a rule. You know, with my sound it's almost like you have to make it sound like it's not chorus. So even though it sounds chorused, there are ways of setting it to get it to sound as unchorused as possible, and as unflangy. I just mess around with it until I can do it – I'm still not sure how it works, actually. A guy called James Farber, who engineered the last few records I've made on Blue Note, is somehow able to get a stereo chorus sound out of my pedal, out of the two amps and everything, and sort of balance it so it doesn't sound too flangy.

**So it's mainly the stereo split that's doing the work?**

Yeah, even when it's mono. It's really weird. I'm not sure how, but it just fattens up the sound somehow. It's guitar straight into the rack and the chorus. I use various reverbs and two Sundown combo amps that they don't make any more – they were made in New Jersey for a couple of years, but the guy went out of business. On the road, if I can't bring my Sundowns, I bring Boogie Mk IIIs.

**How long have you been using your Ibanez guitar?**

I started out with a Gibson ES-335 that I had - a '58, a real good one. I found it in the mid or early '70s I guess, and I played that up until '79 or '80, when I went to Japan and the Gibson needed some work because the neck was warped – it was a little under the weather – and Ibanez came to a gig and gave me the guitar that I play now. It's a copy of the Gibson and I started to play it and liked it. There's something about it that I liked more than my old Gibson, and I've been playing it ever since.

**Have you made any modifications to it?**

No, it's the original pickups. The old Ibanez pickups are good. I don't like the new ones as much, but the old ones I like.

**Did you have anything to do with the design?**

Absolutely nothing! Actually, they've designed a whole bunch of guitars for me over the years. Guys who've worked there have said, 'Well, you want to try the George Benson with a tremolo bar and we'll make a neck like yours...' and I have all these other guitars, but I like this one the most because I think when you play an instrument every day for years something kind of magical happens. Scientists talk about how wood ages when vibrations go through an acoustic instrument for so many years and how it tunes itself to certain pitches, and I really believe in that. So I've just worked on this baby for 14 years or so, and I'm pretty hooked on it. I have all kind of guitars at home, real good ones, but when it comes down to it, I keep going back to the same old guitar. I'm not averse to change. A lot of times I think, 'Well I'd like to get a different sound just for a change…' Then I'll go out and buy some other guitar and I'll like it, but I won't like it as much, and I also won't feel that I can do as much with it.

**Have you ever felt tempted by guitar synths, like Pat Metheny?**

Yeah, I had a guitar synth and I couldn't stop playing it for about two weeks. But then I thought everything I played sounded like something that Pat had played on one of his records, or something that some synthesiser player played.

**Do you get asked to do seminars?**

Yes, I do.

**What do people want to know?**

Well, they want to know how to get a record deal! [Laughs] I tell them to forget it – well, not forget it, but keep plugging away. But on one level it's, 'What scales do you use?' and I tell people, 'Well, I haven't studied scales for a long time, so I'm not sure what actual scales I'm using…' A lot of times it's not a scale; it's not just seven notes over and over again, it's tonalities with chromatic passing tones and all kinds of stuff. I tell them to use all the scales, all the tonalities and all the little phrases they can learn. But it's not that simple. I think the modern approach to playing, the way a lot of jazz is taught, is a little misleading. Even though these scales exist, it's not really how to play music – it's just playing a scale, and I think that the emphasis on the scale is a little too strong.

**So you think people are a little prone to becoming over-concerned with theory?**

Well, I think people are obsessed with music theory. There's one school of thought that states that you can't be analytical about music, it's an emotion.

But learning to play an E chord is an analytical process. Some people are too theoretical, but that's their nature. If somebody's an artist they'll use thought as part of the artistic process.

**Do you write on guitar?**

Yeah, I write on guitar, which is a help and a hindrance. It helps your guitar playing because when you sit around and just practise all your fast licks all the time you tend to miss things. But writing music and putting together songs on the guitar has led me to chord voicings and various kinds of music that I wouldn't maybe do otherwise. I get in situations where I wonder what this melody would sound like over this chord, and you have to slow down a little bit.

**For some of your tunes you use almost a classical approach in terms of right-hand fingering.**

I don't really use classical-style fingering. I like the sound of all the notes in a chord being played at once, and I tend to just put the pick down inside my little finger and play with three or four fingers, or I'll put the pick in my mouth and just pluck with my fingers. I really like that sound – it's really become part of my style. Sometimes I play with pick and fingers at the same time and sometimes, for a funkier sound, I'll just pluck it with my fingers, pulling the strings out like a bass player.

**You have a unique way of voicing chords. How did that come about?**

I don't really see it as too unique. If you listen to a lot of what jazz piano players are doing, I've always tried to get some of that on the guitar. Jim Hall had a very economic and beautiful approach to voicing chords behind a horn player. He made some records with Paul Desmond and one with Sonny Rollins, and I just lived with those for a long time. Sometimes he played two notes in the chord and they were just the right notes, you know? You have to do that on the guitar because you're not a piano; you don't have ten fingers to play all the notes, and so you just try to find parts of the chord that sound good.

# PAT METHENY

*Back in the late '60s, the term 'fusion' was coined as a means to mischievously reclassify a form of jazz that had strayed away from the mainstream towards the outlawed territories of rock music. The younger musicians, influenced greatly by Miles Davis, liked their jazz, but liked it loud. Often hailed as a jazz fusion pioneer himself, Pat Metheny is nevertheless no stranger to the Grab-a-Grammy stakes. His albums* Travels, Still Life (Talking) *and* Offramp *have all seen him walk away with a guitar case full of awards. Our 1992 discussion leapt straight into the fusion debate...*

**Do you consider the fusion tag to still be relevant?**

Well, it's never been one of my favourite words, mainly because it emerged from a marketing concept more than from musicians. I've rarely heard musicians use that term; it's more usually the record companies. When most people hear the word 'fusion', they think of electricity. For me, as a guitar player, the first thing I did was plug my guitar in. That was my first musical gesture. I've been having to deal with electricity since the word go, and I've tried to use it in a musically creative and responsible way. As technology made itself available to people like me, it was very natural to try and use it. It opened up orchestral possibilities for a small group that didn't exist before. I loved the fact that I could have a four-, five-, six-piece group that was capable of making this huge wall of sound in addition to what we did as just a jazz quartet.

**You come from a musical family…**

Well, my older brother Mike, who is five years older than me, was a spectacular young musician. By the time he was 11, he was like a child prodigy, playing the Purcell 'Trumpet Voluntary' in Kansas City churches; he was really something. And so my early music memories are probably hearing him and my father play duets. My dad's also a very good trumpet player and my grandfather, too, is a professional trumpet player. So mostly it's trumpets.

**You've said before that you were put off trumpet, and that you were drawn to the guitar because it was the instrument that your parents most feared.**

That was definitely a large part of it. When I was about eight years old, the Beatles thing happened and the guitar took a place in the panorama of western culture that attracted me. Also, my brother was such a good trumpet player that I knew I would never be as good as he was, so there was that in there too: like, 'God, I don't really want to follow in this guy's footsteps.'

**And of course your parents not wanting you to do something is adding fuel to the flames.**

It's funny, because people talk about rock 'n' roll as the music of rebellion. But to me, jazz was always – and still is – much more rebellious than rock 'n' roll, especially now. Rock 'n' roll has become so totally predictable, and everybody has been doing exactly the same thing now for, like, 25 years. Jazz, to me, was always the music of individuality. There are so many colourful characters within the jazz spectrum and, as a form, it really demands that you get in touch with your own personal self. If you don't have your own sound in jazz, then basically it's nothing. In rock, the more you can sound like everyone else the better. Rock was rebelling against my parents, but jazz was rebelling against my parents as well as all my peers, because they didn't have any idea what I was talking about.

**You do have a unique sound, but that sound has now been very much copied by an awful lot of jazz players. Does that bother you in any way?**

Well, it is a little strange. I don't necessarily feel like I invented anything. I always played what I wanted to play. I saw it happen with Jaco Pastorius – I know what it was like the first time I heard him. There was nothing like that, nothing even close to that before. But whoever first comes up with something doesn't necessarily get the credit for it. It becomes part of the vocabulary, and that's the natural course of events. I see people get very defensive and say, 'Well, that's my shit. People are stealing my shit.' But you can't do that. We're all part of a community and everybody is collectively working to advance the cause, and every now and then somebody gets a little glimpse of something and everybody else thinks, 'Yeah, that's a good idea.' In my case, for four or five years I think I was probably the only person that played with digital delays and two amps and all that, and it was like a 'new thing'. But now everybody does it and I'm not going to sit around and say, 'Oh yeah, well that was my shit and everybody copied my sound.' My reaction to it now is to take all the delays off and play with just the straight guitar – do something different.

**Was there a point in time when your sound actually clicked?**

Yeah, it was kind of an accident, actually. When digital delays first came out, they were very expensive and very cumbersome: five rack space things and they were, like, 8-bit! Anyway, I was living in Boston at the time, but I was in a studio in Oslo and saw a Lexicon there, noticed that the company was in Boston and said, 'Can you put it on the guitar and see what it sounds like?' It was supposed to be used for vocals, for ADT, and the guy said, 'Oh, yeah.' So when I got back to Boston I thought, 'God, there must be a way to do this live.' So I called up Lexicon and said, 'I'm this guitar player...' and they gave me one. I messed around with it and got into this thing of splitting up the amps, because I always thought that the guitar was a bit flat in mono. It seemed like when I heard a saxophone player like Sonny Rollins, the sound seemed to come from all over the place – it didn't come from this one little spot. So I tried it and that was it.

**Does the fact that you have such a distinctive sound confine you in any way? Have you ever wanted to just pick up a Telecaster and rock out?**

Whenever I do play with any kind of distortion, if I go and sit in with somebody, I find it's so easy. It all kind of runs together and you don't really have to make the notes speak. Also, if you play anything fast at all, you sound like Allan Holdsworth! With the kind of sound that I use, if I miss any part of the note, you hear it as a big clang. I find that other kind of sound very forgiving. I can get through it technically, but I can't make it come alive the way somebody else could.

**You write on piano. Is this to create a different harmonic point of reference?**

That, and for me it's just much easier to think on the piano because there is only one version of each note. That still messes me up on the guitar.

**And do you find that if you sit down with a guitar to write, with all the best intentions in the world, you end up...**

...just playing the guitar. Exactly! And you end up writing guitar music which sometimes is OK, but after a couple of records I'd written enough guitar music for a while. And when I started to write on the piano, I found that when I translated it back to the guitar it was better. Sometimes I still pick up the guitar for ideas, but I find that I end up finishing them on piano.

**Your early ECM albums were recorded very quickly. Do you find that now you need the luxury of having longer in the studio?**

Yeah, I do. I need it to get the thing that I want. The ECM records were recorded in two or three days, with maybe a day or two to mix. I still like doing records like that: *Question And Answer* was done in six hours, 15 tunes in six hours. But with the group albums there is a level of detail that I want to get that just takes time. I want people to be able to listen to the records over and over again, and I think for that to happen you have to create a depth of information that's rock solid. And that takes time.

**When I've seen you play, you seem to regard the fretboard from a horizontal point of view, playing along the strings rather than across the fretboard...**

Well, you know why that is? It's because I like the way the note A sounds on the top string better than I do on the second, but I like A on the second string better than I do on the third, and so on. So, if I want to play a melody, I'll think of it along the strings rather than across, to take advantage of that. If there is any way to do it that way, then I will.

**Your playing also incorporates a great deal of chromatic passing tones...**

Well, I think that anybody who studies improvising long enough will eventually get to the point where they find a way to get all 12 notes available all the time. The next step after that is to start using them. A lot of it is a matter of hearing: you just start to hear it that way after a while, especially if you listen to a lot of Coltrane and people who really developed that part of the language.

**I've found with my own teaching that if a player wants to move away from a purely diatonic mode of improvising, their initial steps are dogged by their own reaction to the chromatic tones, by perceiving them as sounding 'wrong' somehow.**

This whole thing of learning to improvise via chord scales is very useful, but it can be deceiving. All seven notes of a chord scale are not equal – some are definitely stronger than others. So I encourage people to play entire solos only using chord tones, not using any approach notes or scale notes at all, but only using the three or four basic notes of whatever the chord is. The idea is to be able to play melodies using only arpeggios, but not making them sound like arpeggios. If you can do that, then you have in your mind what the strong target notes are and you can start going in with the other notes of the scale. When you're hitting the main chord tones pretty hard and you've got the other scale tones as passing notes, then you can start going for the other chromatic tones. It's really four chord tones, three other scale tones and five chromatic tones.

**Do you think in terms of a pure chromatic scale?**

No, I mainly think of the triad. I think if you were to analyse what I play, I'm landing on one of those three notes a lot, mostly on the third; I play a lot of third-based melodies. The reason I started writing tunes was because I couldn't find tunes that set up the kind of guitar playing I wanted to do as an improviser. Some of that has to do with the guitar – we need material that is set up more for the guitar.

# LARRY CARLTON
# AND
# STEVE LUKATHER

JUNE 2001

*When Messrs Carlton and Lukather get together to make an album, the guitar world cocks an ear. The album concerned was entitled* No Substitutions, *and comprised just five live tracks in little more than 50 minutes, and not a vocal in sight. Packed full of scorching guitar, the CD was the result of a mammoth stint that saw the two axe-men playing Japan's clubland together – with the emphasis on 'improvisation' all the way.*

**How did you two meet?**

LC: Way back in 1976 or '77 I was doing a lot of sessions, and my friends at the time were people like David Foster, Jay Graydon and Jeff Pocaro. Steve went to school with Jeff and all the guys in Toto, and so he was the youngster who was hanging out, and that's when I met him. He was probably 19 or 20 years old at the time. We just became friends... The guys and I had a weekly card game where we would take our wives and meet at each other's house and socially hang out, and Steve would hang out with us.

SL: Yeah, we used to play poker and he'd take my money! I was a fan of Larry's when I was in high school and I used to go and see him play with Robben Ford at Donte's. I used to sit there mesmerised. When I heard *The Royal Scam*, around the time I was getting into The Crusaders and all that stuff, Larry was my hero. He still is.

**Did you become a fan of Steve's playing at the time, Larry?**

LC: Actually, I never heard him play during that time at all. He wasn't really doing anything, although he might have just started touring with Boz Scaggs. But I didn't hear him play guitar until many, many years later.

**Was this album something you've wanted to do together for a long time?**

LC: It came about because I've been going to Japan since 1974, and I go back about every 18 months or so and do shows. So over the years I've become very good friends with the promoters. And we've talked about doing special projects and have been throwing names out and thinking about different concepts. When Steve's name was mentioned, I thought it would be really fun to go and play with a guy who plays differently to how I do. So that's how it came about. I called Steve and he said he'd like to do it, but we had no idea that we were going to record it – that was an afterthought.

**Have you played together a lot in the past?**

LC: Nope, only once. I think it was at a NAMM show in the late '80s.
SL: The irony is that we've known each other for about 18 years and this project is the first time we've really played together.

**How did you go about choosing the material?**

LC: We just thought about what songs would be fun and what songs the Japanese audience would enjoy.
SL: I suggested Beck's 'Pump' and maybe 'All Blues'...
LC: 'All Blues' came about because Steve had heard me play it many times with Jeff Pocaro, and then later he used to perform with Jeff at the Baked Potato and do the same kind of approach. So the feel on 'All Blues' is inspired by Jeff because that's the way he felt that tune.

**It's an almost reggae feel...**

LC: Exactly! Then, one of my most successful tunes – which I'm thankful for – is 'Room 335', which the Japanese audience really associates with me. They'd have been disappointed if we hadn't performed that tune. So it was very easy to come up with songs.

SL: Yeah, I said I love all that shit that you did on the first couple of albums when you were turning your amp up real loud and stuff. Let's do some of the old tunes like '335' and stuff.

**Does the album represent the whole set or was there more stuff?**

LC: No. We have enough in the can for another album. I think we were choosing nightly from a list of about 14 songs.

**What other songs did you do?**

LC: We did 'Equinox' by John Coltrane, which is basically a C minor blues, but with a more 'jazz' head to it. Steve would sing 'Red House' sometimes, and we'd do a sort of a Hendrix part in the show. And we did the ballad of Jeff Beck's that was written by Stevie Wonder – 'Because We Ended As Lovers'. So there were just different kinds of songs that we could draw on, depending what mood we were in. The tunes that are on the new CD are just the ones that we felt would represent what went on for a first listening.

SL: We'd do 'Put It Where You Want It' by The Crusaders and 'Freddie The Freeloader' by Miles. So not everything on the album is representative of what we did every set. Some of these tunes are long, y'know? But they fitted in with the format of 'let's just get up and play'. We didn't even think we were going to record it until we were about two and a half weeks into it. Larry's so brilliant that I could start playing something and he would play in harmony with me, and we'd never even talked about it. Every set was different.

**How many nights did you do altogether?**

SL: About three weeks, six nights a week. You get your chops up after that. One of the highlights for me was that, about an hour before we went on stage, Larry and I would just lock ourselves in a room together with our guitars, have a beer or something and we'd just start playing. Larry would give me lessons; he'd show me the chord melody stuff and I'd show him the right-hand technique and all that. For some reason, everyone just left us alone and didn't bug us. It was really cool. I've got a lot more stuff I need to get off of him, though...

**Both of you have a lot of history as top session players. What do you think represents your finest work?**

LC: Well, there's a couple that do come to mind... Probably the *Court And Spark* album with Joni Mitchell. If I remember right that was about 1974, and so I had about four years of studio work under my belt. I think I had grown to a place where I had learned to a fairly high degree how to accompany a vocalist in the studio. So I like where that album went. Then, obviously, the Steely Dan stuff. I'm so fortunate that the timing was right, because the casting of my guitar playing on their songs was a great marriage. Harmonically, their songs are so sophisticated and maybe that is my forte, coming from a pop and jazz background. So I love listening to those records because the harmonies are so sophisticated – and there are no wrong notes on the guitar! [Laughs]

**Becker and Fagen are notoriously hard people to work for – according to rock myth, at least. How was your experience, Larry?**

LC: Honestly, my experiences were only positive. They are very diligent about what they want to do, but they also recognise when good things are happening and they let them happen. People have asked me over the years if I did a lot of takes on those solos, or did they hum licks to me – and no, they let me play, and if we got stuck in a section and I really wasn't sure which approach to take, then sure, they'd have an idea and they would put it out and we'd do some more. But I enjoyed the process and never resented the fact that they wanted to do 30 takes a night...[Laughs] That was all just part of the process.

**What about you, Steve?**

SL: God, it's so hard to say. Playing with Paul McCartney was a big high... Working with Jeff Beck; even though the record never came out, it was still really a gas to work with him. People of that calibre – like Elton John – you get in a room with these people and you're with greatness, y'know. I worked with George Harrison, too – what a lovely guy he is. We didn't get enough time to hang, but I was at a jam with him and Bob Dylan, myself, Jim Keltner and Jeff Lynne, and we just sat around playing Beatles songs and shit – it was pretty deep. It was never recorded, but it was just one of those moments. I just kept thinking where are all my friends, man, I want them to see this shit!

**What qualities would you say are necessary for doing session work now?**

SL: Well, it's a different world now, y'know? There isn't really a session scene now. If you really want to play on a Mariah Carey record I guess you still can, and if you squint you can probably hear a little guitar in there. It's not like the old days, man. Everyone makes records at home and they don't necessarily want you to be real good. With all the Pro Tools and stuff, you don't even have to play good any more. It's like, 'I played a good lick there, let's just fly it in where it needs to be.' The height of the scene when we were all doing it was pre-machines, and they used to hire rhythm sections to play, and they were such great times. You got to play with all your favourite musicians: drummers, bass players, guitar players, keyboard players, percussionists. There were great artists singing in the headphones while you're cutting the track. That shit doesn't exist any more and nor will it. I feel like I got into the last era of all that. Not to say that people don't make great records any more, they do – they've just got a different way of doing it. But the kids don't give a shit. I've got a couple of kids and I know what they listen to: my son's a full-on metalhead and my daughter's a pop singer. So I'd rather hang out in my son's room, to be honest with you...

**Do you think the computer music 'revolution' has had a damaging effect?**

SL: Well, rock 'n' roll was meant to be rebellious to the kids, but I'm not a kid any more. I'm 43 years old. To try to be that would be a joke – it would be embarrassing. I've had a little taste of all that in the heyday of Toto. We sold a lot of records. We got creamed by the press, but so what? Big deal. When it's all said and done, even if people hated the band, they had to admit that the guys were good players. I'm proud of my past, but you have to move on. That's why I feel that I'm in between being a jazz guy and being a rock guy. I'm not a full-on be-bopper like Larry or Pat Metheny, but I can hang with those cats. I can hear it and I can play it, y'know? But I'm still much more of a rocker than those guys are.

**Can we run down the gear you two are using at present?**

SL: I use my Music Man Luke model guitar, just like the one you pull off the rack – the one with the non-locking tremolo. I'm not into the locking trem thing at all any more. That goes through three Rivera Bonehead amps that I helped design with Paul Rivera. One is clean, two wet, with just a little delay from two PCM 70s, just very subtly for a little depth. For the clean sound I used a little bit of compression from a DBX 160X, just to give a little 'slap', a TCG for a little bit of chorus, only on the clean sound, and a stereo Univibe in there, but I don't think I used it much on the songs on the album. That's it. I don't use any of the big shit any more.

LC: I'm using my 1968 335 through a Dumble Overdrive Special and a single 12 Dumble cabinet with an EV speaker in it. I have some kind of small reverb unit in a small rack, and I have a Roland 3000, which I don't use too much, but it's there if I want to hear that sound. That's pretty much it, although I still use the Sho-Bud volume pedal, but Dumble has modified it for me. It's got a device in it that ensures it doesn't lose any of the highs.

**You've gone back to using the 335 after a few years of using solid-body guitars.**

LC: Yeah, it's been almost four years now that I've been using the 335 again. That's since I started playing with Fourplay. I cut their first album with an old

51 Tele, and I liked what it sounded like on the album. But when we came to play that material live, I found I was more comfortable with the 335 for my approach to their whole book.

**Do you have a guitar collection, or have you pared things down to fundamentals?**

LC: It's basics only. I probably own six or seven guitars that I think are very special. I own a 57 gold top Les Paul with PAFs, and I have a 51 Tele and a 51 L5. I have a 57 Les Paul Special with P90s in it that's got a great tone. There are probably one or two more, but I don't remember.

**Do you have an acoustic guitar?**

LC: Yeah, I own one acoustic. It's a guitar I designed with Mike McGuire at Valley Arts Guitars 16 or 17 years ago. It's a one-of-a-kind: we copied a Martin 00, but improved it with double bracing, choice of wood, and so on. It's small, too.

*No Substitutions* **is what could be defined as a 'jam session' in many ways. This seems to be a bit of a dying art these days, which is a shame because there is an enormous value in experimenting live as much as possible. What are your comments on that?**

SL: It's a dying art now, and that's because by the time you get to make a record, you can barely play. There's no jamming, no improvisation and no great soloists, per se. I mean, name me one great soloist under the age of 30 who's made a record in the last ten years. I'd say that Tom Morello is the most important guitar player to come out of that era, because he brought some new shit to it. It's all wacky the way he does his stuff – it's not the way you think he does it.

LC: Well, I think you were accurate in saying that it's kind of a lost art. At least it's diminished substantially over the last 25 years. Getting together, making music and having the aptitude to make it of high enough quality, no matter where the music wants to go, that time or that evening – which is more of a jazz approach. I was kind of brought up doing that and I know that Steve, being ten years younger than me, witnessed that happening many, many nights in his late teens and early 20s, and he related to the fact of how fun and how proficient you have to be to do that. So he incorporated that in his playing and the people he was hanging out with enjoyed doing that also.

**What tools do you have to have at your disposal as a musician to cope with the 'etiquette' of playing with another guitarist live?**

SL: If you're not doing it to make a record, then just go ahead and have fun with it. Be prepared to make mistakes because that's the way you learn; that's how you find new riffs. Just jam with your friends, make mistakes, step all over your own dick – it doesn't matter. Just have fun, go out and play, have a few beers, it doesn't matter. It is a job and it is an art form, but it's also fun. People used to beat on logs just for fun, but music's become such a science, such a business and money, money, money. It's all image – you've got to look right and have the right image. But when Led Zeppelin brought out an album back in the '70s, the only way you'd get to see what they looked like was to go to the show. There was a mystique, and that's gone in rock 'n' roll – and it will never be back. You get everybody's face shoved down your throat, what kind of pants they wear and what kind of food they eat.

LC: I think it's a lifetime of preparation! It all starts with an awareness, and I think that playing on stage with another guitarist is not so different to being the only guitarist on stage and playing with a keyboard player. You have to leave space, you have to have big ears to respond harmonically and rhythmically on the spot and then get out of the way. All you're there to do is to help that soloist perpetuate whatever he's feeling at the time. I think it takes patience and, like I said, big ears and – as I wrote on the album – lack of ego. Your motives have to be pure for the music to really come off.

SL: I used to think that you had to be really good to make it in the music business, but that's not the case any more. But there are a few people left carrying the torch. If we're not careful, be-bop is going to be a lost art. Who wants to put in the years to do that? Now they call 'jazz' that happy smooth jazz, which is like…not really jazz, y'know? You start playing all the weird notes and they say 'we can't play that on the radio'.

# JIM MULLEN

APRIL 2000

*Jim Mullen is no stranger to the British jazz scene. Many will have witnessed his thumb-powered, Telecaster-fuelled performances with the legendary Morrissey Mullen band all over Europe. These days, he's settled to a slightly more sedate pace with an archtop...*

*I spoke to Jim at the time of the release of his* Jimjam *album, but a retrospective on his early years as a player, and particularly how he developed the style of forsaking a plectrum in favour of playing with his thumb, seemed appropriate...*

**When did you first pick up a guitar?**

Before I picked up the guitar, I was the tea-chest bass player in the neighbourhood skiffle group – one of those Fray Bentos corned beef boxes with a broom handle and a piece of string stuck in it. I would have been about seven or eight years old at the time. There was a kid around the corner who had a guitar and everyone was fascinated by it. I used to go round and knock on his door to ask if I could look at it. This was back in Glasgow and I had a paper round at the time, and I persuaded my dad to let me get my first guitar and pay it off on hire purchase. My dad, being a working-class Glaswegian, was very sceptical about doing anything on the never-never, and so he said, 'Well, if you miss one payment it'll go back to the shop.' But fortunately I didn't miss any payments and so that's how I got my first instrument. It cost about ten quid – an Egmond, a sort of plywood body and so on. The action was terrible: you had to be Arnold Schwarzenegger to hold a chord down. I had big black grooves in my fingers from trying to hold down simple little chords. But I had a guitar and I was totally into it, and that marked the beginning of the process, y'know.

**Did you find that you developed a musical ear very early in life?**

I was very fortunate that I always had a very good ear. I've never had any actual musical training, and so I had to hear it and figure it out that way. There was nobody around to explain it to me, and that's the reason I play with my thumb. If there had been a teacher around then, he would have said not to do that. But because there was nobody around to tell me otherwise, the habit stuck.

**This would have been before you'd heard of Wes Montgomery, presumably?**

Oh yes, I didn't know about Wes for years after that. I was only about eight or nine when I started doing that, and I didn't hear about Wes until I was well into my teens. Although he did things with his thumb that I couldn't begin to do: playing octaves at speed with his thumb and things like that. Nobody has really taken that kind of thing further than he did.

**What was your first professional engagement?**

I can remember it, actually. It was at the Highlanders' Institute in Glasgow, and there were all these geezers in kilts and big red noses. We were a band of school kids and we were playing jazz tunes of the day like Johnny Dankworth's 'African Waltz', and these people were all fuming because they wanted to hear highland music – 'The Dashing White Sergeant' and all that – and all we were playing was jazz tunes. They were giving us hell the whole night and that was my inauspicious debut.

**It didn't put you off?**

No, I've managed to survive all those things that are designed to put you off.

**When did you decide to take up music as a career?**

That wouldn't be until I was well into my teens. By that time I was becoming aware of quite a wide range of music. The thing that attracted me to music in the first place was the emotional side. I was always drawn to music on an emotional basis, the feeling of the music drew me in. It was kind of greed on my part, because I wanted to do some of that for myself. I'd always liked the idea of creating a mood and trying to project that to an audience. So that was it for me, and I left school at 15 and started gigging around the local scene in Glasgow. Then, when I was in my 20s, I moved south, following the economic refugee trail as so many do!

**Did the '60s Hank, Stones and Beatles thing pass you by completely?**

Oh, no. I was a big fan of Hank Marvin when he was in The Shadows, and The Beatles were a big influence, too.

**What happened after you moved down south?**

After a few years playing in various rock bands, I met up with Dick Morrissey and we began a 15-year bash with The Morrissey Mullen Band. That was when we were doing all the fusion things and trying to find different ways to bring the music to people's attention. The final album was probably our high point, and so it wasn't as if we ended on a low. It was just time to do something else.

**For a long time you were associated with a Fender Telecaster, which is a fairly unusual instrument for jazz...**

Well, because I play with my thumb I lose a lot of attack. We're talking about the difference between flesh or plastic on steel. So the reason for the Telecaster was to try and strike a balance. It's such a hard, biting kind of a sound, but playing it with the thumb altered that somewhat, but still gave me attack. So, in an electric band I could still cut through, but using an archtop in Morrissey Mullen would have been too mellow. I played a Telecaster for 20 years, but when I started to get my own groups together I started moving into more acoustic settings with piano and double bass, and the Tele didn't work so well. So that's when I moved to an archtop, and I've been playing the Aria Pro II Herb Ellis model. It's a very comfortable guitar to play, and I really like it and use it for everything.

# JOHN ETHERIDGE

MAY 1999

*This particular interview took place after a workshop John Etheridge did at an arts centre in Essex, and so, having taught for most of the afternoon, the idea of passing on knowledge and generally offering a helping hand in all things jazz were still very much at the forefront of his mind. It was common ground for us both, too – I'd actually done some jazz workshops myself at the exact same venue. However, I was surprised at John's opening gambit after my initial enquiry about the nature of teaching jazz.*

*'I think it would do a lot of good if they actually banned people from practising guitar,' he said, laughing.*

*Of course, this doesn't mean that all would-be jazzers should lay down their instruments and relax – that's not exactly what he meant at all...*

**You don't think guitarists should practise?**

People who learn guitar tend to place the emphasis on practising alone in their rooms with a metronome rather than developing their skills by playing together with other musicians. The first-generation jazzers didn't waste their time practising; they jammed together, and in doing so picked up valuable stuff like timing and phrasing. Stephane [Grappelli, with whom Etheridge performed] hated rehearsing – he just couldn't understand it. Neither could he understand why the rest of his band would be practising in their hotel rooms whilst he sat and watched TV. It was just something to him that was a totally foreign concept.

**Having said all that, you are one of a very select few jazz musicians who take part in the teaching of jazz at summer schools or workshops.**

I do quite a few, yes. I usually do some sort of jazz summer course somewhere.

**Do you find that the same sort of questions come up all the time at different workshops?**

Yeah. They haven't really changed since I've been doing them, although there was a period where a higher level of technical proficiency came in, but that seems to have died down a bit. People always seem to have the same problems, like playing over changes and getting jazz timing, or feel – but particularly what you do over chord changes.

**Is there a central point that is missing from many jazz students' studies, then?**

I think a lot of the emphasis on scale study is slightly misplaced, especially when it comes to playing over changes. Something I always mention is that jazz improvising employed no scales until the middle '60s. That's when rock and jazz improvising started merging and became scalar. It was John Coltrane and Miles Davis who, in the late '50s, started using scales as opposed to chord tones. I bought Miles' *Kind Of Blue* album in 1972 and read the liner notes where it talks about scales, and I thought, 'But you play music with scales – that's what you do, isn't it?' I hadn't clocked it at that stage, but basically, before that everybody was playing chord tones and passing notes. If you listen…Joe Pass or Wes Montgomery and guys like that are playing chord tones, and everything else is a passing tone embellishment, really. And that applies to everyone up to George Benson, who is the last player in that tradition – not including the players who have now retrospectively revived it. If you go and listen to a jazz guitarist now, he might be playing in that way, but in the historical sense that line finished with George Benson. Django Reinhardt never played a scale. I used to think that Charlie Parker was playing scales. In fact, Parker's a classic: acres of passing tones all the time, and it's all thought of as chord tones with passing notes, and the minute you clue in to that, there's no problem with it.

**So how can people get out of the scalic approach rut?**

Well, you can get out of that rut quite easily. Say, for instance, you're playing on C minor. Now, instead of thinking, 'Am I playing on C Dorian or C Aeolian or C Phrygian?' you say to yourself, 'OK, I've got a C minor seventh arpeggio tones – C, E flat, G and B flat and, say, the ninth, D – everything else I play will merely be a connecting point.' So you get a totally different sound. That's one way out of that scale/mode rut – if it is a rut.

**Which scales are important to learn?**

Obviously the major scale is important, as is the Dorian scale, the Phrygian not particularly, Lydian is pretty important, the Mixolydian is obviously vital and the Aeolian and the Locrian are less important. It's good to know them all, but you might as well sort out which ones you absolutely must know, and I think you must know the Ionian, the Dorian and the Mixolydian. You really need to know those to get by in most contexts. You wouldn't necessarily have to know their names, either. You could think of them as the major scale, the minor seventh scale and the dominant seventh scale.

**So, when you teach people to play over chord changes, do you first take a simple diatonic chord arrangement and break it down into arpeggios?**

Yes, I suppose so. You'd probably start with a simple sequence and say, 'This is how you can do it... Start with the basic arpeggio and then build it up with extended chord tones and then start using altered tones – sharpened or flattened ninths, that sort of thing. As long as it's logical and clear, people can use it to improvise with.

**Are there any other ruts that you find jazz pupils will get themselves into?**

Phrasing is one. You get a lot of people who can play pretty well, know a lot of scales and a lot about changes, and so on, but they don't have an idea about phrasing. Often it's because they've practised on their own and it's not something that they've developed in a musical context with other people. You find that, if you haven't had experience playing with other people, you tend to play all the time and never stop. That's been a tendency amongst improvising jazz musicians since practice was invented. People play all the time and don't leave any gaps. This has become so common, y'know. Phrasing is about leaving gaps, and if you listen to some of the really great players, like Metheny or Scofield, you'll hear that they leave a lot of gaps. The other thing is that people tend to play on the beat all the time because that's what they do when they're practising. But if you don't play on the first beat and finish on, say, the four-and of the bar, it immediately sounds better, although you could be playing the exact same notes. This is where the obsession with harmony and scales kind of blinds people. Think of any good player from any style who's really popular – Mark Knopfler, Larry Carlton, and so on – and you're listening to good phrasing. It's probably more important than anything we've talked about so far – it's the main thing. If you get a line of jazz guitarists together, what will separate them and make one sound better than the other is not their knowledge of scales or whatever, it's their phrasing.

**It's almost as if the major disadvantage of the guitar is the fact that you don't have to blow in it to make it work – like a sax – because you'd be forced to put in natural-sounding breathing spaces.**

I totally agree. In many ways you should try to phrase like you would speak. You imagine someone talking to you for 20 minutes with no pauses or space for breath – it would sound exhausting. Of course, this is where the thing breaks down. So many guitarists who we admire other people can't stand because their lines go on for ever. Yet it impresses us, because it's technically difficult to do. The early jazz musicians didn't practise; listen to Lester Young, Charlie Parker or Django Reinhardt. They don't sound like they'd done loads of practice, whereas a lot of jazz musicians today go through their practice routines on stage and it cuts off the audience. Guitar players might listen to a guy like Mark Knopfler and say, 'Well, he's not doing anything special…' but listen to the guy's phrasing, and that's partly why audiences love to listen to that stuff.

But phrasing is a difficult thing to teach, which is why people will teach harmony – because you can systematise it. You can't do that to phrasing. You just have to advise them to think about it: leave spaces, use rhythmic devices, don't play on the beat all the time…things that will make even a trite little scale passage sound more interesting. And the whole point is to create interest when you play. You're trying to get people to listen to you.

# the
# ACOUSTIC
# PLAYERS

# JOHN WILLIAMS

APRIL 1994 AND APRIL 1999

*Today's popular guitar, whether it leans stylistically towards rock, jazz, grunge or country, enjoys a very grand and long ancestry. The vihuela and cittern, of which today's classical guitar is an evolved form, were to be heard in the chambers, halls and royal courts of Europe more than 400 years ago. The electric variety has always been regarded as something of a wayward child of the guitar family. Spurned publicly as an abomination by contemporary classical guitar's principal architect, Andrés Segovia, the instrument has remained almost mutually exclusive from its classical relative, despite sharing so many characteristics. John Williams has always demonstrated a healthy disregard for the prejudices of both sides, eager at once to experiment and expand the repertoire of the instrument, no matter which stylistic boundary he has to cross in order to do so.*

**Your father was himself a jazz guitarist...**

He was known in those days – we're talking the '30s and early '40s – as a jazz and dance band guitarist. We'd call him a session guitarist today, because the style of music and places of employment have changed. He had always played classical and jazz guitar in the 1930s in London and used to edit a magazine called *Fretted Harmony*, which you've probably heard of. He used to do a column called 'Tips for fretsters' and there is a copy that I have somewhere which was his signing-off copy when he left for Australia, where he wrote a farewell to the readership. He was in Australia by 1939 and so that is where I learnt.

**Did you have the choice between moving towards either jazz or classical guitar yourself?**

Not really, no. At that stage he was keener on the classical guitar than jazz. He'd always played classical, having had lessons during the early '30s from Mario Maccaferri, the designer of the famous Maccaferri guitar. That was his background. He heard Segovia play in the Queen's Hall in London. So he taught me because classical guitar was his great passion, I suppose. And he was still teaching and earning a living from playing jazz guitar, but he taught classical guitar at a big music store in Melbourne. And then he brought the family back to England in 1952 to open the Spanish Guitar Centre. He then pioneered the class teaching idea for amateurs of all ages, a tradition that has carried on and one that is still in use today.

**Your father encouraged you from the tender age of four to pick up and play the instrument.**

I can't really remember the earliest time that my father put a guitar in my hands, except that I've seen photographs of it. I can't remember anything from the age of four; my earliest memories are from around the age of eight. I can remember practising and the house we were living in then. I had a daily half-hour routine, and my father told me not to wiggle my thumb and to keep my fingers in position. I remember, too, a tape I made around the age of eight, which I sent to my grandparents in England; just a few little pieces, but it was actually quite good. So I was obviously playing fairly well by then, and it's a kind of irony that I can't remember what led up to it.

**At that age, you must have had to overcome many physical problems in order to play.**

My father realised that the guitar has got some awkward arm and hand angles to get round – like with the violin and the cello, I suppose – and children who start on those instruments need to get the mechanics of forming themselves around the instrument, holding the instrument and feeling comfortable with it at as early an age as possible.

**You must have started on a much smaller-sized instrument...**

Oh yes, very much so. I was playing on old 19th-century guitars, which were smaller anyway. I wasn't doing serious practice at the age of four – my father didn't stand over me with a whip and make me do an hour of scales. His idea was just to get me to feel at home with the instrument. He played it, so it was in the family, and I took to it in a friendly kind of way. I didn't have to be made to do it, but I wasn't desperate to do it either and I think he was just very, very good at encouraging me to stay in contact with it without being too fanatical. It wasn't until the age of seven that I started serious practice, which was half an hour a day. But it was proper practice, supervised some of the time and with constant teaching from my father. A very good friend of mine, Sebastian Jorgansen, was also learning guitar, so that was something we did together from the age of seven to ten, when we all came to London. Seb and I used to have odd joint lessons with my father, and he used to practise at his place and I'd practise at my place. But it made it a little bit more of a social activity than it would have been if I'd just been one poor little kid sent into a cold room to practise on my own.

**The classical guitar has always been a very solitary instrument, though...**

Certainly out in Australia there was hardly any ensemble music, and therefore hardly any experience to be had playing with other instruments. But that has actually blighted the whole history of classical guitar playing. This is why guitarists are by and large bad sight-readers and bad ensemble music players, because they don't have the ensemble experience that other instrumentalists have.

When my family came to London, my father opened the Spanish Guitar Centre and he was doing arrangements of classical chamber music; so even at that stage he was trying to get an ensemble going. We had a guitar trio and a guitar and string quartet. Then it was all standard repertoire: Tárrega, Giuliani and the Aguado method – a very good method, full of very good studies and exercises. I used to do a lot of that, Sor, Coste and later the basic Segovia repertoire. That really took me up to the age of 14.

**What happened in between having lessons with your father and your studies with Andrés Segovia?**

Well, it didn't work out exactly like that, because my father was teaching and guiding me all the way through. Likewise when I met Segovia in London in '52, it was my father who was keen to get me with Segovia and spent a lot of money doing so, and it was tough when we got back to England because there weren't a lot of spare shillings around. Nevertheless, he saved up to send me and my mother to Siena in Italy. But he continued to oversee my practice and learn himself, really, because he was an admirer of Segovia and knew that he could learn a lot as well. Actually, one of the few specific memories is coming home in 1952/3 sometime, and he had been to the Piccadilly Hotel to see Segovia and had actually written down in long hand Segovia's scale system. I remember one of the funny details is that Segovia used to call an open string 'empty', which is quite sweet.

**What sort of things did you learn from Segovia?**

Well, in terms of having lessons, not a lot to be honest. The main benefit was the inspiration for a young kid, which I was then, coming from the great master. Plus, doing summer schools in Italy, meeting a lot of international students of all ages – it wasn't only for guitarists, it was on many instruments. So that was what was important, much more than any specific ways of playing a piece of music that I might have learnt from Segovia. When it came to specifics, his way of teaching was kind of 'play it like I do'. [Laughs] Whether it was a bit of fingering or vibrato or expression or whatever, it was do what he does. It was not very illuminating – and this is not only to do with it being traditional and old fashioned – and he didn't have a style of teaching that was very encouraging to students, unless he was happy that you'd imitated him. So it wasn't a kind of teaching that would encourage your own feelings or your own style, and it wasn't very illuminating about the music. If you were young and raw, he didn't help you understand what a piece of music was about and give you some idea of shape. A lot of that was to do with the fact that the guitar is made up of miniature or shorter pieces, compared to the repertoire of the violin or the piano. So the guitar didn't have a lot of music that called for design analysis or shape construction. I'm not necessarily someone who believes in a lot of that anyway. I'm not saying that you shouldn't look at how pieces are constructed and put together, but I think that can be overdone in classical music. I'm not a fan of that approach.

**The deconstruction approach?**

Exactly! However, you'd expect some idea for guitarists who are pretty backward musically, especially someone like myself who was pretty young in those days. Also, you'd expect some sort of encouragement that gives you confidence in your own will or need to express things.

**Was this something that you decided you should include in your own teaching, principally because you found it lacking with Segovia?**

I think at the time I didn't notice. But after I attended the Royal College of Music in London doing general music studies, I made a lot of contacts and ended up doing a lot of chamber music with other instruments, playing what pieces there were with various ensembles and doing work as an accompanist on BBC radio. All that gave me an experience that I hadn't got on the guitar with Segovia, and so I started to make up for that lack very quickly after I left college. But, in terms of my teaching, ever since then, I'm a different generation with a different attitude. I wouldn't say it was a reaction, because I didn't react at the time. In fact, while I was teaching back at the college, I suppose I unwittingly continued a bit in Segovia's shadow. I took over his classes a few times in Spain, but he asked me to take them over because he knew I would carry them on in his spirit. I think teaching styles have changed a lot since then, although there are those who still…a lot of guitarists who ape that particular style. That's pretty tragic, because there are a few around who give masterclasses and belong to the faculties of various universities and colleges – especially in the States – and they keep the Segovia flag flying. But it's getting much, much less and certainly I actively encourage the total opposite approach.

**So you would subscribe fully to the concept that there are many ways to interpret a piece of music and not only the one way, which is perhaps what Segovia advocated?**

Absolutely. I think that if we're talking about classical European music, there are certain things to do with style: whether it's Renaissance, the style of dances which gives the music its rhythm, the Baroque style, much of which grew out of the Renaissance, which itself used a lot of traditional and folk music. Over the last couple of years I've learned a lot about the early 1800s, Giuliani and that period. There are still little bits to learn. Giuliani wrote in the operatic, bel canto tradition, and we now know through a lot of research that his music should be very vocal, flexible and expressive, and not the kind of practised, fuddy fodder that it is often interpreted as being. His arpeggios were a harmonic filling and not an arpeggiated technical filling. The tunes were very broad and expansive, and that the tempo varied enormously within movements, depending on the melodic line, etc. So, when it comes to teaching, I'm all in favour of understanding and learning certain factual things to do with style, but I think, beyond that, you'd be better off to take as a model either jazz or folk music and try to play with the idiom or style, but let the interpretation be totally personal.

The guitar, through being a lesser instrument in terms of repertoire, suffers even more from a very precious, rather pretentious, over-particularised book of rules in terms of interpretation. Most of the criticism you read of performances and things like that don't mean anything. You often read about the way so-and-so controlled their tone in the transition from the first to the second subject and the beautiful transparent textures in the change from G flat major to...whatever, when all they're really saying is that they played it really nicely!

**People regard the electric guitar as a phenomenon of the last 40 years, but the classical guitar has only been recognised as a serious musical instrument in the last 50.**

Yes, since Segovia made it a concert instrument, if you like. He created the framework for anyone who wanted to be a classical guitarist who gives concerts. We came to this country when I was ten and, by then, Julian Bream had really done all the spadework. I don't mean to devalue what Segovia did – after all, he went back much further and almost created the thing in the first place – but in terms of what's really happening musically and socially in this country, Julian really created all that. Segovia came over every year or two and did a concert and, because of his personality, he established himself as a figurehead. But when it came to applying that to the musical life of England in the '50s, Julian created all that. He had been to college at a time when guitar wasn't allowed, but had persevered with it. He persuaded the musical establishment in this country to accept the instrument because he played it so beautifully.

**It's a common misreading of classical guitar that it may have started around the Baroque era and maintained a constant course since then.**

Yes, that's right. The Baroque guitar was a different instrument that had a life parallel to the lute. The lute's popularity faded with the onset of bigger instrumental forces and changes in social and cultural life during the 18th and 19th centuries, and so did the guitar. But the guitar regained short periods of popularity at the time of Sor, Paganini and Boccherini. Composers liked it, but it was clearly impractical when played with other instruments because it was so quiet. You'd find that even people like Berlioz and Schubert used to write for guitar, but were restricted in terms of blending it in well enough with other instruments. There have always been a few aficionados of the instrument and you've always had little guitar societies in different countries – sometimes it was Paris, in the mid-19th century it was London – but it wasn't really until Segovia that it was lifted to modern thinking. But I think the irony there is that Segovia and a lot of his disciples have been imprisoned by this achievement and failed to take in the social and cultural changes in music that have, in turn, changed the guitar, and I think that's a shame. If you look back over the last 20 years, there has been this generation of classical guitarists who have been pretty well blind and wanted to remain blind to all other areas of music, because they've been so taken with the success of the guitar as a classical concert instrument. They've said, 'Right, we've got to paradise, we've got to hang on to it and resist anything else.'

**Learning classical guitar is a hard slog to start with, far more disciplined than electric.**

I think there are different degrees of awareness of what the different problems are. The classical guitar is, in a way, an artificial technique; artificial in the sense that it's not naturally how you would move your hands on an instrument. I think you could describe the piano as a natural instrument, whereas the violin is not. I'm talking now about the playing position – it's just not natural. For rock music on the guitar, the position in which you hold the instrument and the way your arms and hands are put on the instrument is fine. I'm not saying that it's less demanding. What I'm saying is the kind of thing that you play on it is different. With classical hand positions it is impossible to stand up and play a Bach fugue, but as a rock player, you're not playing Bach fugues anyway! It is impossible to get the right rhythmic feel into the arm and right hand for fast single-note improvising unless you're in the position that a rock guitarist is standing with his or her instrument. It's no good the short-sighted, classical fanatic saying, 'It's just chords and single notes' or 'It's easy stuff'. That's a very limited way of looking at it, because if you're sitting like a classical guitarist, you couldn't play those things like that. They're totally different techniques and cultures. When we get down to specific things it gets very interesting because – and I'm now talking about classical playing – if you get into the styles of all different periods of music in the classical field, you find that there are limitations in our classical technique that prevent us from understanding the musical spirit and the rhythms of early medieval Renaissance music, because the guitar of those days was strummed very like popular guitar technique today. It was a natural up-and-down stroke of the fingers, not plucked by groups of fingers simultaneously like a modern classical technique, but they were strummed exactly as if you had a pick in your hand – you just did it with your fingernails.

**Would that be why a lot of Renaissance guitar music from composers like Luis Milan looks very sparse on paper? There wasn't the harmonic movement that was present in the later Baroque era. In the early Renaissance they used a quill as a kind of precursor to the plectrum...**

Absolutely! One of the most exciting pieces I ever heard was Jim Tyler playing a cittern – with metal strings – and I think he played it with a quill.

**This would suggest that some of the established concert repertoire is now performed incorrectly, from a historical point of view?**

That's right. I've got a Baroque guitar, I had one made, and around about the time I had it made, I started listening, and there are so many people that do that period on the Baroque guitar – it's a specialised technique. I can do it, but I can't do it as well as a lot of people can. But what I was saying about different styles, whether it's jazz guitar or rock guitar, it's a different technique. It's the same instrument and I can do it, but it's not my speciality so I just don't. Jim Tyler is the best, because I think that a lot of the old music people are still a little bit emotionally constricted, although they play with the right techniques. But Jim Tyler, being a fine bluegrass banjo player as well, has obviously got an aptitude for music, and so when he plays these old things either with a quill or fingers, it really bounces. It swings terrifically, and I'm totally sure that was how it was meant to be.

Throughout your career, you have earned a reputation for breaking moulds by crossing the perceived boundaries between classical, pop and jazz, and even occasionally writing for the guitar – 'El Tuno' from *The Height Below*, for instance. Why haven't you written more?

I might do, actually. It's one thing to think of nice catchy little formulas on the instrument – I suppose they reflect your own personality and the harmonies you like. The sort of pieces I write are a little like whistling in the bath. Proper composers like to be able to develop material and make something substantial out of it. I have got a very keen interest in the organisation of composition and improvisation, and the link between the two, but I'm not very good at it so I don't do it.

How did your relationship with Sky evolve?

In terms of doing different things, I would have to go back further than that rather than just pick up on Sky. I first played at Ronnie Scott's club in 1969/70, although I just played classical repertoire. I've always played a fair bit for films, and I like the mixture of the way musicians socialise personally and musically. I like a bit of that world. Sky was not substantially different from the things I had been doing anyway, because Francis Monkman, Herbie Flowers and myself had all been working on most of the tracks of a record I did called *Travelling*. There was this mixture of acoustic and electric sounds, which interested us, and that was the beginning of Sky. Francis and myself were the prime movers for the first couple of months. Kevin Peek I'd met and heard play, and Tris Fry was the last; he needed a few months to think about it before he joined. There was no clear policy – I think that the first and second albums we did followed very much on the basis of the original idea, which came from Francis and myself. I think the rest was just a combination of circumstance, luck and image that followed. We never sat down and said, 'This is the path we want to follow…' But I think, unfortunately, over the subsequent couple of years we went off. Frankly, the last record I was on I really was going through hell, only staying with it out of loyalty. *Three* and *Four* were bad albums – not terrible, but patchy – and the sixth was beyond the pale. I remember sitting in the studio and thinking, 'This is everything that we said we would not do from the very beginning. It sounds like jingles.'

**Was Sky your first encounter with the electric guitar?**

No, I tried electric guitar long before Sky. I had a Gretsch – it was awful. I didn't really know what guitar to use properly then. Then I got a Gibson Les Paul. I only used it with Sky once or twice, on a couple of tracks where we needed two electric guitars. Kevin Peek was the clever one. He was terrific on both classical and electric.

**Will you go back to experimenting with an electric guitar?**

I wouldn't say either way. If a contemporary composer in any field were to come up with a piece of music that needed it, then I wouldn't say no. But it's not my speciality. I might be good enough at it, but it's not my instrument. You know, once when I played with Sky, I played it standing up with a strap, and the whole crew burst out in applause!

# BOB BROZMAN

JUNE 1998

*How does bottleneck slide vibrato relate to female anatomy, and just how do you date a Mateus Rosé wine bottle? Ladies and gentlemen, Bob Brozman... The name may not be familiar, but anyone who has attended a Bob Brozman gig and had to scoop their jaw up from the floor afterwards will attest that he's one hell of a guitar player. He's damnably difficult to categorise, too: a typical Brozman solo set will draw on blues, Hawaiian, calypso, slack-key and slide pieces using a collection of National and Weissenborn guitars. Then there's the humour... Try to imagine Groucho Marx with a guitar and you're just about there. He can also do things with a slide that defy most of the known laws of physics. So where do you start? Well, when I tracked Bob down on a date during his 1998 British tour, I decided that the beginning was probably as good a place as any...*

**How did your interest in guitar start?**

I stumbled on this Johnny Winter album where he was playing resonator guitar, and I became fascinated with the sound and by the look of the thing. I went into town and bought one in 1967, and that's the same one I'm playing now. Once I realised where Johnny Winter was getting his source material from, I just went to the source. That was it. So basically the first time I listened to Johnny Winter was also the last time. From then on I went diving into the usual Mississippi suspects...

**Did you take up slide straight away?**

From the age of 13. The bottleneck I carry with me is the one I made in 1967. I use the neck from a Mateus Rosé wine bottle, but unfortunately, they changed the bottle in 1973 and so they're not as good any more. Every once in a while you'll go into something of a hippie environment and see one being used as a candle holder. Hold it up to the light, and if there's a bluish cast to it, it's pre-1973.

**You have quite a breadth of style, taking in not only blues, but also a lot of the world's exotic music forms, too. What stylistic sojourns have you been on recently?**

I've been recording a lot with some Hawaiian slack-key players, Ledward Kaapana and Cyril Pahinui. Ledward and I released a duet record last year. Slack key and steel are two separate traditions, they've never been done together before. I've also got a record that I just finished in Calcutta with Debashisha Bhattacharya, and this is music that I feel is really two things. One: it's a real blending of east and west and not two blokes sitting there doing their own thing; and, two, we're really doing some revolutionary things like harmonising raga melodies and playing blisteringly fast slide melodies in parallel. The music draws on Indian classical music, Indian folk and Goanese music. There's blues-influenced things, modal things and some Hawaiian things all blended together. I've also been recording a project in Athens combining blues and Rembetika music, which is kind of like the indigenous blues music of Greece. Other than that, a lot of solo concerts, sometimes going with a band called Thieves Of Sleep, doing stuff stemming from Django, African and Madagascan guitar. We set up hip-hop grooves and I play ethnically confused slide guitar over the top.

**You recently became the proud owner of your own signature National steel guitar.**

I've been working with National for some time as an artist endorsee, but also as a consultant, designer and test guy. So they're going to do a limited-edition signature model, which is nearly a baritone guitar, built on a standard tri-cone body, which has some special tuning done to the metal that brings out the bottom end. The neck is 27-inch scale and the tuning is dropped so that the bass string (a 0.76 gauge) is tuned to B. It sounds like a lap piano – you can still get bright, clear high notes from it, but the bottom end will break up kidney stones at 50 feet. I've also got a Santa Cruz guitar coming out, which combines the attributes of a 12-fret Martin Dreadnought body shape, but tapered back like a Weissenborn. The reason why I've done that is to get more treble. It's braced under tension like a Larson guitar, so that the braces are slightly curved and the top is forced to it. This gives a kind of springiness to the top and the purpose of that is to speed up the response. The way I measure guitars is how fast the note gets out: archtops are pretty fast, Nationals and Weissenborns are fast. Martins are very slow, especially the treble. It rolls around inside and then it sort of dribbles out of the sound hole. So this guitar combines the bass of a Martin Dreadnought with the treble response of a Weissenborn.

**How did your interest in Hawaiian music start?**

In America, blues people are extremely narrow-minded and they don't quite know what to make of me. Firstly, I'm funny and they don't like that – I'm supposed to be suffering or something. Secondly, for some reason the fact that I play Hawaiian music de-legitimises me as a blues player, but that's bullshit. The pre-commercial ethnic Hawaiian music is as emotionally deep and sad as any blues I've ever heard. What makes it unique is that it's in major keys and still sad. I started laying the guitar in my lap when I was about 18. But in 1980, on my way to the recording studio for my first session of my first album, I was a passenger in a Volkswagen and we got hit head-on by an American police car, and I broke my back. Basically, I was out of commission for about a year, and during that time I was obliged to wear this horrible metal cage around my torso to keep me straight. Every time I tried to play guitar, the cage would scratch it up. And so that's when I really put my energy into playing lap-style because I could still play that way. I figure that the accident was God's way of telling me to practise more before recording...

At the time I started playing Hawaiian, there was really nobody left playing acoustic steel, and electric steel had almost died. I was getting it from old 78s. In the late '80s I had the good fortune to meet one of my heroes, Tau Moe, who made records in 1929, toured the world for 57 years, and retired to Hawaii. Since that time, working with some of these guys, my slack-key playing has taken quite a jump, because steel is not an accompanying instrument – it's the lead instrument. However, we take turns playing lead, and so I've had to develop a whole new vocabulary of playing steel; all these rhythmic things, damping things, things to do with the bar to make chords. Then, going over to India was another shot in the arm for my steel playing, because what the Indian slide guitar players are doing make us all in the West look like children. It's so articulate and expressive. They strike the string once and get 30 notes out of it.

My whole attitude is one of perpetual curiosity and studenthood. As much as I love all the music I'm doing with these musicians, equally I love the process of meeting them halfway and seeing how I can approach the thing respectfully and build something beautiful. I'm also finding some interesting things out about master musicians. For one, none of them has any ego. The real masters are totally relaxed with no ego or insecurity. And it doesn't matter if they're from Hawaii or India, they've all got this hilarious nine-year-old boy sense of humour. At one point I had Debashisha and his brother playing tablas in Hawaii with Ledward Kaapana, and these two guys hit it off great. They were telling fart jokes within the first five minutes!

**What advice do you have for someone taking up slide guitar?**

Get the sound in your head by listening to records. Find the music you really like, listen to it all the time, and then one day you'll be walking down the street and the record will just play itself back in your head. Half the battle is knowing how it goes.

**What would be your recommended listening?**

The number one man for me is Charlie Patton. Then there's Robert Johnson, Bukka White and Tampa Red, Skip James, Son House, Garfield Acres, Willie Brown... My leaning is towards the Mississippi side of things.

**What about slide technique – vibrato, for example?**

I tend to think of vibrato like holding a bowl of jelly and throwing it back and forth. When you're on the right-hand side of the wiggle, the jelly is still on its way over from the left. Kind of like cupping a globular female part and moving it back and forth. And having said that, I should say that slide players do make more sensitive lovers...

**How about tunings?**

I use G tuning a lot [D G D G B D, bass to treble]. The guitar playing on The Beatles' 'Blackbird' is basically an exercise in diatonic harmony in G tuning. I also use altered tunings where I might go to G minor or G suspended; the D family of tunings like D major, which is D A D F# A D; sometimes I use D A D G A D. I also play in a family of C tunings. There's C G C G C E, but the E can be E flat, or D for a Celtic sound. The top string can sometimes be C, too; double-C tuning, which means that you've got no minor third, and that cuts away a lot of the bullshit.

**A lot of players who are new to playing in different tunings find it hard to come to terms with the new chord shapes they throw up.**

The way I learned is that I plunked my fingers down into a chord shape, listened to it, if it sounded good, then I did a mirror image of it, and if that sounded good, then great. That's got to be your only criteria – does it sound good? A lot of regular acoustic guitars are set up with light-gauge strings and a low action, and this will not make a good slide guitar. I recommend you should get a jumble sale guitar and string it up with medium to heavy strings. My normal string gauge for G tuning is .016 .018 .027 .040 .050 .066, but that's a little bit in the category of 'don't try this at home' and so a more normal set might be something like .014, .018, .027, .036, .046, .059. You need at least a .059 on the bass string because you're detuning to D all the time.

**A lot of people will want to know how long you think it takes to become a good slide player.**

Talking about how to play slide takes about five minutes, learning how takes at least a year, and that depends on whether you have a day job or not. It's mainly about getting a good tone first and then learning some riffs.

**And finally?**

In a world where everyone wants to be the lead player, there's a big deficiency of rhythm playing going on. If I'm in a jam session, I'll take solos if I'm invited to, but my preference is to play rhythm. So I strongly emphasise don't just solo, get the groove going.

# JOHN HAMMOND

MAY 2001

*John Hammond has established himself as a central figure in the blues' ongoing struggle for survival. A 40-year career has seen him stick to the traditional route and remain uncompromisingly true to his chosen music form, winning him awards and accolades from all around him.*

**When did you first start getting interested in blues?**

My dad took me to hear Big Bill Broonzy when I was nine. He was a friend of Bill's and I just felt completely awed by this giant of a man who was so gentle, and his playing was just unbelievable. Then, when I was 10 or 11 years old I got a Sonny Terry and Brownie McGhee album and it sowed the seeds, I suppose. When I was in my early teens I heard Chuck Berry, Ray Charles, Bo Diddley and Little Richard on the radio. Then in 1957 I got an album called *The Country Blues*, which was a compilation album of artists from the '20s and '30s. There was Robert Johnson, Leroy Carr, Blind Boy Fuller, Blind Willie McTell, Blind Lemon...

**When did you become interested in playing guitar?**

I didn't play an instrument until I was 18 and then I started professionally when I was 19, so it kind of hit me all at once. But there had been years of this thing festering inside me, and so when I got my first guitar, that was it.

**So what was the first guitar?**

I got a Gibson. I was told that it was called the Sailor model, like a J100 size. It had a hole punched in the top – it was not a great guitar – but it was just what I needed to get started. Then I got a Gibson J45 in 1961 and that was the guitar I used until I got a J200 in 1963, but the neck warped the wrong way and I couldn't get it fixed. I was in a guitar store in New York and they had a 1947 Gibson country and western that had been owned by Josh Graves. I got it for 400 bucks and I played that guitar for 20 years.

**How did you first come to terms with the Mississippi Delta style of blues guitar?**

When you first hear it, you think that it sounds fairly simple. But then when you get actually inside it and try to make those sounds, you find that it's actually impossible. I am very fortunate to have worked with a lot of these 'rediscovered artists' – from 1962 to '68 I was on shows with Fred McDowell and Bukka White, Son House, Lightning Hopkins and John Lee Hooker when they were playing solo acoustic – and when you see something done, you know that it's possible.

**How communicative were these guys about what they were doing?**

I was too shy to ask anyone to show me anything, I just watched real well when they played. I found that the guitar enhanced the song as opposed to taking it over. So I tried really hard not to overplay notes that weren't necessary. If it supported the words and made the song clearer, then I felt that was more important.

**Did you start playing slide way back then?**

Yes, I did. I played harmonica on the rack and slide style from the beginning.

**How did you work out all the different tunings involved?**

I had a friend named Bob Silverman at college, where I went for a year, and Bob was a much more accomplished guitar player than I was, and he showed me an open D tuning. It was like a revelation – so that's how they get that sound! Just odd things like that. I'm sure every guitar player says the same things. We all have a friend called Harry who shows us things.

**Do you use glass or metal slides?**

I use metal. It's actually a ratchet from a wrench – like a socket wrench, y'know? They're very cheap and easy to come by, although they're a little heavier compared to the ones available today.

**Do you have a guitar set up for slide?**

Yes, the National Duolian that I have is the one I like to use for slide.

**What sort of tunings do you use?**

I use open E and open A. It's like a D tuning taken up to E and a G tuning taken up to A. I do that for my voice; it's the key that will enhance my voice better.

**What about your right-hand style?**

I use a thumbpick, a fingerpick and my third finger as well. I used to use two fingerpicks, but I would always lose the third one in the sound hole and the guitar ended up becoming a giant maraca. So I'm down to two. I learned that way and I don't know how to use a flat pick.

**Where did the idea to use fingerpicks come from?**

Well, I saw Dave Van Ronk play in the Village in '61 and I saw that he used fingerpicks. I'd just begun to play guitar and I thought that a thumbpick seemed to make it so much louder, and the fingerpick was a little harder to get used to, but I was driven at that point to get it down and so it all came together.

**Do you use mainly upstrokes with the fingerpick?**

Yes.

**So it's almost like a conventional fingerstyle, with the fingerpicks added?**

Exactly.

**Have you got any tips for someone who might be venturing into the style of acoustic blues for the first time?**

Know the song. Know the song first, the words and what it means to you, and then the guitar will come in behind it. I don't think that the guitar is more important than the song. So if you can accompany the song and enhance the words, then that's the best technique. The guitar will come as you know the song better.

# ERIC BIBB
JULY 1999

*Eric Bibb's story is anything other than traditional: he learned from his father, Leon, numbers Jazz Quartet pioneer John Lewis amongst his close relatives and had Paul Robeson as a godfather! An average party at his father's home when Eric was growing up would include people like Bob Dylan and Pete Seeger. 'It was really my dad who introduced me to music,' he told me when we spoke. 'He was quite prominent during the '60s on the folk scene, although it was really what we would call "world music" today. It had everything. Folk music then was Reverend Gary Davies, it was Skip James and the Clancy Brothers, Odetta, Josh White and Pete Seeger – y'know? I came into it through all that. It wasn't until I was a teenager that I got into the Chicago stuff. But it was the folk blues that really had the pull on me as a performer.'*

**The guitar bug bit you at a comparatively early age.**

I was eight. I had this horrible guitar that cut my fingers all up. It was a cheap old steel-string guitar that frustrated me no end. But for some reason I stayed with it. Fortunately, not so long afterwards I had access to the guitars that my dad had around the house.

**Do you think that starting on an instrument with a high action actually helps strengthen the fingers and actually winds up helping with technique?**

Probably, because first of all you really have to persevere. I must have been really stubborn about wanting to play the guitar because I was not encouraged by the instrument I had. It was painful. But in hindsight it was good, and the people who were our heroes also played on primitive and very difficult to play instruments and ultimately made glorious music, and so there's something to it.

**Was there an early interest in playing with bands?**

I started basically accompanying myself and performing. I had my father as a role model and so I knew all his songs. Very early on I started to look for songs in my father's record collection that would work for me. It would be anything from Odetta to Joan Baez, and later it was Richie Havens – I loved his stuff. The lineage is really like this: my first role model was my dad and I learned his repertoire, and that was everything from spirituals to work songs – basically American folk material from the South; then it went from my dad to Odetta – she was the next big role model who I emulated; then it was Richie Havens and then Taj Mahal; somewhere along the line, this guy called Eric Bibb emerged…

**Pretty soon, your diverse musical influences began to draw together.**

I always had a very eclectic musical palette: everything from mainstream radio, y'know – Stax and Motown – to Skip James. And for me, it was natural that it reflected itself in my performing. But the trick was getting it to the point where it wasn't just playing musical ping-pong, it was something more cohesive.

**As you progressed as a performer, did you start to look back for the roots of the music you were playing?**

Yes, very much so. Actually, I came to Sweden as a pretty young guy and ran into a record store owner who had one of the most fabulous record collections of pre-war blues I think I've ever seen. I just dove into that for about a year and listened exclusively to blues. For a while it was about just trying to find out what they were doing, but I would say that I just gave up trying to physically clone stuff. I discovered that, for me, osmosis worked better. I just basically listened and I knew that, sooner or later, everything would just come back in my playing. And that's basically what happened. I gave up ruining records trying to work out every note Robert Johnson played.

**Do you find touring enjoyable?**

Mostly I do. You can't really get too far in this business if you don't tour. I've been touring for so long that I've got an infrastructure behind me, and I don't have to get it all together by myself. It's a wonderful change, having management and a whole system behind me; it's freed me up to concentrate on the music. I do enjoy it. It can be a little gruelling, but really gratifying.

**Particularly gruelling when you're in one place and your luggage is in another.**

Oh, it is... You realise how vulnerable you are. I mean, it's a miraculous system, this whole thing of international air travel... I don't understand how anything works, there are just so many people involved. The fact that anything arrives at its destination at all is a wonder.

**What guitars are you using at present?**

My main guitar is still a Levin acoustic jumbo. It's about 30 years old. I also have a wonderful Gibson J45, which is what you hear on the solo stuff.

# TIM ROSE

AUGUST 2000

*I first met Tim Rose at a gig in Cheltenham. We got talking about guitars and I suggested that we did an interview shortly afterwards. Tim was one of the very few guys I talked to for* Guitar Techniques *magazine who kept in touch with me afterwards. He'd phone me from time to time, just to let me know of something he was doing, or a guitar he'd picked up. The last time I heard from him I was in a meeting, and so I told him I'd call back later. I did so and we had our customary 'catch up', including the news from him that Led Zeppelin vocalist Robert Plant had just recorded a version of Tim's song 'Foggy Dew' on a new album. He was excited about the new version and I was pleased for him. A couple of weeks later I heard that he had died after an operation for cancer.*

*Tim Rose's 'Foggy Dew' has become a staple of the folk music scene, but few people know that he also enjoyed the distinction of having introduced a certain Jimi Hendrix to a song called 'Hey Joe'...*

**How did you come across 'Hey Joe' in the first place?**

It was 1959 and I was waiting backstage to go on, and the band before me was a five-piece who eventually became The Stoneman Family, and they did a version of 'Hey Joe'. It was bluegrass-sounding, some of the lyrics were different, but the pattern was there. I thought the chord pattern was mesmerising, and after I left the air force I heard a guy called Vince Martin playing it and I asked him if he'd written it. He said he'd heard it from some woman in Appalachia a few years before. So I just started developing the song just based on the first line of the lyrics, 'Hey Joe, I heard you shot your woman down…', and building it up, taking the bare guts and updating it. I added some lyrics and recorded it with a drummer, and the whole thing came together. I never copyrighted it because I was told that it wasn't worth anything. However I should have gone against the advice I received and done it, because I'd be a little bit more well off today than I am.

**There's probably a whole generation of people out there who don't see the song as having any folk origins at all. Moreover, they possibly think that Hendrix wrote it.**

Well you know how Hendrix's version came about? Chas Chandler was in New York, having discovered Jimi maybe six months or so before, and he was already working live, but they needed a record. Chas was in a disco in New York and they played my version of 'Hey Joe'– although I never considered my version being a dance track, but the DJ played it anyway! Anyway, Chas went out the next day and bought my record, went back to England to where Jimi was rehearsing and said, 'This is your single.' At first, Jimi said he hated it, but Chas got his briefcase, took out Jimi's passport and said, 'Go home.' Of course, Jimi didn't, they put my record on and played virtually what I'd done on my session – the backing vocals they kept the same – and they put it out.

**Did you ever get to meet Hendrix?**

Oh yeah, but I'd met him before when he was playing cellar bands as Jimmy James. But I don't think he'd ever been to see me perform or anything like that. When I came to England, let's say I was less than graceful about things – I was pissed off, although not at Jimi. I'd play it at gigs and people would ask me why I was playing a Jimi Hendrix song. CBS never put out my version and so it never had a chance here, nobody ever heard it. They didn't put out my version of 'Foggy Dew' until Version Six had recorded it, either. They were less than stellar in their performance in those days.

# MICHAEL CHAPMAN

OCTOBER 2000

*Michael Chapman's first album hit the shelves in 1969, establishing him as a significant voice on the acoustic guitar scene. Active in folk music during the early '70s – in the days when everything that wasn't electric was immediately categorised as being 'folk' – he quickly became known for his quirky and individual approach to his instrument. The interview we did was to back up a song we had transcribed in* Guitar Techniques *magazine called 'Lumpy McBumpy', which was dedicated to his pet Labrador dog.*

**So how did it all begin?**

I started playing at the age of 15 in history lessons at school to annoy the teacher who, in later years, turned out to be a bit of a hero of mine. I started off basically because I had noticed that guys who had guitars were accompanied by girls who were a hell of a lot better-looking than the ones I was getting. From the guitar players I've talked to, that seems to be a universal reason for wanting one. People as diverse as Mick Ronson and John Fahey have said the same thing.

**What were your early musical influences?**

There wasn't really anybody to listen to. I couldn't pinpoint exactly why, but guitars just seemed absolutely fascinating to me. I would walk into the middle of Leeds just to have a look at one in a shop window. I had no real idea what they did, but I'd walk all the way into town and stand in front of Kitchen's window, and I remember they had a Gibson Charlie Christian: it was that lovely dark sunburst colour. It was £87 – and this was in 1955 or '56, and we'd never even heard of £87 where I came from!

**Did you get caught up in the Hank Marvin revolution a few years later?**

No, never. I was caught up with skiffle, though it was more Ken Collier than Lonnie Donegan with me. I loved the first 10-inch Lonnie Donegan LP released – I've still got it. It had Denny Wright playing lead on it and it was a fabulous album. Someone should put that album out on CD.

**What was it like learning back then? These days we take it for granted that there is a tutor on almost every street corner.**

Well, there just wasn't anywhere to go. There was one guy in Kitchen's shop in Leeds who taught classical guitar with a bit of flamenco, if you weren't careful, and that was it. As long as I could play E and A and B – and then when I got to G and C and D – I thought I was king of the world. Then someone said, 'You can mix them up a bit, if you like... I think that's what this guy's doing', and he played me a John Lee Hooker record. He was only playing E and G if you were lucky, and sometimes it was just E, and so I thought, 'Well, that's all right.'

# TOMMY EMMANUEL

JULY 2000

*In Australia, Tommy Emmanuel is a household name. He has toured endlessly and won just about every award imaginable, having recorded a shelf-full of albums – some of which have gone platinum. He has been nominated for Grammys, recorded an album of duets with fingerstyle legend Chet Atkins, played Sydney Opera House and even taken part in the closing ceremony for the Olympic Games in Sydney. When I interviewed him, he was still an unfamiliar name in the UK, but more recently he is gaining a reputation as one of the finest acoustic guitar players on the planet – it's well deserved, too.*

*Tommy started playing guitar when he was four years old and toured with his family in travelling shows, playing all over Australia. He discovered the playing of his mentor Chet Atkins when he was still very young, working out some of Chet's complex pieces alongside those of Jerry Reed, and stunning audiences with his virtuosity and skill on the instrument.*

**Tell us about those early learning years...**

I was born in a place called Muswellbrook, which is a coal-mining town about three hours above Sydney. I started playing in 1959, when I was four years old. My mother showed me my first few chords – she played a little bit of lap-steel guitar and sang a little, and so she got me started by buying me a cheap guitar and showing me a few things on it, and that kept me inspired for a long time. I think that the first thing that I heard that I really loved was Marty Robbins singing 'El Paso', which had Grady Martin playing guitar on it. Then I heard Chet Atkins and George Barnes playing on some of those early Hank Williams records, and I really loved them. Then there was Hank Marvin, too. When I was seven years old I heard Chet playing a solo piece called 'Windy And Warm', and that was a real turning point for me because, even at that early age, I realised that he was playing everything at once, and that it was a self-contained style. So I set about trying to work it out when I was a kid. I started playing fingerstyle using a pick as well, because I didn't realise that Chet was using a thumbpick, and so I worked out a few tunes when I was a kid, like 'Freight Train' and 'Trambone', but using a plectrum. Then, in '65, I was given the *Best Of Chet Atkins* album by a friend of the family and of course, there he is on the cover with a thumbpick. So I took a look at it and thought, 'That's it!' That helped me to get better at playing that style, by utilising the thumb properly.

**Have you always played solo or were you in bands at all?**

I've always enjoyed playing solo and I make a career of it now, but I draw on many influences when I play and I've had a lot of experience in band playing. All through the '60s I played in travelling shows, mostly playing country and rock 'n' roll. Then, in the '70s, I was well into the Merle Travis, Chet Atkins style, as well as George Benson and Earl Klugh, Eric Clapton and BB King, and other styles of music as well. When people ask me to describe what I do, I usually tell them I'm a songwriter. I wrote my first song when I was nine years old and I'm still doing it. So I write songs on the guitar and I'm a guitar nut through and through – always have been and always will be. I only know one bigger guitar nut than me and that's Chet.

**Describe the travelling shows you were playing in.**

Well, we were playing in little town halls and school halls and things like that.

**Obviously when we talk about 'travelling' in Britain, you can drive nearly anywhere in under a day, but it's a different matter in Australia.**

That's right. When you go into the outback, you allow three or four days in between towns and carry extra fuel and water with you and things like that. When I was a kid we had to go across what we call the Nullarbor Plain – which is between Southern and Western Australia – which was a seven day and night journey across a treacherous part of the country. Many flat tyres, broken axles and broken springs, but you just had to fix the vehicles by the side of the road and keep going.

**When did you make your first record?**

In 1960 we recorded an acetate at a radio station, and it was played on radio and got very worn out. Unfortunately it got broken about 20 years ago and so now there are no copies. But from 1960 until 1963 there was the Emmanuel Quartet, with my sister playing Hawaiian lap-steel and my brother playing drums. Someone made a tape of us playing 'Wipe Out', which was originally by a band called The Surfaris, and we recorded it calling ourselves The Midget `Safaris. I used to play the drum solo on that, because I was a drummer as well. I don't know how to get hold of the tape; someone's got it, but I don't know who.

**What was the next step in your career?**

When I came to Sydney in '76, having been on the road for most of my life, I started getting studio work. Most of the established studio players thought I was pretty unusual because I had no theory whatsoever and couldn't read a note of music – and still can't. But there I was, playing acoustic guitar and fingerstyle, knowing a lot about country music and living in the city. In Sydney back then everybody was into Larry Carlton, Lee Ritenour and George Benson. I came along and…I was so different, had a good ear and could adapt to any style of music, and so I got a lot of work. Quite a lot of the time I was booked to do soundtracks for films and they knew I couldn't read, and so they would have the backing already done and just tell me to play something over the top. They knew I could improvise and had a natural ear for it. When I discovered Django Reinhardt and Joe Pass, it suddenly dawned on me about improvising and that really helped me along. I had also already learned pieces by Chet and Jerry Reed – people who play interesting solos – and so I had got a taste for it when I was still quite young. It's one of my favourite paths now – to play a song and then improvise.

**What was the music scene like out in Australia back then?**

I think it was fantastic. It was small in its own way because we don't have a big population, but in the '70s I took work in bands playing music I'd never played before, and I bluffed my way through it. But there was a lot of good music around – a lot of good jazz, funk and rock bands. Guys like Air Supply were coming up and doing a lot of studio dates and singing together and things like that. There were musicals like *Jesus Christ Superstar* and I played in the pit for a while in that, having learned all the songs from tape and making out that I was reading them every night.

**Did you do club work?**

Yeah, I took a job in a club playing Friday, Saturday and Sunday, and had to learn all different kinds of music for people to dance to. Also there was always a guest entertainer – three on a Sunday – and so you had to go in and sight-read the music. I put myself in the deep end to gain the experience and I really enjoyed it. The only person who pulled me up for playing not what was written was a guy from The Seekers, and then one of the other guys chirped up and said, 'I like what Tommy's playing better!' Then in the '80s, I was doing so much studio work – about 30 dates a week – and I was teaching and playing in bands. So the time between 1980 and 1986 was just a blur. But I've always done things for the experience, where you have to sink or swim.

**Did you teach in a college?**

No, I used to teach from home, although I did teach through the Conservatorium. Because I couldn't read music, they were always a bit funny about me there. And so some of the guys who wanted to learn from me went to the Conservatorium and set up a course called Advanced Fingerstyle. Then they approached me about it and allowed me to teach from home on Saturday and Sunday mornings.

**In the later part of the '80s you started to record your own albums.**

I'd been touring the world with different bands and things, and felt that I was ready to do something myself. I was approached by a record company in America to make a new age-type album. They gave me this brief and said that they wanted it all original and gave me an awful lot of freedom to go ahead and do whatever I wanted. So I recorded 22 pieces that I'd written and some of them were fairly commercial sounding, and when I played the demos to them, the record company said that they really liked the more commercial tracks. So I wrote a few more and did a medley of Beatles tunes, and then the album came out, which was called *Up From Down Under*. The album went into the top ten – much to everyone's surprise – and I ended up, ten years down the track, with ten albums out.

**And, of course, you recorded and played with Chet Atkins.**

It's been a bit sad because Chet hasn't been able to play recently, but we had so many plans when we were together. We hired a publicist and the record company was really going to go for it. Chet had a new lease of life and was really enjoying it, but then they found a brain tumour and it just stopped everything in its tracks. I see him as often as I can, but it's just so hard to see that he just can't play. But it's great to be there with him because we're just like family.

**Do you use alternate tunings?**

It's mostly standard tuning. The only time I change is tuning the bass E string to D occasionally. I've yet to discover D A D G A D and things like that. I love the sound of it, but I'm having enough trouble with standard tuning!

# ACKNOWLEDGEMENTS

This collection spans over 12 years, two magazine titles and two publishers. So, in very rough chronological order, I'd like to express my undying gratitude to...

Everyone at Music Maker Publications in Ely, Cambs, UK, particularly Neville Marten, Eddie Allen, Rick Batey, Gibson Keddie, Danny Eccleston, Debbie Day (née Taylor), James Cumpsty, Richard Ecclestone, Cliff Douse, Phil Hilborne, Chris Francis, Terry Day, Dennis Hill, Alan Goodes, Jeff Hudson, Tim Slater, Jordan McLachlan, Gareth Smith, Alison Clark, Adrian Clark, Dominic Hilton, Simon Bradley, Jane Bird, Rob Last, Helen Bavester, Martyn Booth, Clive Morton, the art department, Sarah Clark, Sally Hilton, Zoe French, Cathy Eastwood, Steve Brendish, Chris Brennand, Steve Collingwood, Kev Lowery, Richard Page, Stuart Catterson, Mike Stapleton, and anyone I might have forgotten.

On *Guitar Techniques*: Dave Kilminster, Geoff Whitehorn, Shaun Baxter, Guthrie Govan, Lee Hodgson, Richard Stockerreit, Frank Evans, Martin Taylor, Jamie Humphries, Eric Roche, Sara Clemenson, and our enthusiastic archivist and good friend Dr James Cameron.

Future Publishing in Bath, UK, notably the various *Guitar Techniques* editorial teams: Sue White, Lilly Blackmore, Chris Lee, Lewis Brangwyn and Colin Nightingale; publishers Simon Haisman and Kathryn Raderecht; and all the support staff who helped us put a great little magazine together every month.

All at Sanctuary Publishing for letting me get this project off my chest, including Iain MacGregor, Dicken Goodwin and Albert DePetrillo.

There is an additional cast of thousands I have to thank, including PR people, record companies, hotel and restaurant staff, airlines, patient taxi drivers, impatient taxi drivers and everyone else who was instrumental in putting the right people in the right place at the right time.

Special thanks to Roland Gower for helping me find some hitherto untraceable material.

To my two sons, Timothy and Toby, who have taught me that the best way to communicate with one's children is to resist the urge to grow up yourself!

On a personal note, I'd like to thank Carol for the endless help and encouragement she gives me on every venture I undertake, whether it be writing a book or creating music, doing clinics, performing or recording. Thanks, Toots!

# INDEX